W9-AAR-195

FLANAGAN'S

SMART HOME

The 98 Essentials for
Starting Out, Starting Over, Scaling Back

BY BARBARA FLANAGAN

WORKMAN PUBLISHING

NEW YORK

~~~~~~~~~~~~~

For my children, Gillian and Nat,
now at home in Santa Barbara and Brooklyn
And for my mother, Irene

~~~~~~~~~~~~~

Library of Congress Cataloging-in-Publication Data is available.
ISBN 978-0-7611-4460-1

Workman books are available at special discounts when purchased in
bulk for premiums and sales promotions as well as for fund-raising or
educational use. Special editions of book excerpts can also be created to
specification. For details, contact the Special Sales Director at the address
below.

Design: Gary Montalvo
Art Direction: David Matt

WORKMAN PUBLISHING COMPANY, INC.
225 Varick Street
New York, NY 10014-4381
www.workman.com

Printed in the United States of America

First printing September 2008
10 9 8 7 6 5 4 3 2 1

Contents

CHAPTER ONE
SLEEPING
— PAGE 1 —

CHAPTER TWO
BATHING &
DRESSING
— PAGE 36 —

CHAPTER THREE
COOKING
— PAGE 59 —

CHAPTER FOUR

DINING

— PAGE 127 —

CHAPTER FIVE

CLEANING & FIXING

— PAGE 162 —

CHAPTER SIX

READING, WRITING, LIVING

— PAGE 181 —

Introduction

I live in a very small house. What's small? Picture a bright, well-crafted sailboat—but one that feels larger than it looks.

What makes it smart? Much of the furniture is built-in: maple cabinetry with deep drawers and strong hardware.

Lighting is hidden: low-voltage, fitted with white and amber color filters layered like watercolors to make the house feel warmer or cooler as seasons change. During the day, skylights bring in the sun.

French doors open from the big kitchen/dining room to the garden. The tiny living room sits only six, intimately. Although the sole sleeping area isn't much bigger than the bed, the bedroom suite feels roomy, with its wide sitting room and closet. Two spacious bathrooms have seamless porcelain tile walls, and floors sloping right to the drain as in Italian showers.

This house wasn't really supposed to be mine. As a product designer trained in architecture, I'd redesigned and reconstructed what used to be a grim, brick Cape Cod for my aging mother. A bachelorette pad of "universal," "barrier-free" design—useful to anyone, fully mobile or not—it was supposed to be the home where she could age in place, near her family, instead of being carted off to a nursing home. Sadly, a series of strokes took her there anyway.

I never imagined I'd one day be the beneficiary of all that design—a labor of love I'd never build for myself—nor had I really understood how living in such tight quarters might squeeze my life into a new shape.

My first real domestic inventory was acquired to fit the scale of a much grander home. "Buy the biggest house you can afford," accountants, financial advisors, and realtors have advised for the past decade. And so we did, and we filled it. My then husband and I bought a gorgeous, three-story Victorian manse in a lovely historic neighborhood. Perfect for two writers working at home and starting a family, right?

Actually, it was too big. Scary big. And predictably chilling. Every winter, dry air from the monster furnace swirled up to the twelve-foot-high ceilings as cold air pushed in from the tall windows and icy brick walls. In summer, bats exploring our six-story maple trees would swoop indoors to terrify us. And every year, visiting repairmen pronounced something dead or defunct: the maples, the slate roof, the kitchen.

Fearing his own demise, perhaps, my husband eventually decamped for a California makeover, quit-deeding the bats and the mortgage to me and leaving two stunned preteens in his wake. The big house got bigger.

Next, everyone dispersed. I moved one block west into my mother's empty house and my kids were packed off to their colleges.

Hard as I'd worked to fill our behemoth with over-scaled antiques and curiosities, it had never really felt finished. As I watched all the furniture parade out the door, I realized that I loved very little of it and needed still less. Only the valuable things had kept their value. Anything made thoughtfully or beautifully—piano, carved mirror, Italian torchère, clay bunnies clumsily sculpted by my kids—seemed worthwhile, along with all the good, solid household tools used every day. But things with cosmetic or theoretical appeal looked more and more worthless: fancy cooking equipment, uncomfortable chairs, wobbly bookcases...

It wouldn't be the last time I'd be forced to confront household possessions.

As I helped my children set up their first households, and, with my sister, reduced my mother's household to smaller and smaller quarters, I handled a whole lot of stuff. I bought it, U-hauled it, moved it upstairs and down, stuffed it into elevators, stored it, boxed it, UPSed it, donated it to charities, refinished it, sold it at yard sales, filled dumpsters with it, cursed it and cried over it.

Moving into my small house turned into an experiment in living with less. With no room for mistakes, I could bring in only things I really needed for a nice life—no more, no less.

As a design-aholic addicted to rescuing "pieces"—cool but unusable furniture—curbing my impulses was no fun at first. I could no longer harbor chromed factory lamps or moderne steno chairs. Everything had to offer some degree of comfort and utility. As I winnowed down my stash, I began asking more questions: "Do I need it? Want it? Admire it?" Eventually, I discovered that useful things could have lots of interesting virtues. I stopped feeling deprived and began to feel surprisingly good, even a bit preachy. It wasn't too long before I got the urge to spread my newfound gospel.

Defining my creed turned out to be surprisingly thorny. How many possessions would it take to make a comfy household? Fifty? Five hundred? I was hoping for a cool 100, but 98 turned out to be the actual count. Defining my list of necessities was hard enough, but finding an exalted example of each was quite a long haul. I sought out specific products and furnishings that would inspire so much affection I would want to use them often, and keep enjoying them for a very long time.

First, I figured out which parts of daily life deserved better equipment (sleeping), and which were filled with bad habits that had gotten out of hand (hanging out—namely, TV watching). Most people I knew were mounting radically new televisions on their walls but enduring substandard, old-fashioned mattresses in every bedroom. Wasn't deep sleep more important than thin TVs? The quandary made me buy an excellent, thin mattress, disconnect my TV from the satellite signal, and use my free evenings to see friends more often.

It turns out I knew a whole lot less than I thought I did about how the commonest products were made, how they actually worked, and how they affected the people who made and used them. Once I began to ask questions, every product opened up interlocking realms of information leading from physics to chemistry, or from history to politics. The subject of pots and pans raised questions about how heat moves through molecules of pre-treated metals. The subjects of sofas and coat hangers uncovered hot debates about using corn to make bio-plastics.

What I was really looking for was a deeper, smarter kind of materialism than the one we've been practicing lately. We're hearty consumerists. We shop with emotional fervor, but we scoop up the merch too fast—we're too trusting of marketing claims and hype. We aim to be self-sufficient by owning at least one of everything under the sun (leaf-blower to espresso maker). We're obsessed with low prices and mesmerized by new "features" and "options," but unable to calculate value: performance over time. When the products disappoint, we toss them and start over, hoping for more exciting relationships but not really expecting our purchases to endure. Where do all of those mistakes go? Underground, incinerated, and out to sea. There has to be a better way.

What would it look like if we found pleasure and pride in living with a small and finite collection of "durable goods" (an economic term for consumer products that last longer than three years)?

Certainly we'd be able to afford better stuff—functional, lovely to look at, easy to maintain, and long-lasting. Remorse-free ownership is a beautiful thing, and in the long-run, it's cheaper for us. And it's just plain urgent for our planet.

How do we get there? By not buying into market frenzy. By thinking before we buy, and by caring for what we have. Home is where we care for ourselves, after all, where we repair our bodies and minds from the damage wrought by the outside world. A home that's filled to the rafters with junk can't be a place of solace. We all know we should be putting better stuff in our bodies. Let's get smart about what we bring into our homes.

How to Use this Book

WHATEVER YOUR LIFE STAGE, it's likely you already own quite a bit of stuff. Do I expect every reader of this book to toss everything they own and follow every one of my recommendations to the letter? Of course not—I would never recommend junking something before its time was up!

What I hope, instead, is that you'll be informed by the spirit of this book as you go forward. Buy well-engineered, gimmick-free products that are built to last. Welcome things into your home with slow, leisurely consideration, using each purchase as an excuse to learn something about the material world. Before you add any item to your virtual or physical shopping cart, ask yourself the following questions:

1. Do I need it?

2. Does it do what I need it to do?

3. Can I fix it myself with common tools and parts? Will it need to be replaced in its entirety if it malfunctions?

4. Can I wash it in household machines or basins? Does it require professional care or fancy chemicals?

5. Does it take up lots of space, or can it be folded, deflated, collapsed, or used for double-duty?

6. Is it safe for my family, my neighbors, and all the people who helped make it?

7. Does making it, or using it, use up a lot of endangered materials: petroleum, natural gas, or ancient trees?

8. Does it improve with age? Or will it need to be tossed after a short life span?

9. After its useful life, can it be repurposed or reconstituted into something else?

10. Does it make me happy for reasons I can or can't describe?

If the answer to most of these questions is "yes," you're well on your way to a smart purchase.

CHAPTER ONE

SLEEPING

INVENTORY

- Alarm Clock
- Bedside Lamp
- Floor Lamp
- Flashlight

- Nightstand
- Mattress
- Bed
- Pillow
- Mattress Pad

- Sheets
- Electric Blanket
- Bedspread
- Rug

The bedroom is the most important room in the house. In theory, it's the place where you make love, fall asleep happily, dream deeply, and rise tall in the morning, free of back pain and grudges. What more could you want from a room?

Although a good bedroom can't guarantee romantic and somatic bliss, a bad bedroom can certainly hamper it. Worst-case scenario? Two sleepless people tossing around under cold sheets in a rock-hard bed night after night become brain-addled and sore. Unable to think straight, they lose their jobs and their friends, go bankrupt, and get divorced. Each party, still as clueless as ever, ends up having to furnish yet another bad bedroom.

Why not get it right in the first place?

Buying bedroom stuff is scary. Sex and sleep are among the most mysterious and elusive of all human activities. Medical advice and prescription drugs can't guarantee them. Money can't buy them. But when merchants remind us that we spend one third of our lives sleeping (or trying to sleep), we feel compelled to upgrade our dreams by upgrading our bedrooms.

Even if we're ready to throw money at the problem, though, who knows which way to aim? Expert advice—on everything from sex, sleep, allergens, and stress—changes so quickly that outfitting the simplest bedroom can be maddening. You're pushed to one extreme or the other: Forget the whole thing and just grab the cheapest stuff you can find, or take a risky bet on the most expensive.

Fortunately, there are answers, and they come from Europe: svelte beds and mattresses, practical textiles, and intelligent lighting. The structure of the mattress and pillow will provide muscular support; highly functional layers of bed coverings will create epidermal comfort; and adjustable lighting will lend optical and psychological ease.

The cautionary news is that a bedroom can swallow up a small fortune without looking particularly swank. The fully clothed bed is going to cost more than you expected to spend. And no one will know! The bed platform will be obscured by a mattress, mattress pad, layers of sheets and pillows, the whole covered by a blanket and bedspread or quilt. So much to buy, so little to see for your trouble.

Get the sleeping and waking equipment right, however, and what you will see is a new, lovelier version of you: wide awake, rested, and less caffeinated than ever before.

~~~~~~~~~~

Alarm Clock
Wake Up Happier

The first alarm clock was built in 1787 by an American clockmaker. Unfortunately, the gadget was set to ring daily at 4 A.M., and the enforced early wake-up time didn't catch on. Sixty years later, a Frenchman patented an important improvement—an adjustable timer—and the thing took off. Hammered brass became the new, sophisticated sound of morning.

Without alarm clocks rousing city workers inside darkened rooms, the industrial age might have lagged; an agreed-upon start time for the workday made the assembly-line factory possible. (The connection will be apparent to any seasoned traveler; the less industrialized the country, the more fluid the concept of time.)

Hammered brass was just the start. For two hundred years, alarm clocks have been growing more complex. Loud clocks with clanging metal and electric buzzers were followed by dual-purpose clock/radios blaring hyper DJs and traffic reports, then trumped by tri-purpose clock/radio/CD players. For a few decades, consumers believed that an acoustic kick in the head was as indispensable as a jolt of morning coffee, part of the macho routine of going to work and getting ahead. As alarm clocks advanced, however, their users began to show wear and tear.

Through the 1990s, biochemists studying patterns of sleeping and waking found that our habits of rushing, competing, and worrying were wreaking havoc with our internal chemicals—too much adrenaline. Lousy nutrition and too little exercise didn't help. Suddenly there were too many identical beeps announcing unlike urgencies: time to wake up, your car is stolen, the roast is done, your daughter is calling, and the security system is armed. It's not surprising that the alarm clock and the cell phone are the two inventions most reviled by the general public, according to MIT researchers.

As we discover more about the biochemistry of stress, we're also learning more about the chemical mechanics of waking up. Left alone, the human body awakens gradually

An abrupt wake-up call triggers the same reaction as the roar of a grizzly.

and silently when the first light of day penetrates the eyelids and stimulates serotonin, the chemical that rouses the sleeping brain. The brain in turn speeds up the body's metabolism: heart rate, breathing, and so on.

An abrupt wake-up call triggers the same reaction as the roar of a grizzly: spiked blood pressure pumping adrenaline and other action chemicals. This sudden workout unnecessarily stresses the heart and other organs.

In a few years, the notion of a gradual, nonviolent waking device will seem obvious. To wit, inventors are currently developing a new generation of "natural alarm clocks"; they aim to wake with gradual stimuli that enter not through the ears, but through the eyes and epidermis. The "dawn simulator," for instance, combines a small light with a timer and clock radio. One apparatus features a normal, dimmable lightbulb encased in a translucent globe, set atop a standard alarm clock packed with the usual options. The light starts brightening, gradually, thirty minutes before the wake-up time you choose, then the fail-safe alarm sounds. And prototypes of glowing light pillows, embedded with dawn-simulating LEDs (see box, below), have been circulating for several years.

Another category of waking machines uses silent vibration, a gentle rumbling under the pillow or mattress. (These are probably not appropriate for earthquake-prone areas.) Both sorts of devices, light and vibes, are marketed with plenty of biochemical-speak about "natural waking."

Until these and other such products become affordable and widely available—they will—a couple of basics will take care of you. To wake up with light, you'll need three components: a standard lamp timer, a normal table lamp, and a simple alarm clock as a backup. That alarm won't shock you out of a sound sleep—it's the light that nudges you awake—but it will prevent you from oversleeping until you become accustomed to the new routine.

I. LAMP TIMER. The perfect lamp timer would turn on your lamp by increasing its brightness as slowly as the sun rises. What's available right now is a standard household lamp timer. For just a few dollars, the donut-size device will automatically turn on a bedroom lamp at the same time every day.

Any lamp timer will do, as long as it has an override switch to let you sleep late. Set it for thirty minutes before you plan to rise; plug it into any outlet; and plug the lamp into the timer. The sudden dawning, though more abrupt than a real sunrise, will perform the same function: the stimulation of those brain-waking chemicals and the warming up of your body for the athletic task of leaving the bed.

A bonus for gloomy winter mornings: The light also helps heat up the room by changing its "color temperature"—a technical term for visual warmth—from a cold blue/black to a happy, caloric yellow. (Tests prove that people actually feel warmer in yellow than in blue light.)

Summer presents a different challenge. If the bedroom floods with sunlight long before you intend to

A BRIGHT FUTURE

I've recommended three lamps and three different lightbulbs to get you ready to sleep and to wake you up gradually. But prepare to eventually jettison them. In a few years those sorts of lamps and bulbs will be replaced by crisp, energy-saving, infinitely adjustable LEDs (light-emitting diodes); made of a semiconductor material that glows in response to an electrical current, LEDs create light in a more streamlined process than traditional lightbulbs. (Those heat up a thin filament in an oxygen-free environment, the bulb, to produce incandescence— much in the same way fire works.) LED bulbs will eventually take over, so don't overspend on lighting now.

rise, you'll probably need to layer the windows with drapes and blackout shades.

If the light doesn't do it for you, experiment with its location and intensity. It needn't be right in your face, interrogation-style, but it should be intense enough to brighten the whole room.

2. WAKE-UP LAMP. Just about any dimmable lamp can serve as a wake-up lamp. But a versatile choice is a table lamp small enough to stand on a chest of drawers or nightstand, yet big enough to brighten a whole room. The details: A "three-way lamp," rated for bulbs that pull a maximum of 100 to 150 watts of electricity, can be used with a three-way CFL (compact fluorescent lightbulb) with low, medium, and high settings; because a CFL uses less electricity than a standard incandescent bulb, the CFL should be 32 to 42 watts. A lamp with a diffuser—a light-colored lamp shade will do—will soften the bulb's light and send it around the room.

3. ALARM CLOCK. The smaller the alarm clock, the easier it will be to swat around, lift, and adjust. A digi-tal model, thin and spare as can be, will do the job without hogging the nightstand or other surface. Choose the smallest font size you'll be able to see clearly from your pillow when you're groggy and bare-eyed. And by all means, shop around for a tolerable tone that starts faint and becomes louder when ignored.

Today's clocks will trigger anything from brass "Zen chimes" to a choice of bird calls or songs personally chosen from your cell phone, CD, or MP3 player. So why not create a soundtrack for waking up? The movie *Groundhog Day* answers that. Music used as a disciplinary tool becomes tainted by association, especially when repeated day after day.

Since the wake-up lamp will be operated by the timer and not by its own switch, the bedroom will require two additional lamps, for adjustable reading light and for ambient light. That may seem like a lot of light sources for a room dedicated to darkness. But it's a question of sensitivity and texture; between dressing, waking, sleeping, and whatever happens between the sheets, there's a lot going on in the bedroom.

Bedside Lamp

For Your Reading Pleasure

In bedside reading lamps, the choice is clear: There is one source of intense reading light that far outshines the rest. It's the beetle-size halogen bulb. No other bulb concentrates such a bright beam into a book-size pool of light, allowing you to finish your book while your bed mate dozes.

Halogen bulbs are about 20 percent more efficient than standard lightbulbs, though still functioning through incandescence (essentially, heating). Pressurized halogen gas makes them burn brighter, crisper, and longer. They also burn very hot—so hot that manufacturers recommend they be kept out of kids' rooms, away from bedsides, and at least eight inches away from everything, especially your fingers. (The skin's oil can cause the bulbs to shatter.)

Used with caution on a well-designed bedside, the halogen lamp is safe for careful adults. An articulated lamp, called a task lamp or work lamp, should have an adjustable arm long enough to reach from the nightstand, over the bed, and safely over a book. The arm should have smooth, moveable joints at the base, elbow, and head, giving you the ability to position the thing in a variety of ways: away from your head while you sleep, up-lighting the ceiling when you dress, or grazing the walls with gentler light.

The lamp head will ideally have a protruding rod or heat-proof cover for maneuvering—the metal gets hot. A heavy base supports the out-stretched arm and prevents tipping. A switch easily found from the bed in the dark also helps.

There's no need to buy a deluxe halogen reading lamp now that LED lamps are about to take over. So, if you start reading *War and Peace* under halogen light, prepare to finish it under LEDs in the next few years.

Floor Lamp

From a Restful Glow to a Vibrant Gleam

Before you choose a floor lamp, choose a lightbulb. Your choice will depend on the length of your morning and evening rituals. If they're abbreviated, use a screw-in halogen bulb; if they're drawn out, use a CFL. Compact fluorescent lightbulbs (CFLs) are lauded for their stunning efficiency stats. They use 75 percent less energy, last ten times longer, and give off 75 percent less heat than standard bulbs. But you may not know that CFLs need to stay on for at least fifteen minutes at a time, or several hours per day, to achieve that kind of performance.

If CFLs are your choice, find a three-way (low, medium, high) bulb. Its highest intensity should be about 23 to 52 watts. Next, find a three-way lamp rated for the incandescent equivalent—100 to 150 watts. (A dimmable CFL lamp is ideal but harder to find.)

From a design standpoint, look for a classic floor lamp: a translucent lampshade on a pole supported by a heavy base. Turned up high, its light bounces off the walls and ceiling, providing an even, overall glow. Switched to low, it exudes a more romantic or restful atmosphere.

The bulb and lamp will be easy to find. The most direct route is the local lighting supply store. Use the customer-service counter person as your lighting consultant. Ask for a three-way CFL in "soft white," the warmest possible color temperature at about 2700°K. Request the latest, best-quality bulb available; lighting companies are in fierce competition to produce the best CFLs at reasonable prices, so the odds are stacked in your favor at higher-end stores.

If halogen is your poison, see bedside lamp, opposite page.

Flashlight

A Beam in the Dark

Doesn't it seem like emergencies have a way of happening in the middle of the night? Those creeping monsters and bursting pipes have nocturnal habits. That's why it's a good idea to keep a flashlight handy in a nightstand drawer. But must it be handheld? Consider a compact headlamp instead.

The headlamp started out on miners' helmets, a giant lantern powered by heavy batteries. Then the outdoor gear industry took over, refining the clunky tool into a streamlined jewel mounted on an elastic headband—handy for campers feeling their way around in the dark. Lately, that band has been further reduced into a set of nearly invisible retractable cords, designed to wrap around any body part or piece of equipment.

The newest headlamps use rugged LEDs to produce a piercing, high-intensity light fueled by very few batteries. The lightest version weighs about 2.3 ounces, lighter than the lightest miniflashlight.

More good news: Each year the price of a no-frills, high-tech headlamp decreases as the fancier models grow more sophisticated. Some of the new features make sense: a color gauge that reveals how much battery power remains, and a choice of brightness levels that lets you use the least amount of juice necessary for the task at hand.

The best part of owning a headlamp is finding unintended uses for it. It doubles as a wearable safety light for night exercisers or commuters on foot or bike. But it has festive uses as well. It can illuminate a snowy path for Christmas carolers; on Halloween, it makes small trick-or-treaters visible as they teeter-totter along in their Spider-Man masks.

Nightstand

For Easier Fumbling

There's nothing like tent camping to show you the true value of a nightstand. You don't realize how many accessories you wear (watch, jewelry, glasses, contacts) or how many bedtime items you need (book, water, pills, snacks, alarm clock, light source) until you bunk on the ground minus a safe, level surface.

Of what should that surface be made? A natural material like wood or bamboo gives the nightstand a tactile warmth appreciated on cold mornings and softens the alarm's vibrations. A durable, water-resistant finish should protect the wood from spills.

Dimensions matter. Choose a nightstand—one for each sleeper—after measuring the height of the mattress installed on its frame. The top of the nightstand should be flush with the top of the mattress, so the sleeper can smack his alarm or fumble for glasses, eyes closed, in one easy maneuver.

A drawer in each nightstand can also contain a selection of leisure accessories: bedwear and potions too personal to leave in a medicine cabinet. Some things just need a hiding place, and nothing is more convenient than the nightstand's drawers: his and hers.

Mattress

The Most Complicated of Bedroom Purchases

"**B**uying a mattress is like buying a car," bedding sellers like to say, nudging customers to take their time, study the options, and pay a large price. While mattresses and cars are approaching each other in size and price (with cars shrinking and mattresses gaining), they are distinct opposites. One is designed to stimulate all the senses, and the other to turn them all off. And, most important, you can take one out for a test-drive, but not the other.

Every car buyer gets to test-drive several models to see how those techy performance specs translate into what the TV ads call a "driving experience." Sitting behind the wheel of a Lexus LS Hybrid, for example, you get to corner with the Active Power Stabilizer Suspension System and accelerate with the Electronically Controlled Continuously Variable Transmission before deciding that one Lexus is worth, say, four Hyundais.

Alas, the only way to sample a mattress is to spend a few months rolling around on it with a sleep mate (if applicable), in a wide range of sleep postures and sexual positions influenced by different seasons, hormonal cycles, mood swings, and stresses.

The winning mattress will be the one that makes the sleepers feel as little as possible: comatose all night and pain free the next day.

The standard testing ritual is short, ludicrous, and inconclusive. Shoppers enter a hospital-like showroom full of identical white slabs where somber salespeople invite them to pantomime sleep in public. The shoppers perform a few butt bounces, lie flat, flop around, and poke the outer layers, as if kicking a tire. Unable to understand why one mattress costs ten times more than another, the shoppers ask for some technical measures of quality.

"What do doctors buy?" the shoppers ask, thinking themselves clever. "The firmest mattress around?"

"Not anymore," merchants answer. "Firm is out. Comfort is key. Doctors now recommend buying for comfort and proper support."

"What's proper support?"

"Let's just say you get what you pay for," goes the misleading response.

Salesmen hand the flummoxed shoppers chunks of mattress to palpate like stress balls. The cross sections reveal the mattress innards. The more expensive the model, the more layers it contains: ticking, quilting, padding, batting, more padding, and more batting, all made with a dizzying assortment of materials that fall into two categories—unnatural (petrochemical foams and fibers) and natural (animal hair and plant fuzz).

Elaborate layering is the current farce of the mattress trade. Isn't a tall, expensive sandwich of ingredients better than a short, cheap one? "You deserve to reward yourself with the experience of true luxury," say the advertisers of everything from spa showers to wide-screen TVs. Combine shopping delirium with a fervent desire for sound sleep and you get an excellent mind-set for buying an absurdly expensive mattress.

In a way, the stacking of every material ever invented into these mattresses is a response to customers', and manufacturers', confusion. The ad hoc stacking solution means that you don't have to choose: You just pay for the confidence of covering all bases.

Certainly, the super-sizing of food and home has coincided with the over-sizing of mattresses. The more people eat, the larger they grow, and the more accommodating a many-layered bed may seem. Bigger suburban houses with baronial master suites demand more imposing beds; the deeper the better. And since there's got to be something inside the volume, it might as well be lots of layers.

These days there are two kinds of layering: vertical and horizontal. Vertical layering bulks up the mattress evenly from head to toe; it typically involves a soft "mattress topper," a semisoft "mattress surround," and a firm core material wrapped in still more padding. (Each of these sections may contain multiple layers of its own.) Horizontal layering gives each sleep partner his/her own mattress density, or gives each sleeper a variety of densities along the length of the body: firm under the torso, softer under the head and feet.

These layers turn up in various guises. They're in the bouncy all-American quilted mattress and box spring sets we grew up with and trust. Similarly manufactured by the

"Blessings on him that first invented sleep . . . meat for the hungry, drink for the thirsty."

—MIGUEL DE CERVANTES, *Don Quixote*

Big S's (Sealy, Serta, and Simmons, and suppliers they share), the sets are sold in department stores and mattress chains, under many brand names, in many tiers of quality.

The layers are in those specialty mattresses—the ones your friends won't stop talking about—intriguing new inventions advertised on TV, fussed over online and in the press, and often sold in dedicated stores. We think they might transform our lives if we had the guts, and the cash, to bring them home. And we're haunted by their enticing claims. Visco-elastic memory foam molded by the body's heat. Inflatable plastic

---

No metal springs. No heat-activated molding. No air chambers. No weird materials. No layering.

"number" beds with dual controls that let you choose your favorite firmness, nightly, for *your* side of the bed. Masterpieces of Swedish craftsmanship, expensively stuffed with fluffed black horsehair.

Beyond the land of layers and hype lies one simple product: the basic foam mattress. It has no metal springs, no heat-activated molding, no air chambers, no weird materials, no layering. Although it's wrapped in protective quilting, the cellular structure of the foam itself does all the work. No box spring required!

Some foams are petroleum based: standard polyurethane foam, memory foam, and all-synthetic latex foam. Some are hybrids: polyurethane foam, made with a percentage of corn-derived oil as a replacement for some of the petroleum, or foams that mix synthetic and natural latex.

And then there's the pure, all-botanical foam known as natural latex, tapped as latex milk from trees (*Hevea brasiliensis*) in hot places like Sri Lanka.

The substance is whipped into a frothy batter and poured into mattress-shaped aluminum molds to form perforated slabs, or "cores." The cores travel to mattress factories to be shaped into standard sizes, encased in textiles for comfort and hygiene, and branded with product names—but these are only technicalities. All the mechanics you really need are in the cellular composition of the latex core. No obsessive layering is necessary.

The mattress supports the whole body, evenly distributing weight so as to avoid those blood-vessel-squishing pressure points. Since latex, unlike memory foam, doesn't hold an impression, the sleeper can move smoothly from one position to another; latex also lacks memory foam's well-known retention of body heat. A hypoallergenic substance, natural latex is pleasantly lacking in irritants; it won't off-gas, grow mold or mildew, or harbor dust mites.

Latex mattresses can also travel longer and more gracefully than many other mattresses. Flexible and lightweight in comparison to mattress sets, they're easily moved from room to room or house to house, rolled up and stored, or even recut as upholstery foam. Merchants promise twenty to twenty-five years of use, but some owners report that their mattresses have stayed supple for thirty to fifty. After that, the foam gradually hardens. Beyond its life span, it's biodegradable.

The most pleasurable route to a natural latex mattress is a long visit to a natural latex mattress store: a showroom run by earnest entrepreneurs specializing in organic sleep products. Most of the mattresses are made by American companies that import the latex cores, then encase them in proprietary envelopes. The Big S's have started to catch on too, but their offerings tend to be stuffed with unnecessary gimmicks.

Bring a pillow and blanket. You will be invited to nap on several models, starting with the firmest and ending with the softest, each one identified by a standard ILD (indentation load deflection) number. In natural latex,

"Soft" starts at about 25, while 40 is "Extra Firm." Ask for the simplest model: a latex core, six inches deep, wrapped in a slight, protective layer of cotton. If they don't offer that, find your ideal ILD and purchase online from a wholesale latex distributor.

The natural latex mattress ends the agonizing search for the perfect mattress. It puts the owner to sleep secure in the knowledge that she has bought neither fetish nor lemon, and is neither overpaying nor underindulging. But most beautifully of all, she might never have to buy another damn mattress.

Bed

Keeping Mattress and Sleeper Aloft

The foam mattress needs nothing more than a flat surface to hold it up. In other words, it doesn't really need a bed, as such; it can work on anything from a floor to a platform to a "slatted bed." It's an independent entity, not a *system*, and that's something you need to know before searching for a mattress holder. You'll want to raise the mattress above the floor for the sake of convenience and hygiene, but you need not spend lots of money to enhance the life or comfort of the foam mattress with complicated contraptions.

The simplest bed surface is a platform bed, a continuous surface designed for a single mattress. A platform can be built into the wall or be freestanding. It can look streamlined, like a low table, or traditionally bed-like, complete with headboard.

Slatted beds, common in Europe, are versions of platform beds. The mattress-holding surface is not a continuous plane but a series of wood or plastic slats, slightly bowed to

> Since the foam mattress is an independent entity, it requires nothing more than a flat surface on which to perch.

add some resiliency to the mattress. Foam mattresses feel more inert, and less trampolinelike, than traditional mattress sets, and slats lend some additional flex for those who prefer it. More important, a slatted bed provides ventilation to keep the mattress bottom dry, which is especially useful in humid climates.

An excellent platform bed will be made of solid hardwood, using durable wood joinery—parts are connected by interlocking pieces of wood, rather than nailed or screwed together.

The more "show wood" (wood that's

still visible when the platform is covered by a mattress), the more expensive the bed. If a headboard is desired, a slight angle will provide comfort for reading in bed. Because the headboard should last as long as the rest of the frame, it should be all wood, not upholstery. While a tall headboard is impressive, it should really be as low as possible to reduce strain on the joinery where it meets the frame. Inspect the quality and construction of the joinery, slats, and show wood.

Before you shop, decide how high you would like the overall bed-plus-mattress to rise. If you desire a sleeping height of 20 inches, subtract the mattress thickness (say 8 inches) from the total desired height, and you have the height of your bed platform (12 inches in this case).

To find a platform bed whose personality you like, you must visit the bed in person, and roll around on it, preferably using your foam mattress of choice. (If the bed and your mattress are not in the same place, try to use a test mattress with the same firmness number as your own.)

A SHORT HISTORY OF BEDS

To better appreciate the minimal "modern bed," consider a brief history of its evolution, and that of its American cousin, the mysterious box spring.

The Egyptian pharaohs of 3500 B.C. were the first known people to sleep on dedicated pieces of elevated furniture. Before that time, beds were essentially portable—all-too-organic constructions of straw, leaves, fleece, or animal skins spread out on the hard ground. In Europe, raised beds weren't common until the sixteenth and seventeenth centuries; stationary but adjustable, their wooden frames held grids of ropes that could be tightened as needed.

A raised bed suspended sleepers over a cushion of air, which was far warmer than a cold, damp floor. It kept floor dust off the bed linens and discouraged pets and critters from nesting. Height also made it easier to change bed linens and climb in and out of bed.

The earliest modern mattresses were simple sacks of straw or down, and eventually of cotton and wool. But in 1871, industry spawned the innerspring mattress, a bouncy entity filled with a field of vertical steel coils; its companion, the box spring, was invented soon afterward.

The box spring literally *is* a box: a wood frame holding a series of heavy steel coils, upholstered with an outer layer of foam and fabric. Its purpose

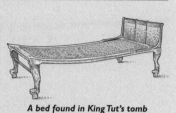

A bed found in King Tut's tomb

is simple: to ventilate the mattress and lift it to a convenient height. Manufacturers claim that it also prolongs the mattress's life by absorbing some of the sleepers' weight and movement, and they insist that each mattress be supported by its companion box spring and no other. If you buy a mattress without its box spring, its warranty is invalidated. (Read the fine print.)

As early as the 1920s, excellent latex foam mattresses were being produced as an alternative to factory-assembled steel coil mattress sets. But the latex mattresses were expensive, and confusion was rife. Low-quality foams gave all foam a bad reputation, while innerspring mechanics proved easier to explain, illustrate, and advertise. Steel sounded like a better, more progressive investment than a product made of whipped tree sap.

So we kept on filling our beds with those coils. The only change? The beds got wider and deeper, enhanced with thicker and thicker bedding (comforters, decorative pillows, and so on)—outsized monuments to comfort and grandeur. If only grandeur could guarantee a good night's sleep!

Pillow

The Real *Pea in the Princess's Mattress*

With sleep being such a huge part of life, you'd think evolution would have given humans head cushions by now. Or that humans would have invented something on their own. They did. The pillow. Only none of them seems to work. To begin with, legions of body experts, from orthopedic docs to ergonomic engineers, can't even agree on what a pillow is supposed to do. Should it cradle the neck? Support the head and the neck equally? Support the neck and/or head firmly in one position, or allow the sleeper to assume several positions while he tosses and turns? Furthermore, should the pillow heat the head, or cool it? Ventilate? Cure snoring? Prevent allergies? Save the earth?

Motion is the thorniest problem. Shy of using a video camera to document a night's worth of tossing, one can't know what one's favorite sleep patterns and positions really are, and no pillow provides ideal support for all poses. Someday sleep gear will probably be dispensed from a sleep lab, just like eyeglasses are prescribed by an optometrist. Experts will measure their clients' quirky sleep habits and fit them for customized mattresses, head supports, sleep climates, and sound environs.

But until that time, confusion reigns. Scientists study the dynamics of sleep, and manufacturers capitalize on the information they provide, flooding the marketplace with pillows promising to deliver new, improved states of unconsciousness.

Which pillow is the comfiest? Most ergonomic? The one that will deepen your sleep, color your dreams, and electrify your waking hours? Again, experts are unanimous in not really knowing. Not only do they disagree on the subject of pillow form and density, but they also differ on issues of pillow substance. Some are profoam and antifeathers, promoting firmness over fluff. Some are just the opposite.

If there's any consensus, it seems to be this: Only your body knows what it needs. Comfort (i.e., lack of pain) is the only real measure of a pillow's efficacy.

Sadly, finding your personal comfort zone isn't as simple as it sounds. You won't necessarily be able to tell how your pillow feels when you first bring it home: A change in sleeping posture, even for the better, may be painful for a time (a few days to a couple of weeks). And if it turns out

INSIDE A PILLOW

Contrary to popular belief, most pillow-related allergies are caused by dust, from both inside and outside the pillow, rather than by pillow materials. Unwashed pillowcases harbor exterior dust, and natural pillows may contain interior dust due to incomplete processing of feathers, fur, or vegetable matter. Add to that dry ingredient some human essence (100 liters of sweat per average sleeper per year, according to one British researcher), and the mix creates the perfect landscape for dust mites, culprits for 95 percent of human allergies. The upshot: If your pillow of choice isn't washable, double-encase it in a regular pillowcase over a sealed pillowcase, and air it out once a month.

For clarity's sake, here's a rundown of common pillow ingredients:

 Synthetic fills, each with proprietary names like *Dacron Hollofil II,* mimic the fluffiness of natural materials but offer better washability at lower prices; some synthetic fills are specially engineered for sensitive sleepers, but all are made with oil-derived chemicals—ingredients some prefer to sleep without.

 Feathers comprise a vast and confusing realm of varying quality, from the softest Hungarian down to flat, pointy goose feathers. If you're not already a feather expert, you'll need a tutorial. Buy down pillows directly from sellers of down products to understand what you're getting, and how to maintain it. A feather pillow can feel very luxurious, but it isn't the best choice for anyone with orthopedic issues, as it won't hold its shape through the night. Sensitive sleepers should seek out pillows with the cleanest down content, then seal their pillows in protective cases that keep dust out of the pillow core.

 Organic fills like cotton, wool, and silk are grown and processed without pesticides and bleaches. Buckwheat hulls, made of seed pod shells and used in Japanese pillows, fall under the organic category as well. Though they're somewhat unusual, hull-filled pillows are adjustable; you simply add or remove hulls to change their size. And as they're naturally ventilated and can be warmed in the oven, hulls are the ultimate temperature regulators.

not to be right, returnability is an issue—pillow manufacturers usually ban returns of opened merchandise. The determined pillow-seeker must get creative. One option is to buy a pillow, encase it in a pillowcase without removing the packaging, try it out, and return it if necessary. Or test the pillows of friends, relatives, and hotels.

B ut first, here's some pillow geography. The pillow marketplace is segmented into three parts. The first produces the traditional, pillow-shaped "comfort" pillow found in department and bedding stores. There's also an expanding world of alternative products labeled *organic, natural,* and *hypoallergenic,* where it's the materials that count. The last, most specialized category comes from the medical products trade, enticing older customers with terms like *ergonomic, therapeutic,* and *sports medicine.*

If you have time for a science project, try to sell yourself on a *cervical pillow* or *neck pillow.* You'll first need to accept the notion of a pillow as a personal therapeutic aid, as opposed to decorative accessory. It may take a few tries before you find the right fit.

The cervical area is the potentially stiff, achy zone between your skull and shoulders, comprising the first seven vertebrae at the top of the spine. Proponents of cervical pillows believe that the primary role of a pillow should be to support this natural, anatomical curve.

Standard cervical pillows come in myriad shapes, each of which promises to outperform the other in fitting the sleeper's particular neck length, neck curvature, shoulder width, and head size and weight. There are Tootsie-Roll shaped "neck rolls," butterfly shapes, and wedges pleated into "waffle bubbles" to circulate air. The shapes are made of plain polyurethane foam, visco-elastic polyurethane foam (aka "memory" foam), latex foam, polyester fiber, vegetable hulls, cotton, wool, or even water encased in various plastics. They're generally a lot harder than traditional pillows. (In a strange cultural reversal, Americans are warming up to solid pillows while Chinese sleepers are switching to fluffy Western products after centuries of using famously hard box pillows.)

If you cannot warm up to a neck pillow because of a lifelong attachment to "real" pillows, you can still be a discerning shopper.

The search starts with size. Ditch the notion of symmetry. If you buy king-size pillows just to fit your king-size bed, you're paying for lots of filling without ensuring a good fit for your body. And though matching his-and-hers pillows may look nicer on the bed, they won't do anything for your individual gripes.

Consider density. Some pillows are made with multiple materials to create dense, neck-supporting centers under fluffy, cheek-caressing envelopes. Comfort pillows may all start out looking about the same, but they can be squished and fluffed into different shapes, depending on the density and texture of their filling (unlike cervical pillows, which retain their shapes). Synthetic materials tend to retain their shape better than natural fillings.

For all pillows, comfort or cervical, a few criteria apply. First of all, ignore the issue of so-called sleeping style: side, back, or front. For want of a better formula, salespeople will try to match your "favorite sleep posture" to the right density. But since the average person tosses through dozens of unknown sleeping positions throughout the night, it's a ludicrous proposition.

Climate, though, does matter. Figure out whether you are a hot or cold sleeper—do you prefer a hot or cold room? Hot heads and tropical climates fare best with ventilated materials that don't retain heat. Ease of care matters too. How easily and safely can the pillow, or its protective envelope, be laundered? Some pillows are designed for frequent washing; some are not washable at all.

All in all, you're probably much more opinionated on the subject than you'd like to believe. Anyone suffering from specific allergies, allergy paranoia, or plain old phobias (feathers, rubber, or off-gassing foams) will be able to speed up the process by immediately eliminating some materials (see box, page 17).

Finally, you must figure out how much time you're willing to buy. An expensive pillow that washes well may thrive for ten years or more; a cheap pillow may last for one uneasy year. Although a high price guarantees neither comfort nor longevity, a very low price tends to buy too little of each.

If the idea of pillow shopping is too much to bear, just take this advice: Go to your local purveyor of natural bedding and grab a nice, perky pillow filled with shredded natural latex. Unappetizing as it sounds, it's the best of both pillow worlds—comfort

> "A ruffled mind makes a restless pillow."
> — CHARLOTTE BRONTË

and cervical—at a reasonable price. This pillow will conform to your sleep positions without getting squished, and it never needs to be fluffed up or otherwise reanimated. It's also reassuring to know that the usual household scourges—mold, mildew, and dust mites—leave latex unscathed. You don't need to wash the whole pillow; just launder its protective cotton case and occasionally air out the latex core in bright sunshine.

And remember that the only guarantee for a good sleep may be the absence of worry. After all, a pillow can only put you to sleep once you've turned off your brain.

THE SCIENCE OF BED-MAKING

While mattresses and platforms provide a structure, bed fabrics create a contained climate: eight hours of fluctuating temperature and humidity under the sheets (and blanket and bedspread) and over the mattress pad. Like the science of sleep, the technology of sleep textiles remains somewhat of a mystery. It's all about microscopic fiber behavior. While we've learned a lot about clothing—how to layer hi-tech sports duds, and how to choose low-maintenance wardrobes—we're pretty clueless in the bedding department. Luxury has been the operative marketing lure, not function.

It's too bad, as the right textiles can not only improve our sleep, but can also do global good by supporting green agriculture, cutting down on power and water used in washing and drying, and keeping us comfortable with less heating and air-conditioning. It's simple: Use the leanest and lightest amount of easily washable textiles, and use the largest possible amount of sunshine and fresh air to dry and freshen them. (Clothesline advocates claim that clothes dryers use 6 percent of the total power consumed by American households; they're also proven to shorten the lives of all fabrics.)

Mattress Pad

The Bed's Foundational Garment

When you buy a pair of jeans, the subject of underwear never comes up. The salesperson doesn't say, "Remember that underpants will protect your skin from the rough texture of the denim as they absorb stains and perspiration, allowing you to launder these jeans less frequently." Underpants are to fashion what mattress pads are to bedroom linens.

Both are traditionally white, fitted, stretchy, designed for protection and comfort, never sold as a package deal with the textiles they protect, and seldom discussed. But while most adults have exacting specs for their knickers, many have no idea what a mattress pad is supposed to do, let alone how to buy one.

After the exhausting chore of choosing a new, wildly expensive mattress, springing for a mattress pad feels as extraneous as buying the after-market "underbody rust protection" on a new car. Some young mattress buyers end up "going commando"—putting sheets on bare mattresses. No good.

A mattress pad has a very specific, if icky, function. It's the layer that keeps the mattress from getting soaked by accidental spills and by the oozing of various bodily fluids; it also keeps sheets from sliding off the smooth mattress surface. (If mattress surfaces were waterproof plastic or rubber, they could be easily sponge washed, but they need to be porous enough to allow air circulation and discourage mold—hence the need for protection.)

A mattress pad should be designed for easy washing. If the pad is too fluffy to fit in the washer, or so dense that it hogs the dryer, then its utility is null. If a so-called mattress pad is too bulky for home laundering, it's really a "mattress topper," the newest cushy layer to complicate the bedding scene.

The topper started out as a "featherbed" or "pillow-top," a sort of poofy down quilt designed to be slept on, not under, for warmth and snuggliness.

Marketed at first as a luxurious indulgence, toppers became so popular that retailers began to offer them in every conceivable material: lamb's wool, sheep's wool, alpaca wool, wool fleece, organic wool, cotton, organic cotton, real down, fake down, silk, polyester fill, latex foam, and memory foam, in addition to "super-luxurious" or "all-organic" combinations of many layers.

What caused this bed-topping phenomenon? The topper satisfies

> "The bed is a place of luxury to me! I would not exchange it for all the thrones in the world."
>
> —NAPOLEON BONAPARTE

two markets, high and low. People who pay vast sums for mattresses often suffer from buyer's remorse. For those unhappy folk, the topper adds the missing adjective they seek: supple, supportive, responsive. People stuck with nonluxury mattresses use toppers for the same reason. In other words, the topper diverts blame from the mattress and makes the comfort issue seem controllable. After all, you can always replace a topper.

The problem with the mattress topper is that it acts like a mattress pad—absorbing sweat and other stains—without the benefit of easy washing. The result? It's often left unwashed. And that's the dirty secret of American bedrooms: the unwashability of it all. Much as we obsess about antibacterial, hypoallergenic, dust-mite fighting, organic products, we're piling our beds with stuff that never gets washed because it's just too damned luxurious. Too big to wrestle on and off the beds, too big for our big machines, and too big to lug to the dry cleaner's on any semi-regular basis.

What do you really need? A mattress pad that washes well. The idea is to buy the least amount of bulk with just enough top quilting and just enough elastic to do the job. If the bed is the family rec room, where piles of toddlers or teenagers eat, sleep, and hang out, the pad should be heavy duty. The pad of a lone Arctic scientist may be flimsier.

Unless you have laundresses on staff, avoid thick pads that quilt not only the top of the mattress, but also its four side walls. Avoid the skimpiest models, flat pads with elastic "anchor straps" for holding the mattress corners. A good pad is fitted, with lightweight quilting on top, snugly held in place by elastic panels that grip the mattress around all sides. (Measure your mattress depth before you buy the pad, and don't buy more than you need.)

For breathability, the top of the pad should be cotton, but the fill will be polyester, and the stretchy sides synthetic. It needn't be top-of-the-line, as the stretchy part will eventually lose its elasticity.

Sheets

Old-World Is New Again

S heets were once thought of as practical, hygienic dry goods and sold in a bleachable, sanitary white. At some point in the 1960s and '70s, manufacturers began pushing seasonal collections of colorful bedding "fashions" designed to be bought, retired, and replaced with the latest styles as fast as possible.

Sheets, once utilitarian and uncomplicated, have been upgraded into household fetishes. We not only want fancy sheets, we want lots of them. Household experts tell us to buy at least three sets per bedroom: one set for the bed, one set for the closet, and one set for the laundry.

We're particularly susceptible to persuasion in this area; we wear sheets next to our skin, and beds represent all of our most fervent wishes for relaxation and escape. So we go ahead and make choices based on indicators of luxury that we don't really understand. Does anyone know the difference between Egyptian cotton and pima cotton? Between pima and Supima? Does buying organic actually help? Compared to other crops, cotton requires a huge amount of irrigation. What about alternative fibers like bamboo, beech wood, soy fiber, or corn fiber?

The fact is that natural textiles are complex goods, closer to agricultural products than to hardware—more like tomatoes than cell phones. In that way, they're not easy to label. Two tomatoes may belong to the same family, but their taste and texture depend on the soil, the weather, and other conditions of their cultivation. And the only way to prove a tomato's true worth is by taking a bite.

Similarly, sheets can be judged only by the person who rolls around in them after a few launderings. Thread count, fiber name, and weave don't predict performance as accurately as we've been led to believe. Fiber quality differs from plant to plant; fiber processing and the weaving of threads vary from one factory to another.

The solution? Linen sheets. Your purchase will be vindicated in a few years, when the rest of the world catches on to the wisdom of growing, eating, building with, and sleeping on flax, the most ancient of natural fibers. It's way overdue for a comeback.

Some linens are rough. Others are crisp and refined. Others still are

> Beds represent all of our most fervent wishes for relaxation and escape . . .

remarkably soft and supple. All weaves soften and improve with age. The differences are easy to see and to feel, and there are no confusing trade names or thread counts to worry about. Linen is also the best textile for handling the serious demands of workaday bedding, which are not so pretty.

The true purpose of sheets is to protect sleepers from scratchy outerwear (blankets and bedcovers), and outerwear from odoriferous sleepers shedding skin cells and exuding various bio-fluids. To that end, sheets should be highly washable and absorbent; linen is the natural choice. Compared to cotton and other natural fibers, flax has a long staple (fiber length) that can be twisted into more durable yarns (threads)—which means it's longer-lasting and can take a beating in the washer/dryer. Its cellular structure also allows it to soak up many times its weight in water and release that water very quickly—key for temperature regulation.

Millions of American sleepers are being smothered in heavy, clingy, densely woven cotton sheets bought under the false assumption that a high thread count equals luxury; some of those heavy sheets are coated with chemicals to create a slick, wrinkle-resistant sheen, further impeding their breathability.

In winter or summer, sleepers perspire according to what they've been eating or dreaming about, or how they are sleeping with whomever. Menopausal women experience sleepless sweat-and-freeze cycles that have them wrestling the sheets off and on. To their rescue comes the lightweight, nonstick texture of linen—surrounding the body without constricting it, so air can circulate between sheets and skin and rapidly wick away moisture.

Cotton sheets may sound thriftier, but they come with hidden costs: On

Millions of American sleepers are being smothered in clingy, densely woven cotton sheets.

warm summer and autumn days, sleepers must resort to air-conditioning, adding a massive electrical load to the price of their luxury sheets. A couple weeks of AC-free nights may not seem like a great fuel savings until it's multiplied by a few million households. Add to that the simpler maintenance and longer life span of linen sheets, along with the sustainable performance of flax fiber crops, and the environmental merits become even clearer.

Linen is one textile that loves extremes of washing and drying.

Cotton, on the other hand, starts breaking down when tumbled wet, or overheated in the dryer. That's why all manufacturers recommend that their cotton sheets be removed from the machine when damp and air-dried to avoid permanent fiber damage. No matter what their pedigree, cotton sheets may begin to show wear—pilling, thinning, or tearing—after a couple years of heavy laundering.

In contrast, linen is famous for lasting forever (think of those Egyptian mummies) and thrives on long, hot wash cycles and lots of dryer tumbling. Its moisture-wicking cellular structure makes for fast drying; it's stronger when wet; and its texture is actually improved by abrasion.

An added bonus: Lightweight and nonbulky, linen sheets help streamline that most arduous housekeeping ritual, the weekly bed stripping, sheet laundering, and remaking of beds.

They may also make life a bit easier for allergic sleepers. It's unpleasant, but true: The second most common allergen is the detritus (shed skin and feces) of microscopic dust mites, those bugs that like warm, humid places littered with human ex-epidermis. To create a hostile environment, doctors recommend washing sheets often, preferably in the kind of very hot water that ages cotton. Linen is also lint free, another plus for the allergy prone.

Now comes the hard part. Linen isn't cheap. Fiber flax takes lengthy harvesting, and only the highest quality crops can be used in the special spinning and weaving machines used to turn it into linen.

The longevity of linen certainly amortizes its price. Sadly, that long-term commitment may be uncomfortable for consumers accustomed to freshening their homes with seasonal dry goods. Since we expect to buy things, use them up, toss them, and buy anew with lively momentum, the idea that our sheets will mellow with age, outlive us, and become family heirlooms seems a bit spooky. But it's time we get over our costly, wasteful prejudice against good things that last.

The more we put flax fiber to use, the less expensive it will become. And prices are already coming down. Over the last couple of years, a growing number of bedding merchants have begun to offer linens far less costly and more rustic and rumpled than those flawless things made by Pratesi and Frette, Italian purveyors of sheets that look best ironed by servants. The more affordable linens are still expensive, but not unreasonable if you limit your sheet shopping. (Ignore the recommended ratio of three sets per bed; try one or two. Use linen all year, and eliminate thick flannels and jerseys.) Although buying sheets online is not the best idea, some Web merchants will send sample swatches at no charge, and some will allow you to return sheets even after they've been washed.

There's one more, local advantage to linen. Although fiber flax became extinct as an American crop once cotton and cotton-processing machines took over, it's making a promising comeback. U.S. agriculturalists have watched European industries using flax, jute, and hemp fibers to replace the wood fillers and glass reinforcement of composite plastics like those used in the interior door panels in Mercedes automobiles. Because they believe fiber flax will yield bio-based products yet to be invented, the Feds are investing in pilot programs that could turn flax into a brand-new (old) crop for American farmers. Their plan is elegant: Plant flax as a winter crop on fallow cotton fields. Grow rural economy and global competitiveness on the same soil.

No wonder the ancient Romans called flax *Linum usitatissimum,* or "maximum usefulness"—a criterion that should be applied to every object you bring into your home.

Electric Blanket

Wired for Comfort

This is a plug for the electric blanket. No, not the creepy old thing filled with bulging wires, tainted by associations with bedroom fires and other sleep-marring events—a new electric blanket (let's call it the NEB), deserving of a good defense even if it *is* thin and synthetic.

The flimsy old-fashioned version snaked regular household voltage through its thick wires. It was lumpy, ugly, and potentially dangerous. In contrast, a low-voltage NEB uses a small transformer to convert heavy AC household current, at 120 volts, into a perfectly safe DC current of 25 volts. The blanket is also more energy efficient, plenty warm at a low setting that pulls about as much power as a single lightbulb.

> On icy nights, turn down the thermostat, switch on the blanket, and climb into a lovely warm bed.

The NEB's thin internal wires are virtually undetectable. Some models are made of the durable microfleece polyester used in fleece jackets, remarkably warm for its weight. Microfleece doesn't collect dust, and it's easy to wash. (Even the widest fleece blankets fit into household machines.)

Geeky as the NEB may sound, it has a certain sensual prowess. On icy nights, you can turn the house thermostat way down, switch on the NEB, wait a few minutes, and climb into a welcoming bed. The sheets will be uniformly warmed; you no longer need to stay curled up in tiny comfort zones maintained by body heat and flannel pajamas. In fact, you can dispense with sleepwear altogether. Freed from bunchy fabric and fear of cold spots, you can stretch out into wider, longer sleep postures. The winter bed begins to feel luxuriously larger, and much more interesting, as you and your sleep partner bare yourselves to each other.

For further harmony between sleep partners, the NEB eliminates the usual blanket warfare. The queen- and king-size blankets are wired into two sections, each with its own computerized temperature control dial. (Both sides shut themselves off automatically after ten hours.)

An NEB also lets you easily adjust to in-between seasons or unseasonably cold or warm fronts. Pull the plug and it feels like the thinnest and lightest of summer blankets; turned to its highest setting, it works like the thickest of winter comforters.

Though an electric blanket may sound like yet another fuel-guzzling extravagance, it's actually quite green, enabling users to save fuel costs at night by keeping the bed warm and the house cold—creating a small microclimate (the bed) rather than warming and cooling a large, empty space (a whole house). The benefits aren't just planetary: Each degree of lowered thermostat saves 1 to 2 percent on heating bills, and a colder bedroom is also better for the nasal passages.

Zoned heating and heated furniture are old ideas. During the Renaissance, the gentry slept on raised beds over pans of embers, insulated by bed draperies. In traditional Japanese houses, diners sat on insulated grass mats and covered their laps with quilts containing the heat of sunken, undertable stoves.

In those days, the prospect of heating an entire room to a comfortable seventy degrees would have seemed unimaginably wanton as well as technically challenging.

Soon NEBs may become still more responsive, able to automatically adjust to the temperature and humidity of both sleeper and bedroom. (Same goes for the mattress, mattress pad, sheets, and pillows.) An NEB might generate its own power through photo-voltaic cells mounted on the windowsill. Or it might be powered by the heat and current of the body itself. NASA already knows how to make this happen in space suits. If we can hand crank enough energy to turn on a flashlight, surely one day we'll be able to harness our body heat to power our homes.

~~~~~~~~~~~~~~

DOWN IS DOWN, THIN IS IN

With the inevitable rise of the power blanket will come the fall of the fluffy down comforter—the favored "blanket" of the last twenty years. Down-filled quilts originated in the rural, goose-filled communities of Europe; heat was costly, feathers were cheap, and families routinely aired their quilts out in the fresh air. In contrast, they gained popularity in North America in part for their mystique and considerable expense. They stood for old-school luxury. Buyers grasped the

(continued on next page)

(continued from previous page)

principle: Down feathers created a lightweight, insulating cushion of air. But they didn't always understand why two identical-looking comforters could be priced so differently—from $100 to $1,000.

The answer has to do with market forces. As demand outpaced supply, the price of premium Hungarian and Siberian goose down skyrocketed. Blends of down and quilled feathers from geese and ducks began to replace pure down. Few buyers had the patience to learn the difference. The end result? Comforters that *looked* like the real thing but failed to perform.

The costliest models pack the best-quality European down with the greatest "fill power" (density) into the best-engineered "baffles" (the interior chambers that keep feathers from clumping). In this tricky realm, however, the costliest models are not necessarily the best. Most are just too hot.

The subject of washing is another source of comforter confusion, and one that must be discussed sotto voce on the selling floor. Comforter manufacturers recommend dry cleaning as the only warrantable method. But most consumers don't want to lug the thing to the dry cleaner's or inhale chemicals through the night, and so choose machine washing instead. Salespeople cannot officially endorse washing, because it voids the warranty and may damage the comforter. Off the record, however, they'll recommend machine washing comforters and drying them in commercial dryers for a couple of hours. Ill-dried comforters become bumpy and mildewy, they warn. (But the cotton fibers of the comforter cover break down when overheated.) "The truth is, most people don't wash their comforters at all," one saleswoman confided.

The complete truth is that consumers tend to buy comforters of barely understood quality or construction; try to squeeze the things into their home washers and dryers; fail, and go out and buy duvets to cover the comforters and avoid washing them; and realize they cannot wrestle the washed duvets back on the comforters.

Over the past few years, a post-down generation of voluptuous comforters with natural fills—wool, cashmere, silk, and even wood pulp (Lyocell)—has entered the market. All are very interesting; none of them is low-maintenance.

Let's face it. Big fat comforters are best left in the mountains of Switzerland, where they can spend every morning basking on chalet balconies, purified by the sunny Alpine cold. Back at home, there's nothing like a dependable, all-season blanket made of recognizable stuff you can buy at a reasonable price and actually wash in your own washing machine.

Bedspread

Streamlined Can Be Cozy

With an electric blanket providing all the warmth, a bedspread need do nothing more than decorate. Unfortunately, true bedspreads are rare in the current world of bed fashions. You may have to define them to salespeople. Try this: A bedspread is not a duvet, quilt, sham, or throw; it's a bed covering made of a single layer of fabric with no insulation at all.

The largest dust-attracting surface in the house (other than floors), the bed functions as a playground for kids and pets and a staging area for clothing, books, and homework. Translation: frequent cleaning is essential. Comforters are undustable, unvacuumable, and daunting to wash or dry in household machines. In sharp contrast, the thin bedspread is easy to launder with minimal water or heat.

The trick is to find a lightweight textile that performs like high-performance sportswear: wrinkle-resistant and quick drying. Tuck it tightly under the mattress military style, or cover the whole bed by letting it drape to the floor.

It should feel soft and look handsome. Ideally, it will be made of artificial fibers (polyester, rayon, nylon, etc.) skillfully woven to feel like cotton or raw silk and to withstand lots of laundering. The perfect textile could also be a blend of natural and synthetic fibers that feels soft but works hard.

Right now, the most common bedspread is the same funky expanse of Indian cotton that once covered all the waterbeds of the early 1970s.

> The trick is to find a lightweight textile that performs like high-performance sportswear: wrinkle-resistant and quick drying.

Time for a new approach. Consider a custom-made bedspread. Find an excellent, noncotton fabric first, then figure out how to make it work. "Contract" textiles, designed for commercial interiors, are engineered with amazing fiber blends and outstanding artistry. They're pricey and must be bought through a decorator, though with a little detective work they can be found online, as mill ends, or through city discounters.

Within that realm, try a washable upholstery fabric—it's extra-wide at fifty-five inches and up—and have your local seamstress/tailor hem it to fit your total bed height (mattress plus bed furniture).

Rug

For a Softer, Quieter Living Space

Fuzzy floors . . . On the one hand, they're cozy and insulating; on the other, they're unhealthy (see box, opposite, if you need convincing). The solution, thousands of years old, is the area rug: a free-floating floor textile that's bigger than a bath mat but smaller than a wall-to-wall carpet. Depending on its construction, an area rug can be vacuumed, hand washed at home, whisked off to a specialist, or refreshed outside, where air and a bit of sun kill off dreaded spores, mites, and other living things.

What kind of area rug is best? There's no doubt that the material should be wool, unmatchable in the way it holds onto dyes and reflects light. Although wool yarns vary in texture, they tend to be soft without being slippery. Wool sheds dirt easily and resists stains.

Best of all, in the care of loving owners, a well-woven wool rug can last a couple hundred years, gaining value as it ages gracefully. (The oldest extant rug—a Siberian Pazyryk—was woven around 300 B.C.) Other natural materials—cotton, silk, sisal, jute—start out strong but don't hold up under traffic. Though wool does have its enemies, including the dreaded moth, bugs won't inhabit a rug while it's unfurled on the floor.

Choosing a particular weave of wool gets more complicated. The quality of the weave depends on the wool and its processing: the dyes, vegetable or chemical; the warp and weft materials; the weaving or yarn-knotting technique; the complexity and appeal of the design; the skill and reputation of the weavers and their working conditions; and the rug's age and country of origin. The higher the price, the more you should know about its justification—but unless you want to be pulled into a complex (if fascinating) dialogue on politics, religion, aesthetics, and animal husbandry, just look for the following at a price you can afford: a flat, reversible wool rectangle handwoven by bona fide adults and sold by a reputable merchant.

These days, courtesy of our vast global economy, there's an amazing supply of solid and beautiful rugs (mainly from India, Nepal, Pakistan, Turkey, China, and Mexico) available

THE PROBLEM WITH WALL-TO-WALL CARPETING

Wall-to-wall carpeting is hard to clean. In fact, it can't be cleaned thoroughly, as it can never truly be aired out. It starts losing value the moment it's installed. And it ends up as landfill, never as heirloom. Still, it was exciting at the beginning. For American homeowners from the 1950s to the 1980s, broadloom carpeting was the only modern, responsible choice of floor cushioning. It insulated the floor, offered the safest play surface for kids, and created resale value along with cachet.

For builders, broadloom was just expeditious. A "finished floor" required skilled labor and costly materials like hardwood, ceramics, or stone; extra-wide rolls of machine-loomed carpeting were designed to be custom-cut on site and semipermanently attached to an unfinished floor with staples or glue. Easy and quick.

What broadloom lacked was long-term value. While a good finished floor might last a hundred years, gaining charm as it matured, bad broadloom began aging fast, looking tired in five years, shabby in ten. The inevitable task of replacing it also entailed the hidden costs of moving furniture, junking old carpet, and installing new nailing strips and padding. Reselling a house posed a special problem. Owners had to choose between leaving an unsavory carpet as is or remodeling with new carpeting that the next owners might loathe.

Over the last twenty years, wall-to-wall lost its appeal. Hardwood floors became fashionable as historic preservation encouraged home-owners to restore the authentic, irreplaceable woods of old houses. Broadloom makers defend their product with the claim that bare floors let dust fly, while carpets hold it tight until vacuumed away. But as asthmatic Americans search for the sources of evil allergens, broadloom is looking nastier all the time.

through a range of sellers from small importers to big boxes. (Target, for example, has commissioned a slew of affordable handmade rugs in reversible flat-woven wool.)

In some instances, benevolent groups—from home governments to foundations to virtuous entrepreneurs—have intervened to sustain old craft traditions while improving weavers' working conditions. A RugMark foundation label, for example, certifies that a rug was made without child labor. (The absence of such a label, however, doesn't necessarily mean child labor was involved.)

Why not just circumvent the labor issues and go for a machine-made rug? It will often look just as good, for less money. There are a few ways to answer. Good rugs made by hand maintain or increase in value while machine-made rugs start depreciating immediately, just like new cars leaving the plant. Under the best conditions, rug making is a skilled livelihood in areas of the world where steady labor is in short supply. And the rug buyer gets the chance to own something made with qualities disappearing in our fast-paced world: patience and skill.

~~~~~~~~~~~~~~~

SLEEPING

T HE SEARCH FOR A GREAT MATTRESS may involve shamelessly rolling around in public, repeatedly. Try to get as close to the manufacturer as
possible: natural bedding stores producing their own brands of mattresses and
pillows. Natural linen sheets can be hard to track down, but that's changing as
new sources of quality linen emerge every few months. Seek out importers and
small companies online, and request swatches. Finding the remaining bedroom
gear should be straightforward; solid wood furniture and inexpensive lighting
are widely available.

ALARM CLOCK

• Small alarm clock with large glowing
numerals and a pleasant, gradual alarm tone
• Find it: Big-box or electronics stores

Cost: About $10

• Three-way table lamp rated for 50/100/150
watt standard incandescent bulbs
• Three-way CFL rated for 12/19/28 watts
• Find it: Lighting supply or big-box stores

Cost: Lamp, under $50;
CFL, under $10

• Lamp timer with an override switch
• Find it: Lighting supply or hardware stores

Cost: Under $10

Note: *The three components listed here*
(alarm clock, wake-up lamp, and lamp
timer) are temporary measures to be used
until gradual, light-based waking devices
are improved.

BEDSIDE LAMP

• Small halogen task lamp with moveable arm
and weighted base
• Find it: Lighting supply and big-box stores

Cost: Less than $50

FLOOR LAMP

• Three-way floor lamp (adjustable
to three levels of brightness) suitable
for screw-in CFL
• Heavy base; light-colored translucent shade
• Find it: Lighting supply and big-box stores

Cost: Lamp, under $200;
CFL, under $10

FLASHLIGHT

· Lightweight LED headlamp
· Try: Headlamps by Petzl, Princeton Tec, or other outdoor manufacturers
· Find it: Outdoor outfitters like REI

Cost: Less than $20

NIGHTSTAND

· Solid hardwood, with a durable water-resistant finish and at least one drawer
· Shopping tip: Measure the height of your bed/mattress combination and purchase a nightstand at a corresponding height. Purchase one per sleeper.
· Find it: Local manufacturers or artisans making solid wood furniture; dealers of used or antique furniture; home design stores

Cost: $100 and up

MATTRESS

· 100 percent natural latex
· 6" thick, with an ILD number between 28 and 39
· Eco-rating: Long life (twenty years plus); renewable and sustainable resource; biodegradable
· Shopping tip: Roll around on mattresses of different densities; the right one should hold up your body evenly—no sagging at the pelvis
· Find it: Stores specializing in natural latex mattresses, online from wholesale latex distributors

*Cost: $500 and up for
a queen-size mattress*

BED

· Hardwood with solid wood joinery; top can be slatted or continuous. (Steel, aluminum, or plastic can work as well; just stay away from particleboard.)
· With a hardwood bed, save on costs by cutting down on the amount of "display wood"; try a simple platform bed.
· Shopping tip: How high do you want your bed/mattress combination to rise? Subtract the depth of your mattress from your desired bed height to find out what to buy.
· Find it: Natural bedding stores and home design stores

Cost: $300 and up

PILLOW

· Pillow filled with shredded natural latex in a size to suit your body, not your bed width. Or, try a cervical pillow.
· Cotton cover
· Eco-rating: Long life (twenty years plus); renewable and sustainable resource; biodegradable
· Find it: Natural or specialty bedding stores

Cost: $50 to $60

MATTRESS PAD

· Streamlined, with a quilted, all-cotton top and polyester fill. (Elastic sides should not be quilted.)
· Find it: Department stores, bedding stores, and big-box stores

Cost: $40 to $80

SHEETS

· 100 percent linen
· Eco-rating: Linen comes from flax, a sustainable fiber source; it's lightweight and compact in the wash and line or machine dries quickly, saving on energy; it's also long-lasting and durable. A little-known fact: Using linen sheets in the summer can actually help you save on air-conditioning costs.
· Shopping tip: Fiber quality varies with price. Texture, on the other hand, varies from rough to fine but doesn't determine quality.
· Find it: Natural bedding stores; online (ask for sample swatches)

Cost: $200 and up for a queen-size set

ELECTRIC BLANKET

· Low-voltage electric blanket (polyester microfleece)
· Try: Chattam & Wells brand blanket
· Eco-note: Using an electric blanket will reduce your energy use on cold nights. And since you'll be plenty warm, there's no need for those washer-and-dryer-hogging flannel sheets.
· Find it: Department stores and bedding stores. Or call Perfect Fit, the manufacturer of the Chattam & Wells blanket, for local retailers (800-299-1378).

Cost: About $150 (queen size), which includes a five-year manufacturer's warranty

BEDSPREAD

· Machine-washable, attractive, lightweight fabric—store-bought or custom sewn—in a mix of natural and synthetic fibers
· Find it: Buy an excellent fabric at a local fabric retailer, or order it online after receiving sample swatches; have a tailor or seamstress cut and hem it as a bedspread.

Cost: About $50 and up, depending on the cost of fabric and labor

RUG

· Wool, handmade, flat woven; try a kilim.
· Find it: Design, department, or retail stores; buy it new or used directly from a rug importer.
· Shopping tip: Always buy a rug in person; if the seller allows returns, try it out in your home. (Rugs reflect available light and colors.)

Cost: $200 and up for a 5' x 7' rug

CHAPTER TWO

BATHING

&

DRESSING

INVENTORY

- Bath Towel
- Bath Mat
- Hand Towel

- Trash Can
- Mirror
- Dresser
- Clothes Hangers

- Iron
- Ironing Board
- Clothes Hamper

I t's a jungle in there (the bathroom, that is). Humidity levels are high after a steaming bath or shower, and they stay that way long after the fact.

The ideal American bathroom is filled with plush cotton textiles that drink in moisture and hold on to it tightly—superabsorbent bath *sheets* (as if towels weren't sufficient), voluminous terry bathrobes, and thick

bath mats. They feel luxurious, and luxury is the driving inspiration behind all bath products. We never calculate its true costs.

In a house without upstairs maid service, the underbelly of luxury is housework. The big textiles act as humidifiers, keeping the air comfortable for fungal life-forms. TV ads tell us you can fend off the invaders with a spray of this or that product, but all the techniques require plenty of elbow grease. Meanwhile, those luxury textiles need hauling to the laundry room for long sessions of washing, drying, and folding.

The same luxury-affliction has beset our dressing habits. The search for extra closet space is endless. How many home buyers beseech their realtors for additional square footage and buy bigger houses, only to fill up their storage spaces and hire professional closet organizers to colonize their garages with new "systems" of interlocking cubbies?

No amount of spending will solve the American crisis of shrinking closet space. And that's good news. To combat frustration, all we need is a new mindset: If we choose our clothing as carefully as we select our household items, we'll have a more functional collection of loveable things we can actually find.

How do Parisians manage to look so magnificent, living out of those skinny armoires? First of all, they don't warehouse the needless and useless. They also prefer to stay lean (in one dress size), and wear a few well-made, form-fitting pieces of clothing in excellent fabrics, maintaining them loyally for a very long time and amortizing the cost with each outing.

In our culture, we shop for fun, not for posterity or practicality. We shop because we're bored, elated, nervous, or angry, and we crave the thrill of the purchase, however fleeting.

Over the past decade, the lure of shopping has been boosted by the impossibly low prices of Chinese and Indian goods. With more variety available at a faster pace and lower cost, we've begun to use clothes in new ways: camouflage, for example. Because overeating, another fun pastime, has made us bigger than we want to be, we buy disposable clothes to hide our bodies until we slim down. Eventually we acquire three sizes of everything—for before, during, and after dieting.

Partly because of this, we expect the closet to hold too many categories of stuff. The clothes we wear occupy but a fraction of its cubic space. It's mainly a warehouse for wearable, off-season clothes; unwearable clothes in need of laundering, dry cleaning, mending, or tailoring; and unusable keepsakes or reckless purchases too precious to jettison.

Forget about enlarging your closet. Shrink your wardrobe. Keep your weight steady, for your health, for your wallet, and for your closet. And set up a simple, good dressing space. (Read on to find out how.) But the best thing you can do for your closet is that hardest thing of all. Stop all the shopping!

Bath Towel

Dry Yourself Faster — with Less

Enough with the fluffy bath towel fetish. Why work so hard taking care of the thing for just a few moments of dermal caress? Along with many of the items in the fantasy home catalog, over the years the ideal bath towel has expanded in size and thickness. Now a 35-inch by 66-inch bath "sheet," it's an absurdly heavy, double-sided carpet woven with the tallest and densest possible nap of loops.

The craze can be traced to the 1980s, era of excess and inflated shoulder pads. Travelers began to covet (and occasionally steal) the impossibly vast towels delivered fresh each day from the hotels' mighty industrial laundry machines. Soon, these luxurious "hotel towels" would hit the mass market.

> The craze can be traced to the 1980s, era of excess and shoulder pads.

There were unforeseen issues, however. The big towels were too big. Manufacturers of large appliances redesigned washers and dryers to handle the unprecedented volume, weight, and tumbling torque. Hampers and closets expanded. Bathroom hardware got meatier. And most significant of all, central air-conditioning became indispensable: without it, sopping towels would stay wet all summer long.

It would be difficult to calculate the amount of natural resources consumed and abused in the process of poofing a single bath sheet to hotel-quality fluffiness: natural gas, oil, electricity, steel, rubber, plastic, refrigerants, laundry detergent, bleach, and softener—in addition to the sheer volume of cotton, a crop that demands plenty of water and pesticides.

Perhaps the most amazing feature of the cherished luxury bath towel is its incompetence at doing one simple job: drying its owner. For that there is only one kind of towel, and it is Italian: a thin, honeycomb-textured cotton rectangle called *nido d'ape* or, literally, bee's nest. (We generally call it a waffle weave.) Its gridded texture is soft, but bracing enough to stimulate circulation and gently exfoliate as it dries. Magically, the towel not only dries *you*, it also dries *itself*, quickly and frugally. That's important in Italy, where metal drying racks are more common than clothes dryers.

Waffle-weave towels come from many other countries as well, including France, Portugal, Pakistan, and China. Like all textiles, they come in varying levels of quality determined by the fiber and weave of the cotton with which they're made. Egyptian cotton yields longer fibers that can be spun into stronger and finer "yarns" (threads), resulting in a silkier, softer feel. (Qualities of Egyptian cotton vary, but let's not go too far afield.)

A word of caution: The first time you dry off with a *nido d'ape*, you'll miss the security blanket–like fluffiness of your former towel. Grow up. Persist. There will be lighter loads of laundry filling fewer baskets and straining fewer appliances. Eventually, you'll come to love your *nido*, and the towel will start changing your life.

Bath Mat

Drip Dry Carefree

Nobody takes the bath mat seriously. It's sold as a horizontal towel for the feet, not as the serious boon to bathroom pleasure and safety it can be. Each morning, the first step over the shower's threshold and beyond

its steam is the hardest step of the day. The floor is ice, the air cold, your mind cloudy, and your sense of balance absent until the coffee kicks in.

At this point, the bath mat can save your life. Even when they aren't lethal, bathroom falls are acutely embarrassing. Because no one likes to be rescued when naked and wet, a good bath mat is essential. It absorbs the waterfall you carry while exiting the shower and gives you a firm footing as you dry off.

Technically, a bath mat is a cushy, nonslippery textile backed by a nonslip surface. Until recently, the best bath mats were tufted or woven minirugs made of cotton. Backed with rubber, or nothing at all, the mats did a fair job of soaking up water but had a tendency to hold on to it, becoming mushy, mildewy bogs.

Washing them was problematic. They became heavy when soaked in the wash cycle and stayed wet through much of the long dry cycle— cotton releases moisture slowly. The heat and tumbling deteriorated both

> The bath mat is a cushy textile that can save your life. (And no one likes to be rescued when naked and wet.)

the cotton fibers and latex backing in short order, and their weight strained the dryer's drum supports.

Now a "new" synthetic boon— microfiber—has made the old cotton mat an expensive nuisance. Woven of extraordinarily skinny strands of polyester and nylon, microfiber mats keep floors dryer, and for longer than anything else. This results from nylon's hydrophilic (thirsty) nature,

but also from the density of the product's ultrafine fibers.

Microfiber can absorb seven or more times its weight in water, and the moisture evaporates fast, eliminating the dankness caused by slow drying. Microfiber mats last longer, since there's no need to machine-dry them—the act that wrenches the weave while melting the backing. The textile also survives machine washings much longer than cotton.

What took microfiber so long to reach the bathroom? Invented by Japanese scientists in the 1970s, then rediscovered by Swedish entrepreneurs in the late 1980s, it started out as a superabsorbent improvement on cotton towels and robes. But consumers were turned off by the slight creepiness of its tactile quality, or "hand." Although microfiber is now being made in nicer textures, most bare skin still prefers cotton. In any case, it's perfect for bath mats as feet seem to be oblivious to "hand."

The most important use for microfiber, however, is only just beginning to be implemented on our shores. More on that later . . .

Hand Towel

Damp No More . . .

Hanging next to the sink on its appointed towel bar, the fluffy cotton-terry hand towel has become a dependable accessory in the American bathroom. It effectively replaced the crisp linen guest towels once draped as a welcoming gesture; they were lovely to look at but too fussy to actually use. (Plus, though linen is very absorbent, it's not all that soft when wet.)

The hand towel is an interesting member of the household arsenal. It's fairly intimate, but shared by family and guests and replaced on a very irregular basis. Its communal nature tends to go unnoticed—until guests come over. Try drying your hands on a damp towel just used by several guests in a row. It's not as weird as sharing a bath towel, but slightly unsavory nonetheless.

Who has the time or money to stock up on single-use towels? That would be wasteful anyway. The remedy? A microfiber hand towel. It's so absorbent that with ordinary use, it never feels wet. Just like that thin bath towel, it's quick to dry, lowering overall bathroom humidity. (It also line dries rapidly when hung on the towel bar fresh from the wash; no need to machine dry.) Best of all, microbes don't thrive on synthetic materials the way they do on cotton.

Granted, it's not a perfect product. Microfiber has that unfamiliar, almost too-soft feel. When it's woven in an imitation of terry cloth towels, its loops tend to droop—it lacks the plush, bouncy feeling of the luxe cotton stuff.

The solution is to seek out towels woven in a waffle weave—just like your new *nido d'ape* bath towel. The 3-D

The hand towel's communal nature goes unnoticed—until guests come over.

pattern offers extra surface area for absorption and gives the textile more of that old-fashioned, full-bodied cottony cushiness that feels so right (even though it's wrong).

Trash Can

Sort It Out

A bathroom needs a serious mechanical trash can, not a girly basket woven in jute or upholstered with ribbons whose plastic liner bag eventually overflows with a strange mix of intimate refuse. A decent trash can, discreetly tucked into a corner, will make daily life sweeter in implausible ways.

Bath bins need to be bigger and sturdier than the coffee-can-size models offered in bed-and-bath stores. Bath trash is not cute. It is biological, in an all-too-personal way that's less appealing than the kitchen rubbish we handle with so much more discretion.

Bath trash involves unlike species of detritus, all of which share one important feature: Once you throw each item away, you don't want to see it again. It may document your recent history: predate primping, recent sexual activity, fertility status. It confirms your physical infirmities (Viagra), insecurities (Rogaine), and diagnoses (Effexor). A common cold can double the amount of refuse.

Doctors' offices and hospitals are the only venues with adequately discreet receptacles. Their infectious waste bins have all the right features: washable stainless steel bodies, tight mechanical lids with foot pedal openers, plastic liner buckets invisibly holding liner bags. Of course, they would make domestic waste look way too infectious.

But anyone who's ever tried to squeeze a shampoo bottle into a tiny flip-top or struggled to hide personal trash in an open bin will understand that our bathroom-trash needs are not being met. The solution? Sort. A huge amount of bath trash is actually recyclable. Rinse out those shampoo bottles and put them out with the rest of your plastic bottle collection. Cardboard and paper packaging should go out with your newspapers and other dry goods.

For the trash that's actually trash, use a diminutive version of the medical bin, with a step-on pedal and a well-hinged lid that contains garbage and odors.

To figure out the proper bin size,

spend a week (or your usual time between emptyings) collecting two kinds of garbage—recyclable and other—in two cardboard boxes. Check out the accumulation, decide whether it's typical, then choose a bin sized to fit your actual trash output.

Yes, this chore is even more loathsome than taking out the trash, but do it anyway. And enjoy the increased privacy and diminished waste for many years to come.

~~~~~~~~

Mirror

Mirror, Mirror, Off the Wall

As the world's most enthusiastic shoppers and gym-goers, we're constantly inspecting ourselves in mirrors —in weight rooms, locker rooms, fitting rooms, and even in the cars that get us there. But, image-obsessed as we are, we settle for mediocre reflectivity at home, where our inferior mirrors are tucked into unreachable corners.

We don't know much about mirrors. Should we buy them like building materials and glue them on drywall? Treat them like art and frame them expensively? Buy them like housewares at the cheapest big-box store? Or consider them optometric aids, important and costly as eyeglasses?

Mirrors belong to a small family of household products that have remained remarkably unimproved for centuries. Since sixteenth-century Venetians devised an exorbitant way to back clear glass with shiny metal, they've been getting cheaper and faster to make, but the principle has remained the same: a heavy brittle material—baked sand—painted with a metallic backing. (There are other reflective materials out there, but all are flawed: Highly polished stainless steel, the costly material used in prisons, scratches easily; laminated plastics such as acrylic and polycarbonate, though shatterproof and light, offer less clarity with more distortion.)

The quality of household mirrors is measured in three ways: the thickness of the glass, the quality of the backing, and the finishing of the edges. A good mirror starts with a quarter-inch thick piece of distortion-free glass. The back of the glass is "silvered" with silver nitrate and then coated with several protective layers to prevent flaking or blackening. Only the newest mirrors are lead free; the rest are hazardous waste when junked.

Think of your mirror as an alter ego. It's the well-behaved version of your three-dimensional self, the one with good posture, a sucked-in stomach, and a pleasant but self-conscious demeanor some call the mirror face. Treat this twin with more respect and it will make the real you look better.

To do that, put a full-length mirror in a decent place; neither a window-less closet (no matter how big) nor a bathroom, where condensation clouds reflections. A bedroom is good.

Women need a bit more space for the choreography of dressing, room enough to flounce and strut. Good illumination, both natural and artificial, is key.

Light yourself, not the mirror. You may have to experiment by moving lamps to bounce light off walls and ceiling until you get the kind of diffused general lighting—as opposed to spotlighting—that creates a good reflection.

Because there's no perfect, permanent location for a dressing mirror—what with sunlight continually changing course—a movable mirror makes more sense than the customary wall- and door-mounted panels.

Consider the cheval mirror, the old-fashioned mirror-on-legs. (In French, *cheval* means "horse," and *chevalet* means "easel" or "support.") The cheval may not be the barest of necessities, but once invited in, it gives the daily dressing routine a more theatrical dimension, in addition to plain old visibility.

Set in a frame suspended from two points, the mirror can be rotated to any angle or flipped over when you don't want it staring back at you. (Some ancient cultures believed reflections contained part of one's essence. Traditional Muslims designed mirrors to face the wall when not in use, to discourage vanity.)

If you're dead set on a wall-mounted full-length mirror, go one better than the cheap versions found in big-box stores by ordering glass from a local glass cutter—you'll get a thicker, better quality mirror in dimensions you choose. The shop will finish the cut sides with a beveled edge or a less expensive polished edge. If you plan on leaning the naked mirror against the wall, a safety backing—plastic film embedded with long fibers—should be applied to keep shattered glass from flying in the event of breakage.

Dresser

Never Toss One Again

Whatever you call it—*chest of drawers, bureau, chiffe-robe, highboy,* or *lowboy*—a dresser is important: It holds all the clothing and possessions that are better off piled, folded, or mashed together than hung in a closet. That's a lot of stuff: underwear, lingerie, socks, panty hose, pajamas, shirts, sweaters, and more. A dresser also provides a casual altar for important things too private or precious for more public display: romantic tokens, maudlin souvenirs, family portraits, and revealing meds.

Too bad so many people choose their dressers based on style alone, sometimes as part of a whole suite of furniture. They deserve more deliberation.

Like sofas, they tend to fall into two categories: long-lived pieces that cost too much and short-lived pieces priced just right.

Disposable furniture is very attractive. No investment or time required. The downside: It depreciates at the speed of light.

Witness the typical dresser. It's made of heavy, laminated particleboard (wood chips) and/or fiberboard (wood fibers). After a few humid summers and dry winters, the veneer chips and peels. The handles drop off. And, most frustratingly, the drawers move out of alignment, once and for all—never to glide smoothly again. (Sometimes they won't even close at all!)

Can the poor thing be rescued, repaired, and refinished? No point. When bad furniture starts to go, there's no stopping it. All that's left to do is pummel it into a pile small enough for a trash hauler's curbside pickup—like most trashed wood, it heads to a landfill, where it will remain intact for many years.

The most efficient dresser would be a sturdy steel filing cabinet, with deep drawers on tracks filled with ball bearings. But such a cold, noisy piece of furniture would turn the bedroom into a workscape—anything but soothing. Real, solid hardwood is a homier choice, warm to the touch and beautiful to look at. As for the ethics of the matter, solid woods have been gaining favor as a clean, long-lasting choice, and respectable sources are multiplying.

Solid hardwood has many advantages over "engineered" wood. There's no top layer, and so no wearing off of that top layer.

Bare, solid wood improves with age, and it holds onto fasteners (nails, screws, and staples) far better than its imitators. The best dressers actually use few metal connectors, instead employing old-fashioned wood joinery—something you certainly won't find in the land of particleboard. Parts that are notched, glued, and

TANSU: THE MOBILE DRESSER

A good piece of adaptable furniture is hard to find—but it may be worth the search. A flexible piece can be moved to a new house, a new room, or to fulfill a new purpose as your needs change. In Japan, carpenters mastered the art of versatile furniture back in the Edo period. Their storage chests, called *tansu,* were presentable and durable enough to travel back and forth from home to *kura*—an unheated, fireproofed outbuilding designed as a storage locker for excess and out-of-season domestic things. The *kura* helped keep the living rooms streamlined.

The *tansu* were boxes made of strong woods, using exacting joinery and beefy, wrought-iron reinforcing hardware. Many of them were modular, designed to be lined up, stacked vertically, or stepped like staircases, and rearranged as needed. The clean, simple forms seem remarkably modern: no legs, feet, carving, or shaping. Stacked, the boxes look still more contemporary.

A modern take on the tansu chest

While Western cabinetmakers were treating rooms with very different degrees of formality—the kitchen as scullery, the parlor as museum—the *tansu* craftsmen built storage units handsome enough to reside anywhere in the house and versatile enough to hold contents from kimonos to onions. Japanese families considered the *tansu* a permanent possession, to be passed down from generation to generation.

Today, American furniture stores are starting to market modular bedroom dressers, either modeled after historic *tansu* or reinterpreted in high-tech materials. Whatever their style, good-quality *tansu*-like chests are good investments. Their adaptability allows you to love them longer. (Japanese homeowners have loved them for about four hundred years.)

interlocked stay fused together, while screws are likely to loosen over time.

Solid wood is also far sturdier than porous "wood products." That's important: In order for dresser drawers to slide smoothly along their tracks, they must remain rigid—no warping or flexing. Examine an antique dresser, assembled with expertly "dovetailed" drawers inside a well-assembled frame, and it's likely to be hardier than any modern factory-made counterpart. (Dovetailing is a method of notching and interlacing two pieces of wood.)

But let's get real. Short of commissioning a bearded Maine artisan to craft a work of fine cabinetry, a compromise is in order. Aim for the best construction you can really afford. A good commercial dresser is a hybrid of solid wood parts (the drawer faces, for example) and high-quality plywood (the frame's back), assembled with some classic wood joinery and some metal fasten-

ers. Good steel drawer runners will help the drawers roll smoothly and silently.

Proportions matter. A tall, dark dresser monopolizes a room, especially if the bed is low; a waist-high piece puts at least one drawer at a comfortable height and creates a convenient counter surface. Drawers should be outfitted with handles you can easily grab.

The drawers' size and configuration are a personal choice, dependent on your particular wardrobe.

Like the clothing with which you should fill it, a solid dresser will prove economical over the long haul.

Do you need many shallow drawers for your collection of diaphanous undies, or just a couple of deep units to pile high with boxers and socks? Do you stuff or fold? A careful choice of dresser will finally reveal the sort of person you've been all along—for better or worse.

THE STORAGE FIXATION

The shipping container was the greatest of American storage inventions. It may not look revolutionary, but the standardized 20- by 40-foot corrugated steel box transformed the global economy. Invented in 1956 by Malcolm McLean, a North Carolina dirt trucker turned shipping magnate, the multimodal container eliminated much of the time and expense involved in handling loose cargo. Goods could suddenly travel all over the world at a ridiculously low cost and with reduced liability. Containers could be neatly stacked on ships and sent across oceans; thus, cheap stuff could be scooped up from far away countries, where labor and materials costs remained low, and brought to our shores.

The modern landscape is blanketed with storage. Along the continent's periphery, ports welcome containerships full of foreign merchandise. Restacked on land, the containers form small city skylines. Loaded onto railroad cars or hitched to truck tractors, they travel inland to exurban industrial parks. There, they are stored at gigantic, digitally mechanized distribution centers—some larger than one million square feet—until they're sent to retailers.

With all the coming and going of goods, we've come to expect merchandise to be cheap, plentiful, and short-lived. We needn't calculate its value over time, because we don't expect to spend much time with it. We even look forward to buying affordable replacements because we so like to shop.

Even the stores we shop in have begun to look like storage units: no-frills warehouse displays designed to cut costs and provide the bare bones, discount experience that makes customers feel like they can afford more. Multiple buildings are joined by outdoor sidewalks, stretched out along fields of parking lots. Everything is designed for speedy access, by car or by cart.

And what we bring home from those giant stores, we store.

Empty spaces have become our fondest longing, the endless quest that drives us to upgrade to bigger houses, cars, consumables, and storage containers—sloughing off the tight ones like hermit crabs seeking ever larger shells.

Houses are built to the newest standards of storage, with three-car garages and huge rooms outfitted with roomlike closets, all stacked at least two stories high over vast "finished" basements.

We fill those basements with yet another stackable modular container—the plastic storage bin. When that's no longer enough, we move our goods into self-storage facilities: chains of attached garages with the look of abandoned villages, open to their invisible renters at all hours. (In an effort to bring public storage back home, some companies have started to produce small plastic buildings—much larger than the usual storage shed—for use as private storage lockers in suburban backyards, where empty land is abundant.) Where will it end?

And what is it that we're storing in our homes, garages, and mini-storage units? Bulk-bought food and beverages sealed in their own super containers; holiday decorations; sports equipment; temporarily unwearable clothing. The bins also hold precious things, expensive mistakes we can't bear to toss, accumulations we've no time to sort, and objects we optimistically plan to use one day to change our lives for the better (exercise equipment, for example). It's a strange mix of expired hopes and fresh aspirations.

Maybe our expansionist history explains our hoarding tendencies. Those early colonists and pioneers, holed up in their own private forests and prairies, had to stockpile enough food and fuel to live in the middle of nowhere in between long bouts of drought, snow, natural disasters, and long-distance deliveries. Puritan settlers believed that God rewarded the worthy with the most wealth; flaunting abundance earned them local respect. In Utah, Mormon pioneers prepared "one-year pantries" in case conditions became apocalyptic.

Precious things, expensive mistakes we can't bear to toss, accumulations we've no time to sort ...

These days our supplies are abundant, but we still tend to see ourselves as rugged individualists: DIY'ers ready to face any and all dangers with our complete sets of tools and appliances and our own fleets of vehicles.

It turns out we spend a great deal of money housing things we seldom use. (And think of the mortgage payments, insurance premiums, taxes, and heating and cooling wasted on all that extra space . . .) There's a psychic component, too. "I feel like my stuff owns *me*," shamefaced homeowners tell professional organizers. Extra cargo is extra weight, and that's something no one needs.

Let us outsource our storage. Let food stores refrigerate fresh ingredients until we actually need them. Let public libraries shelve the books we've already read and subscribe to the magazines we've no time to read. Gyms can store the treadmills we use only occasionally, and contractors can garage the power tools we'll use only once.

You won't miss a thing, I promise.

Clothes Hangers
Tame the Closet-Jungle

The perfect clothes hanger is one of the greatest unrealized designs for daily life. Until it arrives, we have three options: deluxe, downscale, and unconventional. Deluxe hangers are those traditional, furniture-quality hardwood hangers found in five-star hotels. They're lovely for a couple days of vacation, but a closet-full of those space-hogging dinosaurs is expensive and inconvenient. They're heavy too, and unable to hold straps. (Yes, IKEA sells cheap versions, but why carve up virgin wood just to pad shoulders?) As for the bamboo iterations popping everywhere, they're even heavier than the originals.

Downscale hangers, from colorful plastic triangles to flocked wire models, may be practical but look and feel cheap. When they break, as they inevitably will, they end up in landfills with billions of other much-hated hangers.

The coat hanger of the future will be perfectly elegant and a pleasure to use. It will be cast in a weightless but indestructible new material (ingeniously made of transformed consumer detritus) able to lend shape to any fabric it suspends—from a diaphanous peignoir to the sturdiest wool blazer. It will expand and contract to properly cushion each garment, and it will stack away for storage. Its adaptable design will replace all the dozens of hangers shaped for specific garments: coats, pants, suits, shirts, jackets, skirts, dresses, sweaters, blouses, lingerie.

But until that perfect product arrives, don't bring any crummy new hangers into your home. Just adopt recycled retail VICS-compliant dress hangers. They fit the standards set by the Voluntary Interindustry Commerce Standards Association, whose members want to be able to roll garment racks from foreign containerships directly into their stores without any surprises.

A VICS dress hanger is the familiar, clear plastic model with a swiveling steel hook, upper slots for sleeveless shoulders, and lower slots for the loops of pants and skirts. It's made of ribbed K-Resin, a crystalline, lightweight derivative of styrene. (It looks like the polystyrene of CD boxes but is more durable, and a little bit more expensive.)

The VICS hangers may not look gorgeous, but you can feel pretty good about them: You already know they work, and you're lengthening their useful lives. Typically, retailers cycle out their old hangers as new shipments come in. Recyclers gather, sort, and resell the hangers online in batches of a hundred. For less than twenty cents apiece, you can have a highly engineered icon of the modern era of free trade!

Once your shipment comes in, you may want to share your icons with friends and family—unless, of course, you're starting a VICS-compliant store of your own.

~~~~~~~~~~~~~~~

Iron

An Old Chore Gets a Bit More Fun

Ironing, to be fair, is not for everyone. Non-ironers tend to stick to their guns. They also tend to wear their clothing outsourced, wrinkle-free, or defiantly wrinkled. The outsourcers have their wardrobes cleaned and pressed by dry cleaners and/or housekeepers. The wrinkle-free carefully curate a wardrobe of synthetics and knits. The proudly disheveled wear wrinkled or dryer-fluffed jeans and sweats.

Too bad. Practiced with the proper mind-set, ironing is a craft that makes you feel talented and very productive. Turn wads of rumpled linen into rectangles of elegant dinner napkins, and you're transforming rags into riches.

In New Age speak, ironing is a meditative ritual that brings you into harmony with the forces of nature—fire (heat), water (steam), and metal, to be specific.

From a more practical standpoint, there's really no such thing as a decent "wrinkle-free wardrobe." Beautiful, fluid, breathable textiles are made of natural fibers, all of which need serious steaming. That's why Italians look so good—statistically, they're among the world's most devoted ironers. They weave the most sublime fabrics and steam them with affection. It's a way of life for them.

Ironing shows you're being cared

for—even if you're the one performing the chores. It's a sign of self-respect, a hands-on effort to look present-able. Styles may change, but a man in a white cotton shirt, a woman in a smooth silk blouse, and anyone in a crisp wool uniform looks attractive ... because they look pressed.

Though nearly every year iron makers launch new models with ever more baffling features, ironing technology hasn't really advanced since the 1980s (dawn of the auto-matic shut-off feature).

Ironing works through a simple chemical process. The iron first loos-ens the fabric's molecules with water, then realigns them with heat. Steam penetrates fibers more effectively than heat alone.

That means the best iron is really a sturdy, steam-making machine able to shoot out lots of pressurized vapor

> Good glide and the ability to shoot out lots of pressurized vapor are key.

without leaking. Gliding is key to good handling, and a stainless steel "soleplate"—the iron's perforated bottom—glides better than lighter versions made of coated metals.

Unfortunately, irons have tended to vacillate between two extremes: cute little no-brand numbers that are fun to maneuver but don't work hard ($10), and hefty powerhouses of great repute that are hard to lift and no fun

to pay for ($100 and over).

Combining water, electricity, and heat in a compact, handheld device is not easy. You need a dependable thermostat and ample wattage—if your soleplate is too cool, wrinkles will persist and water won't vaporize. Leakage may occur.

What's more, a bad iron's perfor-mance will deteriorate over time. The more water an iron vaporizes, the more minerals accumulate in its steam chamber, eventually clogging its steam holes. Good irons have self-cleaning mechanisms that allow you to drain their holes with steam bursts. But cheap irons leak and sputter their way to untimely deaths.

One last item on the cheap iron diatribe: They gum up. Their metal soleplates, finished with Teflon or other coatings, accumulate scratches caused by buttons and zippers; those scratches attract fibers, and the gunked-up surface leads to "drag." Stainless steel is the answer, preserving "glide" by resisting abrasion.

Whatever the weight and glide of the machine, it's the ancient choreography of ironing that tires out the ironer. While moving the fabric, you must lift the iron, set it aside in a standing position, and retrieve it over and over again, twisting the hand, wrist, and rotator cuff each time.

Fortunately, a newcomer has slipped into the marketplace to change all that: the patented, robotic Oliso with "Auto-Lift." Its claims are dramatic. The response, measured by awards, news stories, and TV appearances, was energetic at first. But some after-buzz, among ironing geeks, labeled it a gimmick.

Not true. The Oliso iron addresses the weight problem in a novel way. The iron stays horizontal. No need to alternate between driving the thing around and repeatedly parking it on its heel. Grab the handle, and the soleplate eases down on fabric. Release it, and the whole apparatus rises slightly on little plastic feet. The distance is just enough to keep the soleplate from heating the surface below. When the microprocessor inside senses your hand, it activates a small motor that lowers the iron and releases the steam. The steam stops when you let go.

Basically, the iron feels like it's alive. It transforms the act of ironing from a solitary task into a strangely interactive delight.

"It freaks some people out at first," admitted its inventor, Ehsan Alipour. "But then they really start to love it."

The Oliso has other welcome features too. Unlike other irons, whose water tanks are filled from the top and constantly bubble over, this one has a side door—it lies flat while you fill it. Even though its soleplate is stainless steel, the Oliso TG-1000 is lighter, at 3 pounds 8 ounces, than many less-animated irons. And the thing actually speeds up the pressing process by eliminating the up-and-down parking motions. It also promises to reduce accidents caused by exposed soleplates and toppling. (For the forgetful, there's extra safety in the automatic shutoff.)

Normally, of course, buying any newfangled product with moving parts from a tiny upstart enterprise is courting disaster. But because this freaky iron is the company's mainstay, it's all pretty personal, and they're committed to replacing any iron that stops working.

Give it a chance, but read the simple directions before you get to work. This is not your grandma's mangle.

THE ÜBER IRON

When iron hunting, you may be distracted by the newest and mightiest of steam devices. One of them is the "steam center," a steam generator attached to a lightweight pressure iron; such machines apply as much as six times more steam than a regular iron, at three to fifty times the price. The units are so powerful that they can flatten both sides of a pant leg at once. Because the actual iron carries no water or steam-making equipment, it's small and light for its ferocity. The steam machine, however, is another matter; it requires a special ironing board with a separate rack. Serious stuff. Unless ironing is your chief passion, the contraption just requires too much cash, space, and caution.

Ironing Board

Space Age Hits the Laundry Room

N ow that I've spoken to the merits of ironing, a question remains: What does one iron *on?* Ironing foes and fans alike complain that the ironing board is a rickety, space-hogging contraption that is prone to toppling and squeals like a pig upon unfolding. Some staunch contrarians refuse to own boards at all. (They'll improvise when necessary by spreading towels over counters and floors.)

It's true that a bad board is a curse. But it is also miraculously cheap (the price of a few pairs of socks), while a great board can cost ten times more without looking any prettier.

A well-engineered board is lightweight and portable, sporting a wide, well-cushioned surface narrowing to a "nose." Topped by a replaceable all-cotton cover, it is well balanced on sturdy steel legs that slide smoothly to standing or sitting positions, with the ability to fold and lock tightly for upright storage.

Sounds boring, right? (And novelty boards disguised as surfboards and cactuses don't fool anyone.)

The Galaxy Plus, from German company Leifheit, is a welcome anomaly—to true ironers, anyway. Packed with features too numerous (and complex) to hawk in its marketing blurbs, the Galaxy Plus seems more like the pet project of an iron-loving inventor than just another item on the corporate roster. Actually, it's sort of poignant to see how a real innovation struggles to tell its story to an impatient marketplace.

The story begins with the board material. Instead of the standard heavy steel mesh, the designers used expanded polypropylene, a nearly weightless semisoft substance developed for the auto industry in the 1980s. EPP has been silently protecting consumers for decades—lodged between their cars' steel carcasses and interior upholstery, the rigid-but-resilient foam protects passengers from impact and shields them from noise, heat, and cold.

Unfortunately, EPP looks exactly like crumbly Styrofoam (expanded polystyrene), the reviled packing material, full of toxic chemicals, that won't easily recycle or biodegrade. Unlike its evil twin, however, EPP is a nontoxic, very recyclable, heat-resistant, resilient material with a structural strength remarkable for its light weight. (And no, it won't off-gas when you iron on it.)

Unlike steel, EPP is warm to the touch, and silent when you bang it around.

Now try fitting all of those great qualities on the label of an ironing board. No dice. So it's easy to see why the company soft-pedals EPP by calling it "thermosoft"—a meaningless term.

Too bad. That foam board accomplishes two major tasks. First of all, it provides a deep, wide work surface (15 inches by 49 inches) at half the weight of all-steel ironing boards (11 pounds rather than 20 plus). Supported on tubular steel legs, the board is brilliantly bottom-heavy, with a sturdy, well-balanced feel seldom found in even the best models.

The foam also defies the principle held sacred by all ironing board makers since the switch from wood planks to perforated steel: The Galaxy Plus does not vent the iron's steam through a porous top. Instead, its water- and heat-proof surface acts as a heat sink and vapor barrier, returning heat and moisture back through the pressed fabric—ironing it "from both sides," as the company likes to say. The warm cushion of air under the clothes also improves the iron's glide.

Like conventional ironing boards, the Galaxy Plus is covered by a machine washable, padded cotton cover stretched over the board like a shower cap. But the GP's cover is a "metalized" cotton made to reflect still more heat back into the clothes. When the cover wears out, you can buy another. Or you can use the board with no padding at all, as it's resilient and rounded enough to act as a naked ironing surface. For anything but shirts, that is: Created with an eye to storage, the board's rectangular shape is too blunt for the tight curves of cuffs and shoulders, so Leifheit includes a narrow collapsible sleeve-ironing board you can piggyback comfortably onto the big board.

> Real innovations may struggle to tell their stories to an impatient marketplace.

And there's more. No more enforced standing—the GP's board slides on a quiet, continuous rail to an adjustable height from 39 inches down. Its bowed legs allow you to sit comfortably or stand tall without hunching. No more dangling cords to trip you up and potentially send the hot iron flying—an embedded electrical outlet allows you to plug the board into the wall and then plug the iron into the board. For an extra safety bonus, a holster-like steel holder lets you park the iron safely.

All very thoughtful, but perhaps not convincing to the non-ironer—especially when you take the price tag into account. So here are two options. If you iron, amortize the GP's expense by using it as an all-purpose table. Experiment. If you don't iron, consider this alternative to the emergency towel-on-floor method: a compact, metal "tabletop ironing board" equipped with a small surface (about 14 inches by 24 inches), short folding legs, an all-cotton cover, and a wall hook. It will be there when you need it. And need it you will.

Clothes Hamper
Storage, Luggage, or Furniture?

In bed-and-bath land, there are hampers of every conceivable material at every price range. Some are sculptural objects of leather or woven teak. Some are pretend antiques, mini-armoires made of veneered particleboard.

Many are traditional wicker baskets with hinged tops. But none of them do a very good job of storing and transporting damp laundry.

The ideal clothes hamper is not a hamper, of course, but a wall chute leading from the bathrooms to a spacious bin in the laundry room. Barring that, dirty laundry needs a lot of space and ventilation in order to stay relatively pleasant. When humid bathroom hampers keep sweaty clothes and damp towels mashed up and airless, bacteria thrive and odor penetrates the hamper's materials.

Since there's no such thing as machine washable furniture, the hamper should not try to be furniture at all. It should be breathable and nearly weightless. Luckily, a new generation of hampers has arrived: the inexpensive pop-up hamper, in light polyester mesh supported by a flexible steel wire frame. The pop-ups are not particularly pretty, especially when stuffed with laundry. So hide them in a louvered laundry closet or a bedroom closet. They're easier to use than conventional hampers, and *almost* nifty enough to make kids haul laundry downstairs without complaint.

Almost.

BATHING

&

DRESSING

~~~~~~~~~~~

A PART FROM THE MIRROR, DRESSER, AND HANGERS, most of the items in this chapter are best bought new. Get the soft stuff—towels and mats—directly from websites; mainstream stores are just beginning to carry waffle weave, so you'll find a better selection online. To avoid shipping costs, buy the hardware—iron, ironing board, hamper, and trash can—in person, using the Internet to locate dealers near you.

BATH TOWEL

- Thin, all-cotton waffle weave
- Eco-rating: Uses minimal cotton (a resource-intensive crop), and saves power by taking up less space, water, and time in the washer and dryer. Quick to dry on a clothesline.
- Find it: Online, in bath and bedding stores, or in stores selling European linens

Cost: $20 plus per towel

BATH MAT

- Latex-backed microfiber with short, dense pile
- Eco-rating: Quick line-drying, long lifespan
- Find it: Online or at specialty bath stores

Cost: Under $40

HAND TOWEL

- Waffle-weave microfiber
- Eco-rating: Quick line-drying, long lifespan
- Find it: Online or in bath and bedding stores

Cost: $5 to $10

TRASH CAN

- High-quality, 3 to 5 liter step-on bin with an inner liner
Try: Brabantia's "Pedal Bin"; see page 120 for more information
- Eco-rating: Long life
- Find it: Department stores, bath and bedding stores, online

Cost: $40 to $80

MIRROR

- Full-length cheval mirror
- Distortion-free glass
- Pivoting or rotating hardwood or aluminum stand
- Find it: Department stores, specialty furniture stores, online bulletin boards and auctions

Cost: $100 and up, or buy used

DRESSER

- Solid hardwood
- Wood joinery, dovetailed drawers, smooth steel drawer runners
- Find it: Department stores, specialty furniture stores, online bulletin boards and auctions

Cost: $300 and up, or buy used

CLOTHES HANGERS

- VICS-Compliant Dress Hangers
- Eco-rating: Recycled from retailers; durable and long-lasting
- Find it: Online, by searching for "recycled VICS hangers"

Cost: Under 20¢ per hanger

IRON

- Try: Oliso Iron with Auto-Lift
- Find it: The Oliso website (www.oliso.com) features a list of stores.

Cost: Approximately $100

IRONING BOARD

- Galaxy Plus Ironing Board, by Leifheit
- Life span: Expect the Galaxy Plus to far outlast its five-year warranty.
- Eco-rating: EPP top is 100 percent recyclable and nontoxic.
- Find it: Call 1-866-MY LEIFHEIT or e-mail leifheit@intergest.com.

Cost: Approximately $140
Note for non-ironers: *Choose a steel tabletop ironing board, with folding legs and a padded cotton cover, widely available online or in big-box stores for less than $15.*

CLOTHES HAMPER

- Pop-up model in synthetic mesh with a flexible steel frame
- Eco-note: Look for a mesh gardening container made without vinyl or PVC—it's better for the environment, and it'll last longer, too.
- Find it: Bath and bedding stores

Cost: $10 and up

CHAPTER THREE

COOKING

INVENTORY

- Chef's Knife
- Paring Knife
- Bread Knife
- Cutting Board
- Measuring Spoon
- Measuring Cup
- Mixing Bowl
- Salad Spinner
- Mesh Strainer
- Saltcellar
- Pepper Mill
- Can Opener

- Scissors
- Cooking Spoon
- Tongs
- Spatula
- Vegetable Peeler
- Grater
- Wine Opener
- Meat Thermometer
- Fry Pan
- Dutch Oven
- Stockpot
- Saucepan

- Broiling/ Roasting Pan
- Microwave Oven
- Toaster Oven
- Kettle
- Teapot
- Dish Drainer
- Dish Towel
- Coffeemaker
- Pot Holders
- Trash Can

A little of this and a little of that. The average cook should be able to prepare just about anything with the thirty-four items included in this satisfyingly utilitarian kitchen inventory. (Major appliances—oven, cooktop, fridge—aren't covered, as for most homeowners and renters they come with the package.)

If you already own a mishmash of kitchenware, paring down to the basics will let you easily put your hands on the things you need to cook the food you *actually* eat. So, go ahead, give yourself permission to clear out what you never needed all those years: the aspic molds, the boning knife, the zabaglione pot.

Just remember the essential rules:

Steer clear of sets. No piece of cookware needs to match anything else. Do not buy a big hunk of wood speared with a dozen knives. Run away from collections of matching pots. Reject colorful families of utensils. Choose every single piece of kitchen equipment independently, for its specific merits, and never for its group discount.

Most of the items covered here are made to last at least one lifetime, and some pots and pans can last a couple. So choose them carefully, even ceremoniously. Flea market hounds and heirloom hoarders take note: Many kitchen items don't need to be purchased new—or at all. Those dated and patinated pieces rescued from a relative's attic have character on their side, as well as history.

This kitchen gets a little heated—politically, that is—in the area of nonstick cookware and microwave ovens. Microwave cooking deserves overdue respect for its ability to cook healthy food with minimal fuel and scant danger. It's safe, and it's newly green. However, nonstick cookware, along with all the soft utensils designed to avoid scratching it, should be banished from the kitchen altogether. According to the FDA, nonstick coatings are safe under most conditions, but worrying about them isn't worth the trouble anymore. (You'll find out why.)

When it comes to the kitchen, dare to be a contrarian: Say no to nonstick. Yes to cast iron. Yes to microwaving. No to matched sets of anything.

Enjoy your new freedom!

~~~~~~~~~~~~~~~~~~

Chef's Knife
The Helping Hand

The chef's knife is the centerpiece of the kitchen arsenal, emotionally cherished as an indispensable personal assistant by professional chefs, researched and fetishized by the rest of us. People spend a lot of money on their knives, partly because of the labor-intensive process through which they are hand forged.

It all begins with a malleable lump of hot steel that is pressed into a mold, cooled, hardened, sharpened, and polished through many steps. The technique can create a sculpturally beautiful knife, with blade and handle formed from a single piece of naked steel. (But most knife handle extensions—called tangs—are sandwiched and riveted in another material, or completely encased in it.) Forging also creates a bolster, the bump that separates blade from handle, acting as ballast to balance the knife and stop fingers from slipping down the blade.

There's a new(ish) game out there, and it's called stamping. Stamped knives start out as sheets of cold-rolled steel. A machine stamps out multiple knife outlines from the sheet, just as cookies are cut from dough. The finished product is lighter than a forged knife; the metal tends to be thinner, and the tang doesn't extend all the way through the handle. Most stamped knives also do away with bolsters.

Conventional wisdom holds that forged knives are better than

Should a knife be forged or stamped? It depends.

stamped knives—they're certainly far more expensive. But do you really need a bolster or a full tang? Some cooks believe that a bolster impedes sharpening; some like the detailing and solidity. Some cooks think a full tang improves handling; others dislike its weight. Just remember that the presence of either or both hallmarks of the forging process does not guarantee a good knife.

Truth is, it all depends. A good stamped knife may turn out to be more agile, comfortable, and downright likable than a precious forged model. Fans of stamped knives prefer the lighter weight, thinner blade, and more casual, sometimes resilient handle. (Forged knives tend to have hard, serious handles.)

A good chef's knife is indispensable—and it must be picked out in person.

Go ahead. Try to research your way to the perfect chef's knife. En route, you'll cross a bumpy landscape of folklore, myths, celebrity testimonials, and the boldest of Internet misinformation. You will find universal agreement on two facts, however: A good chef's knife, with a blade 8 to 9 inches long, is absolutely indispensable. And you have to pick out that knife in person.

The quality of cooking knives is both contradictory and subjective. The right steel alloy needs both hardness (for holding an edge) and some degree of malleability (for resisting fracture); but the hardest blade will be too brittle, and the bendiest one will be too soft to stay sharp. Thus, a good blade is a compromise: a hard-but-flexible alloy skillfully heat-treated to strengthen it further.

Today most blades are made of high-carbon stainless steel; various brands use slightly different alloys. To become as fiercely opinioned about steels as chefs are, you must abuse knives then lovingly sharpen them, repeatedly and relentlessly, over several years, to see how the edges behave.

Are they dependably sharp enough, or temperamentally ultrasharp and too hard to maintain? There is no shortcut to subjectivity here. You just have to earn it.

Short of culinary school, the best way to choose *your* ideal chef's knife is to find a kitchen supply store, preferably an eccentric little place frequented by real chefs as well as wannabes. Seek out the resident knife maven there, and tell him your story. Are you a vegan graduate student slicing occasional cukes, or a national barbecue champion hacking up fowl? A burly meat fanatic should try out the heavy, brand-name knives (and cleavers) made of forged stainless steel in Germany, and priced well over $100. Most other home cooks, including jobless vegans, can be very happy with a lightweight, stamped stainless steel knife made in any number of places: Italy, Brazil, Australia, the U.S.A., Taiwan, or Germany too.

If price is any indication of quality, shouldn't we all just buy the toniest knives and call it a day? Well, it turns out that not every household needs a chef-worthy chef's blade. As one knife expert put it, "Why buy a Mercedes if you don't have to?" Certainly, a costly forged knife will outlast a stamped knife if it's used correctly, stored carefully, and sharpened with skill (preferably on a waterstone or ceramic stone). But you may end up treating that precious thing more gingerly than it deserves. The über-knife may become the focus of the kitchen, carefully hand washed and polished, poised on the countertop as a trophy, cushioned in the drawer as an art object, wrestled from the kids slicing pizza. "Not that knife!"

As for me, after cooking with famous German and Japanese knives—from workhorses to stream-lined works of art—I found the humble stamped knife, under $50, to be the nicest of all. It's plenty sharp, able to hold its edge for years and respond to inexpensive sharpeners. But it's also friendly: lightweight, thin, graspable, and occasionally colorful. Compared to forged models, the stamped knife uses thinner steel and less of it. The lighter overall weight and bouncier handle make it easier to toss around; the thin blade meets less resistance; and the lower price inspires more confidence in handling. (Who hasn't ruined a costly blade by dropping, chipping, or mal-sharpening?)

Once you've conquered the choice between forged and stamped knives, you may find yourself beset with a host of other options. Pay no mind. While celebrity chefs may hawk their favorite knives like branded fashion accessories—new shapes, new colors, new *concepts*—there's not much newness in the old knife trade. Every manufacturer offers a series of signature blade shapes, but there are really only two major camps to consider, each with a long history of craft: the classic European tool, with its tapered, double-edged blade, and the Asian knife (such as the *santoku*), with a straighter,

single-edged blade. Knives go in and out of style, acquiring and losing certain details as they go but never reaching evolutionary perfection.

The good knife is the one that fits your hand for what you cook, the way you cook it. So don't be cowed by knife salesmen and Web prose pushing more expense, heft, and worship than you want to expend. Ownership needn't feel like initiation into some fearsome samurai cult. There is no enemy, just a lot of onions to be liberated.

One good-natured liberator is the Sanelli chef's knife in the Premana Professional line, a series of stamped knives with two-tone plastic handles. Designed in 1985 and originally produced for chefs, the collection is still made near Lake Como, Italy, in the same Alpine town where the company's founder started his knife business in 1864. Today, Mr. Sanelli's great-grandson is the company president.

Premana's plastic handle makes chopping feel fun, not surgical. It's a friendly combination of materials, safe and warm in the hand and quiet on the counter, where its bright colors stand out in the chaos of cooking.

Two lightweight layers of plastic form the handles—a hard core of red polypropylene peeking out from under a sleeve of green Santoprene—for a pleasantly grainy, nonslip texture that's soft, but not too soft. The knife is designed to weather the dishwasher, although it will last longer hand washed and dried.

But does it actually slice? Sanelli says the stamped Premana knife, backed by a lifetime warranty, is just as sharp as a forged knife, at half the price. I've only put a few years on mine, but it has made me happier than all of my old pretentious knives put together.

~~~~~~~~~~~~~~~

Paring Knife
The Jack of All Trades

A pocketknife was probably the first knife you owned. Its small blade folded away into a handle, and the whole thing disappeared into your pocket, safe from confiscation at school. Owning it was a rite of passage.

Using it was a revelation. Suddenly, you could emblazon your name everywhere, whittle wood into anything, and de-crust any sandwich.

The right paring knife can renew the affection we felt for our first cute-but-dangerous tool.

Before launching into a long-term relationship, it's a good idea to handle as many as possible. The differences are visually subtle but manually significant. Some feel cold and stiff, others warm and lively. Choose an endearing knife that inspires attachment, at a sum that allows you to treat the thing casually, and experiment freely.

The paring knife is the shortest member of the trio of indispensable kitchen knives. Its duties are small scale and lightweight: scraping a carrot; skinning an orange or other thick-skinned species; slicing or sculpting a radish. It's also a popular tool for ad hoc chores like opening a parcel, peeling a label, or mortaring plaster onto a small igloo for a fifth grade science project.

Given a choice between a costly, forged stainless steel paring knife (with a bolster between the blade and handle), and a decent stamped stainless steel version, take the latter for one-fifth the price. Choose a lean, nonbulky handle in a material—wood, steel, firm plastic, cushy plastic—that feels good in your hand, for inexplicable reasons, just like a loveable pen.

And if the knife disappears, commandeered by the kids building those plaster igloos, you can replace the thing pretty painlessly.

Bread Knife

The Master of Ceremonies

I t's a rite practiced on family dining tables all over the world: the slicing of bread, often using a special porcelain-, fused glass-, wood-, or silver-handled knife. Be it a religious or secular occasion, in these bread-lazy days a whole fresh loaf of bread is a rarity meriting a ritual instrument. A distinctive bread knife can help remind us to take pleasure in the product of a bygone artisan craft.

Tough as they are, chef's knives have their limits. The world's costliest chef's knife cannot split a fluffy cake, or a dense bagel, as effectively as the cheapest bread knife. The trick is in the teeth. A serrated blade cuts horizontally as well as vertically, and can slice a porous, cellular confection without squishing it. Bread knives (9 to 10 inches) tend to be longer than chef's knives (8 to 9 inches) in order to span round, rustic loaves and wide cakes. They are also thinner and narrower.

Sharp is good, but the tool should look friendly enough to visit the dinner table for communal bread-breaking. Avoid all bread knives shaped like the sword of Damocles. There's no reason for the bread knife to mimic a machete, or to match a mighty chef's knife in brand, style, or quality.

Beyond shape, teeth have personalities too, and some are meaner than others. A blade with a series of deep, sharp points looks more menacing than one with a wavelike, or scalloped, profile of rounded serrations. The latter may not slice quite as efficiently, but it looks a lot more sociable.

Likewise, the handle should be appealing. Unlike a chef's knife, which must be carefully hand washed after chopping raw flesh, the bread knife could stay unwashed pretty much forever without causing casualties. So there's no reason not to choose an ornate handle of wood, or another material that feels warm and interesting in the palm of the hand. The more fragile it is, the less you dishwasher it.

> Avoid all bread knives shaped like the sword of Damocles.

Where to find it? Even shopping for your bread knife can be an occasion for ceremony: Visit a neighborhood bread maker, be it an old *boulanger* in Paris or a bunch of kids baking organic in Santa Cruz. Try the local breads, swoon, and buy an indigenous knife.

To recap: A good bread knife is evocative. It has character. It also has a mildly serrated stainless-steel blade equipped with a wooden, or other nonmetallic handle—it needn't be dishwasher safe. It should cost far less than your chef's knife, simply because cutting good bread is not a big production.

Finding that loaf of good bread is the real challenge.

Cutting Board
A Hard-Working Surface

Neither wood nor plastic. That's the answer. Composite is the way to go, and Richlite is the material that ends the debate. Though you probably haven't heard of it, it's been around a long time. You might even own a slab of it without knowing what it is. A wood-derived composite that combines the attributes of wood with metal and plastic, it was developed midcentury by the Rainier Richlite Company in Tacoma, Washington. Layers of paper are soaked with phenolic resin, then pressed and baked into boards. That composite of cellulose fiber and resin is "much like Mother Nature's trees," according to the company, with extra resin for durability.

The super wood, first used to make tooling for the Boeing 747, later became a boat-building substrate. (Boston Whalers still use the material as a backboard for fiberglass-covered boat components.) In the 1960s, it appeared in commercial kitchens as a surface for cutting and baking. Thirty years later, it morphed into Skatelite, an outdoor ramp-surfacing material for skate parks. More recently, the company has been selling the composite as countertop material for residential kitchens—a less challenging environment than factories, oceans, and skate parks.

Richlite is also the material that makes those impossibly thin, Epicurean brand cutting boards seen in serious kitchen stores. The quarter-inch-thick board is thin as an artist's hand palette, with a hole for holding and hanging. Its rigidity and lightness make it easy to throw around, scrub in the sink, dry off, and reuse right away.

The board's label lists an unlikely range of attributes: not only waterproof but dishwasher safe; scratch resistant; nearly stain proof; heat resistant to 350 degrees; with a nonporous, bacteria-hostile surface approved by the National Sanitary Foundation. Its warm color and feel make it presentable enough to double as a bread board or serving platter. And it's long-lasting with no maintenance, taking on a deeper patina as it ages without warping.

D o you still need to be convinced? Okay, let's take this step by step, starting with the alarmists, who claim the cutting board is the most dangerous place in the house, the source of all bacterial scourges. The U.S. Department of Agriculture (USDA) recommends washing wood cutting boards in the dishwasher, but wood board makers ban such destructive treatment. The USDA also advises sanitizing boards with chlorine, the very chemical other government agencies are trying to ban from the household and planet.

This may explain why various home economists recommend stocking a collection of four or five thin, semidisposable polypropylene sheets color-coded to foods: red for raw meat, yellow for raw poultry, white for garlic and onions, green for greens,

The composite combines the attributes of wood with metal and plastic.

and others for bread, fruit, and so on. That's unnecessarily scientific. An Epicurean board made of Richlite has a logo on one side, allowing you to designate one side for plants and the other for animals. Chop garlic off center, lemons on center. A 10-inch-by-17-inch board is big enough for all that, yet easy to wash.

But what about all those beautiful, artisanal cutting boards stocked in foodie boutiques? Or the fun plastic toys in IKEA? Let's review.

A cutting board needs to be soft enough to cushion the knife edge; dense enough to resist gouges and germ colonies; structural enough to resist warping; light enough to toss around with one hand; small enough to hide in a drawer; or handsome enough to hang around as part of the countertop.

Wood? Forget about it. Whether it's maple or walnut, end grain or flat grain, only a thick laminated slab—a butcher block—will resist warping and splitting. That slab is too heavy to wash properly, and its porous surface needs monthly hot-oiling and occasional sanding.

Bamboo? It's a thinner, less porous alternative to wood, but still heavier than necessary, and not cheap.

Rigid plastic (polyethylene or polypropylene)? Easy on knives and easy to dishwash, these boards scuff up quickly, look cheap, and feel synthetic at the very moment you're palpating food and feeling organic. Were it not for the lovelier (composite) options out there, this would be the board to choose, however.

A cutting board should be dense, yet soft enough to cushion the knife's edge.

Flexible plastic? Lightest of all and easy to pour out; but impossible to wash properly in a crowded sink, short-lived, and cursed when it slips and sloshes sliced tomatoes all over the floor.

Tempered glass, or any glass? The densest and most washable of all. But heavy, hard to grip, and hostile to blades, the hands holding them, and the ears of all those around.

A process of elimination brings us back to the Epicurean brand boards made of Richlite, and one last question. Are they green?

Well, pretty much. Though most of the paper used in the board is not recycled, it comes from North American trees. According to the manufacturer, these trees are a renewable resource grown in "managed and sustainable forests." The board's long life amps its green rating. Most of all, the stuff makes the preparation of real, fresh food seem a pleasure instead of a dangerous, salmonella-inducing chore.

~~~~~~~~~~~~~~~~~

Measuring Spoon

What a Scoop It Is . . .

It's rare, but possible: a product that looks like mere gadgetry but is actually real invention. In the world of measuring spoons, that would be the Nuscup, a Swiss tool that turns a plain task—measuring ingredients—into a smooth, appealing movement. Proof, in cute plastic form, that elegant mechanics can elevate any human chore.

Even the most basic of kitchens generally boasts three sets of measuring tools: one for dry ingredients, one for liquids, and one for small quantities. Why the distinction between wet and dry? Bakers and other exacting cooks explain that dry ingredients

---

Proof that elegant mechanics can elevate any human chore.

---

must be leveled off with a knife. Since liquid ingredients are self-leveling—and often used in larger quantities than dry ones—one large spouted, graduated container does the job.

The problem with excess is not just that it's excess—pricey, bad for the planet, conducive to domestic chaos—but also that it tends to be unwieldy. Those measuring spoons linked like a set of keys are hard to use; free-floating in drawers, they disappear when you need them and hog space when you don't. "Dry" measuring cups in nested sets don't often stay in their orderly towers; scattered, they cause drawers to jam and tempers to flare.

At long last, the Nuscup eliminates the need for separate wet and dry, large and small measures. A movable seal—an industrial mechanism completely foreign to household technology—changes the size of the measuring container. The plastic contraption can hold anywhere from two tablespoons to a half-cup of any substance, wet or dry.

Inside the bowl, a tongue-shaped paddle seals off the desired portion. You adjust the bowl size and scoop up the ingredients with one hand. The clear plastic case is marked in both ounces and milliliters. For ease of cleaning, a button separates the Nuscup into two pieces that you stack on a dishwasher's cooler top rack. One final bonus: The Nuscup will never perform a disappearing act. An implanted magnet means you can stick it onto any available—and visible—hunk of steel. In short, the Nuscup does what cool design can't help but do: make all predecessors seem hopelessly clunky.

~~~~~~~~~~~~~~~~~

Measuring Cup

A Classic, with a Twist

Lack of a big measuring cup is bad for your health. In addition to the little Nuscup, you also need a 2-cup measuring "cup" to dole out cooking liquid for all the wholesome grains and legumes that ought to be part of your diet: couscous, bulgur, oats, quinoa, lentils, and all those other foods coming out of obscurity.

Health pitches aside, accurate, quick measuring in semilarge quantities is essential to a great many dishes. Any kind of baking, from scratch or from boxes, requires precise pouring. Actually, just about all recipes call for some measure of liquid.

The Pyrex glass measuring cup was an irreplaceable kitchen tool—transparent! heat proof!—until polycarbonate came along and made a featherweight, microwaveable version in the 1990s. That model also seemed irreplaceable until the OXO company took out two patents (6,263,732 and 6,543,284) to protect an ingenious advancement. They figured out how to take the stooping out of the measuring process.

The standard measuring cup has markings on the side. You use it by filling it with a rough estimate of the amount you need, placing it on a flat surface, then bending at the knees or the waist to get a side view of the cup. You add or subtract liquid, then repeat as needed to hit the mark.

OXO's container, officially named the "Good Grips Angled Measuring Cup," has an angled measuring surface that saves you from having to torque your whole body; you read the numbers from above as you fill the cup. The two-cup version is a fine start to a healthier, more precise life.

Mixing Bowl
Whisk It, Toss It, Chill It, Store It

A 5-quart, stainless steel mixing bowl can do much more than any one person might need it to do. Serious cooks will mix marinades and batters in it and use it to soak spinach and other rough greens. Casual cooks will employ it as a tossing, serving, and storage bowl for salad dressings, salads, and vegetable dishes. Snackers will find it to be an ideal holder for popcorn and all other foods requiring grabbing and shoveling. Little kids will enjoy the ringing sound produced when the bowl is turned upside down over their heads and pummeled on from above. (For resonance, the better the steel quality, the better the ring.)

For most purposes, a cheap, lightweight stainless bowl is just fine. It's more likely to dent, but it's also easier to toss around. Bowls of the highest quality, made with a thick gauge of good steel, can be quite heavy.

A shallow bowl is more storage-friendly than a deep one, which stands too tall in the fridge, cabinets, and drawers. A streamlined bowl is best; handles, bases, and fat rims just get in the way and add weight. Avoid bowls with pouring spouts, since they are too hard to seal for storage, but don't pass up models with lids.

In this case, age has nothing to do with performance: The only difference between new stainless and old is superficial. All steel, stainless or not, will eventually collect scratches. So rather than buying new and paying quadruple the price, even at discount stores, why not score used stainless bowls at yard sales or flea markets?

Mixing bowls come in other materials, of course. Pyrex glass can go into the microwave or oven. Colorful plastics are great as picnicware and storage. Both glass and plastics tend to be heavier than stainless, however, and not entirely crack-proof.

A stainless bowl is one of the few consumables that lasts, intact, forever, while acquiring no cachet or value as it ages (unlike, say, vintage ceramics). But it will never lose its usefulness—especially as a percussion instrument.

FOR BAKERS ONLY . . .

It's often said that there are two types of people in the kitchen: bakers and non-bakers. Bakers need an array of tools that just clog up the kitchens of non-bakers. (Translation: If you bake only in your fantasy life, you don't need the following items!)

Food Processor. For the serious cook as well as the baker, the processor mixes, chops, liquefies, and purees. Cuisinart is the tried-and-true brand.

Stand Mixer. Modern bread making requires a powerful kneading machine. The tool of choice is a KitchenAid stand mixer; it features a powerful motor and a heavy base.

Hand Mixer. For casual bakers and whipped cream devotees, the hand mixer (a motorized egg beater) can replace the stand mixer. Serious bakers use it in addition to the stand mixer for small tasks.

Scraper. A flexible silicone spatula transfers ingredients from one basin to another. (The stainless steel spatula on page 85 won't do for the precision transfers required in baking.)

Rolling Pin. A French rolling pin—a wooden stick tapered at both ends—is easier to wash and store than the more common pin with handles.

Bakeware. Are you a cookie cutter or a pie baker? Both? Whatever the dish, professional bakers forgo nonstick for bare aluminum, glass, or ceramic bakeware.

Salad Spinner
A Lean Greens Drying Machine

The Zyliss Easy Spin Salad Spinner does five things well. It dries food, replaces a metal colander, doubles as a salad bowl, serves as an airtight storage container, and makes centrifugal force feel like a good time. Any one of those services is well worth the price of admission. But the spinner also works as a case study in design, demonstrating how important it is to deploy shape, color, and materials for usefulness *and* delight.

The Spinner may not cure cancer, but it does give busy people an incentive to eat the healthy foods that can help prevent it: fresh, leafy green vegetables. None of those floppy veggies are particularly fun to wash and dry. Blot them with towels, and you bruise them by crushing their fragile cell structure. Spin them in flimsy spinners, and the gadgets skitter all over the place and whirl out of control. Even good salad spinners have always hogged too much storage space, unable to nest or stack nicely with other utensils.

Not surprisingly, a faction of the population remains devoutly anti-spinner. They prefer to swaddle their kale in tea towels or stuff plastic bags with layers of paper towels and lettuces and swing them like lassos. Some citizens ban *both* spinners and lettuces from their homes.

Time for a conversion. In 2004, Swiss housewares company Zyliss announced that it had designed the "Porsche amongst salad spinners." What makes it so high-tech? Well, for one, its looks—it's a showcase for its spinning mechanism.

Like other spinners—including the modern clothes dryer—the Easy Spin uses centrifugal force to throw off water, rapidly rotating contents in a perforated container balanced in an outer bowl. Those rotations become spectacle when viewed through a transparent plastic in a vivid hue—red, green, orange, or blue.

But it's not all for show. The use of a glasslike plastic for the outer bowl gives the contraption further utility as an attractive salad bowl. And as the lid is engineered to create an

Leafy green vegetables have never been fun to wash or dry—until now.

airtight seal, the salad bowl is also a chill-able storage container. The plastics are made to endure the intense heat of a dishwasher, so the components are also adaptable to a variety of kitchen tasks. For example, Zyliss recommends using the sturdy inner basket as a colander or pasta strainer. (The product's press release also recommends its "misuse" for the drying of ladies' stockings.)

The stuff that makes it all happen is the "Easyglide" system of gears, powered by a retractable cord. One linear motion—a swift tug on the cord—creates a blur of fast revolutions. The pull replaces motions required by other spinners: the palm-of-the-hand button push of Easy Spin's nemesis, the OXO-brand salad spinner, or the Model-T cranking of previous spinners. To keep the Easy Spin under control, the designers installed a stop button with disk brakes and a circle of nonslip plastic on the base.

Let the green revolution begin!

Mesh Strainer

For a Bit of Culinary Finesse

Whether or not homemade chicken soup is truly a cure-all, it certainly makes recovery comfier. That's why every house should be equipped to make a real soup, which requires a fine mesh strainer. After everything has simmered in a big pot, the drama comes in separating the hot broth from the sodden ingredients, all of which tend to slosh out of the pot in one slimy avalanche.

Both chicken soup and pasta share the need for draining devices that separate liquids from solids. Pasta can be drained quickly in a big colander or colander stand-in (see previous entry). In soup making, however, the liquid is the stuff you want to collect, and the challenge is to direct the flow from the pot into another container while trapping the spent ingredients.

A colander sends liquids pouring out, in all directions, through 180 degrees of curvature. A mesh strainer aims better and filters more finely. It's also virtually indestructible.

For longevity, the basket and its rim should be stainless steel. The basket's diameter should be about six inches. The handle can be made of any material, provided it is strong and firmly connected to the rim, the point of greatest stress. A hook on the far side of the rim is helpful.

In addition to its indispensable work on soups, the strainer also serves as a miniature colander for rinsing and straining small quantities of grains, beans, or berries. It removes the lumps and debris from gravies and sauces. And it can perform decorative tricks like the powdering of desserts with sifted snowfalls of sugar or cocoa.

A mesh strainer also comes in handy at urgent moments when no other tool will do. It can actually correct mistakes caused by other tools. For example, should you open a wine bottle with a humble winged corkscrew and shred the cork, it doesn't have to be a calamity. Simply place the mesh strainer over each wineglass, and pour as usual.

Saltcellar

Out of the Shaker and Into the Wild

S haking is over. Pinching is the way to go. The era of chunky salt is here to stay. Consequently, millions of adorable condiment dispensers will become defunct, relegated to the status of collectibles. Among the future antiques:

the ubiquitous diner-style salt and pepper shakers, those octagonal glass bottles topped with perforated, chrome turbans. The pairs match.

That's wrong: Salt is a rock; pepper is a fruit.

Salt lasts forever. Pepper gets old.

Salt needs nothing but an open vessel. Peppercorns need a machine.

Salt, the indispensable crystalline compound sodium chloride, vivifies just about all cuisine and helps electrify the human body. It feels like Caribbean sand and sparkles like diamonds.

Pepper, however, is an optional spice, made of tropical vine berries dried into wrinkled balls, potentially lethal when inhaled as a powder.

Both have been misunderstood and overprocessed ever since they emerged as some of the earliest globally traded commodities. Neither should appear at the table in pulverized, shakable form. Salt should be as

grainy as sand. Peppercorns should stay intact until crushed, at mealtime (see page 78).

The recent rise of salt as an object of culture and cult is partly explained by the rise of celebrity chefs—burly guys flipping chops into the air and making big fistfuls of ingredients

> "Salt is born of the purest parents, the sun and the sea."
>
> — PYTHAGORAS

explode into hot pans on high-definition TVs.

The revelation: They use their hands. Instead of meting out powdery table salt in puny measuring spoons, à la Fannie Farmer, they reach into bowls of Kosher salt with four-fingered pinches and throw the big flakes at the food.

At first, the chefs had to explain their strange, earthy rituals to a squeamish American public. Using bare hands is okay, they said. Salting is not an exact science; you have to add and taste as you go. Kosher salt is not a religious thing, they insisted. It's simply easier to grab and toss, and faster to dissolve.

Around the same time, a reversal in nutritional doctrine began to cast a shadow on refined foods. Flawless, sanitary, and super-white sugar, flour, and rice were deemed nutrition-less, dangerously fattening, or just plain déclassé, while hunks of natural-looking, unbleached foods gained cachet.

The time was ripe for a fresh look at condiments.

Salt connoisseurship has been slow to catch on. Americans have had a unique allegiance to one brand ever since the 1920s, when the Morton company responded to the midwestern goiter epidemic by adding iodine to its refined table salt. The ingredient was printed on their unchanging label—girl under umbrella—and salt, as medicinal condiment, became one of the few foodstuffs that required no comparison shopping.

These days, we eat a wider variety of foods, and enriched, processed salt is no longer as essential to the thyroid gland as it once was. (Fish, for instance, is one good source of iodine.) So it's time we open our minds to the notion that the cylindrical blue container is not, in fact, the only source of salt.

With or without the iodine, table salt has been specifically engineered for uniformity in order to flow through generic saltshakers. That's a lot of work for a little implement. Remove the saltshaker, and you open up a whole world of evocative crystals culled from scenic places.

Salt actually comes from lakes and seas all over the world. Some is mined from ancient bodies of water that dried up and disappeared underground; this is the source of most processed table salts. Some is evaporated from seawater in seaside fields; every coastal nation has its own varieties of sea salt, naturally colored and flavored with the minerals of the local oceans—magnesium, potassium, sulfur, and so on—and farmed through techniques passed down for many generations.

While the health benefits of sea salt, with its additive-free mix of natural minerals, may be a bit overstated on some labels, the allure is real. Would you rather eat salt mined in dank caves and processed in factories, or the trademarked gray Celtic Sea Salt, sun dried and harvested along the wild coast of Brittany by the rugged Paludiers (salt farmers)? The price reflects the labor, but concentrate hard enough and you might catch a glimpse of wind-lashed breakers crashing onto sand, and French artisans raking your salt into white piles tidy as art installations.

Salt snobs prefer the still more arcane form of French sea salt called Fleur de Sel. Flat crystalline "petals" of salt are culled from the crispy film that forms on the evaporating salt fields of Guérande. Yes, a gourmet variety of sea salt seems wildly expensive as a replacement for table salt—unless, that is, you treat it as a consumable souvenir.

Where to store all this newfound bounty? The British have long used "salt pigs" to hold cooking salt at their stovetops; the homely, fire-hydrant-shaped crocks have large circular openings for quick grabbing—but those won't do for the table. Before shakers were invented, formal dining required saltcellars: open containers, big enough for one diner or several, equipped with matching minispoons. Could those be the answer?

Let's face it: Just as there's no agreement about what texture salt should be (powder, flakes, fine, medium, coarse), what additives should be banned or welcomed, or how natural *natural* salt should be, there's no agreement on how the salt should appear in the kitchen or at the dining table.

Each household must take its own stand, testing the new range of available salts and forming its own policy—in much the same way that it chooses certain forms of milk, coffee, or peanut butter based on taste, budget, and superstition.

If you believe that sea salt from the Baja peninsula, home of wintering gray whales, boosts longevity, go for it. If you prefer the sexy Mediterranean salts on the Costa del Sol, enjoy.

But do stay away from refined table salt, for one simple reason: It's just too boring. Find a nice chunky salt with a bit of crunch. Buy whatever quantities you like. Put a half-cup of the stuff into a dispenser. Use the same one for kitchen and table.

The most entertaining salt holder around is a retro-futuristic polished stainless steel "sugar bowl," familiar in Europe as a generic container for sugar cubes. (Stainless is one material

> Gourmet sea salt seems wildly expensive—unless you treat it as edible souvenir.

that won't be eroded by salt's causticity.) Attached to a conical base, the semispherical top resembles a helmet's visor. Open, the container looks animated, like Pac-Man. Closed, it protects the salt from dust.

Whatever container you choose, learn to revere an ingredient you formerly ignored. For an in-depth treatment, try the book by Mark Kurlansky, *Salt: A World History.*

Pepper Mill

Une Machine Extraordinaire

A few decades ago, the only black pepper known to most Americans was the preground powder kept in the pepper shaker (which matched the saltshaker) on every table. Only the most exquisite restaurants offered an alternative back then, one that was scary at first sight. Waiters would appear with their menacing totem poles, hover over the entrées, then surgically crank out showers of black grains until they were dismissed.

There was something dangerous about this pungent spice, so exotic it was administered one-on-one with ritual equipment, untouchable by diners. Who could believe this was

> Peppercorns should be bought whole and kept in airtight containers until ground.

the same foodstuff—dried berries called Tellicherry peppercorns—we used at home?

Today, of course, we're grinding everything in sight (exotic peppers, sea salts, coffee beans, coriander . . .) without knowing what kind of grinding works best, and when we should stop. There's no point milling salt at the table, for example. Because it's a mineral and doesn't get stale, it tastes the same at any age, in any form. But peppercorns, like other dried fruits, should be bought whole, kept in an airtight container, and ground no sooner than needed to keep the flavor intact.

When that moment comes, they should be crushed by a specialized machine that creates the texture, fine to coarse, to suit the recipe. Anyone who's accidently gnawed through whole peppercorns knows that ill-distributed pepper can overwhelm a dish.

Despite their proven powers and faddish omnipresence, pepper mills are no longer respected. They have become tabletop vaudevillians, outfitted with cartoony methods of squeezing or twisting. The newest electric pepper mills look and sound like personal vibrators. Even the most elegant versions tend to grind poorly, clog up, then stop working entirely.

How to find one's way through the labyrinth? Ask the owners of any kitchen supply store or culinary boutique, and they will tell you: Peppercorns must be pulverized in a two-step method, by well-engineered, durable mill gears. They will claim that the only mill capable of this task is produced by a French maker of automobiles called Peugeot.

It's a long story. In 1810, the two oldest Peugeot brothers, Jean Pierre and Jean Frédéric, turned an old mill into a steel foundry, where they began to manufacture saws, springs, corset boning, coffee mills—and, in 1874, pepper mills designed to be used at the table. First produced in white china, that original Z model is still made today. The company kept experimenting in steel, turning out sewing machines, lawn-mowers, watch springs, and other products, including a series of gas-powered vehicles produced by Armand Peugeot in 1890.

Now there are two Peugeot firms, both sporting lion logos: PSA Peugeot Citroën makes cars; PSP Peugeot makes spice mills and handsaws. But only one of them has a reputation for being the best in its class.

We forget that pepper mills are machines. Good machines last longer, and do a better job over their lifetimes. Like a car, the Peugeot pepper mill features a curvaceous shell hiding the ugly steel mechanics inside. First, teeth are cut into the steel by hand. Then the steel parts are "case-hardened"—heated to a high temperature and quickly cooled.

Two sizes of grinding grooves create finer, more uniform particles, also preventing the teeth from grinding themselves into steel flakes—a feature of very cheap pepper mills. When you turn the top knob, the larger grooves line up the peppercorns and crack them into shards. The smaller grooves grind the shards into coarse or fine particles; the size is adjusted by a metal button on top of the mill.

Though the company makes suave shells in modern materials and shapes, its classic series of beech wood, especially in the 5-inch-high Bistro or Paris model, has the best tactile personality. Stained in a chocolate brown, it ages well, especially with the help of continual hand-oiling by diners.

The bottom line, though, is that Peugeot guarantees their pepper mills' steel mechanisms will last forever, backed by an "unlimited warranty." Would that automobiles could offer the same peace of mind!

Can Opener

If It Ain't Broke . . .

Spend a few dollars on the Swing-A-Way Portable Can Opener Model #407 and you get a remarkable bit of Americana, along with a handy tin cutter that just won't quit. If you don't have one already, you'll find it in your local bodega as well as in the toniest foodie boutiques. If you do have one, resist the urge to chuck it. Clean the gunk off the wheels with an old toothbrush, dry, lubricate with vegetable oil, wipe, and keep it going.

After the failure of Swing-A-Way's original signature invention (a hinged wall-mounted can opener), the company used the same cutting device on a handheld, i.e., "portable," model.

> The knob rotates the cog, advancing the blade. The rim works like a railway, guiding the wheels.

Two steel levers were pinned together like scissors, each with a handle on one end and a gear-mounted wheel on the other. One wheel was a circular blade, the other a serrated cog. Using the advantage of the lever—the knob—the user could pierce a can by squeezing the wheels around its rim. The knob rotated the cog, which advanced the blade. The rim worked like a railway, guiding the wheels.

This can opener was a little miracle, its levers and gears cutting steel with steel and minimal hand power. The ballet of one motion driving another—how many children's imaginations has it captured?

Here's a perfect example of a mechanical tool that is preferable to its electric competitor. It also exemplifies the *ain't broke/don't fix it* philosophy. The Swing-A-Way can opener has not been updated, mechanically, since its appearance in 1955. Competing brands have tried to improve the utensil with ergonomic proportions and padding, while the S-A-W has remained defiantly bare.

The can opener is on its way to becoming an antique, what with canning being replaced with other preservation/delivery methods (freezing, freeze-drying, fresh delivery) and new packaging techniques (coated cardboard boxes or plastic contain- ers with peelable lids). But that thing was great while it lasted. And it's still indispensable.

~~~~~~~~~~~~~~~~~~~~

Scissors

"The Good Ones"

S ometimes the choice is simple. A pair of Fiskars No. 8 Bent Scissors (right- or left-handed) cuts more than anyone should expect from a fun-looking tool priced like a toy and praised as an icon. In 1967, Fiskars, a Finnish company, introduced a pair of scissors that looked like an alien artifact. Day-Glo orange and organically curvy, they were so lightweight they felt gravity-free. Plus, they cut things, lots of different things, with an ease and precision never known at that cost.

Designed around 1960 by Olof Bäckström, the "O" series scissors were deemed a "humble masterpiece" by the Museum of Modern Art in New York and added to its permanent collection as a forerunner of ergonomic products.

Now that the much-copied item is everywhere, we've forgotten what scissors used to look like. Since their appearance as hinged shears three millennia ago in ancient Egypt, scissors have been either dull and cheap or sharp and expensive, depending on the grade of metal and method of sharpening. Good scissors were made of carbon steel and hand ground, thus the expense. Though they cut well, they were quite heavy, hard on the hand, prone to rusting and to loosening up over time, and off-limits to anyone but adults.

> "I believe more in the scissors than I do in the pencil."
> — Truman Capote

Early scissors were specialized, like knives. Each purpose—paper, fabrics, hair, homework—had its own model. Misuse, such as cutting paper with hair scissors or vice versa, could ruin the tool. At work on school

AN UNLIKELY MODERN ICON

At 350 years old, the Fiskars Corporation is one of the world's oldest companies and is still Finnish. Fiskars Brands Inc., the subsidiary that makes the scissors and other sharp things, is headquartered in Madison, Wisconsin. Why *Fiskars?*

It's the name of an iron ore–rich village near Helsinki, where in the mid-1600s Dutch merchants built a steelworks that the Finns eventually expanded into a manufacturer of farm equipment, tools, knives, and household utensils.

projects, kids faced an ethical dilemma: risk a bad grade for sloppy work with "kid scissors" or break house rules by borrowing the "good scissors."

Fiskars figured out how to eliminate hand finishing, using fully automated machinery to make its sharp blades. Suddenly, they could produce as many scissors in one day as they had formerly made in a year. They used stainless instead of chromed carbon steel, and light plastic handles instead of heavy, painted steel loops. A strong but adjustable screw hinged the blades securely.

In the sleepy scissors industry, this was radical engineering. But it was also gutsy design, the glamorizing of a normal tool, made cheaper, better, and . . . pleasing. The big orange handles, sculpted like two bone shanks, felt custom-molded to the user's fingers, impossibly light, and warm too. More amazing was the way the thing cut all sorts of densities, hard

or soft, brittle or squishy, over and over again, without dulling or falling apart. Because the stainless steel was easily washable, the scissors could switch from inert household materials (paper, cardboard, fabric, plastics, rope) to living things (flowers, shrubs, parsley, pet hairdos).

Now, after thirty years, the No. 8 Bent Scissors have taken on another distinction: trust. Even back in the day when products were built to last, the No. 8s tended to far outlive their expected life span.

Today, the company offers a big menu of specialized scissors for crafters, gardeners, students, and office workers, but the classic No. 8 lives on as a master of all trades—now available with a new twist: a golden, titanium nitride coating that keeps the blades smooth longer by resisting oxidation and scratches.

An unnecessary addition, but worth a splurge if you're buying them for someone as a special gift.

Cooking Spoon
Stir It Up

The most sensuous part of any televised food show happens when the charismatic chef slurps a Bolognese sauce from a wooden spoon and hums with pleasure, eyes closed. "Mmm... perfect." The ideal utensil for TV slurping is a 12- to 14-inch long beech wood or olive wood cooking spoon, handmade in the same sunny country that inspired the very same sauce it stirs.

The wood feels warm in the hand, sounds nice on metal, tastes good as you adjust the seasonings, *and* makes you look more kitchen savvy.

Natural oils and dense grain will help preserve the spoon over the years as its patina deepens. The older and more fascinating the tool, the more presentable it becomes as an "antique" serving utensil.

The wooden spoon can be a symbolic baton of domestic continuity, passed on from one generation to another, along with the secret to making a decent risotto: time. The wooden spoon is the utensil of patience, and patient cooking is an expression of caring and love.

But lovely as it is, a wooden spoon gets decimated in the dishwasher's superhot washing and drying cycles. It needs to be hand washed and dried, which brings up pesky questions of kitchen microbes. It may be evocative, but it's not really the best tool for the job.

Instead, buy the simplest, smoothest, solid (nonslotted) all-stainless cooking spoon you can find. Used or new. Brand name or off-brand. It doesn't matter. But scoring a graceful, beautifully proportioned spoon can prove worthwhile, since you won't be tempted to replace it unnecessarily.

> "I hate people who are not serious about their meals."
> — Oscar Wilde

In a pinch, however, there are plenty of efficient models to be found anywhere from kitchen suppliers to big-box stores.

The stainless spoon is not only a good serving item—able to lift more liquid and slimy ingredients than a wooden spoon—but it's also the best scraper for pot and pan bottoms, especially when you're turning the fond (golden burnt stuff) into sauce.

Affordable, handsome, indestructible, and efficient, the stainless steel spoon is as simple and useful as it gets. (And yes, you *can* use it to stir a risotto.)

Tongs
Get a Grip

Tongs. Great word. Great utensil: like having robotic hands for handling hot coals, greasy chops, and steaming linguine. No electronics needed. No need to scramble around for the right utensil at the critical moment of flipping or grabbing. Tongs do the work of a dozen utensils, then lock away into a compact shape.

Forget pasta rakes: tongs grab pasta more decisively. Forget meat forks; tongs turn and serve hunks of meat without bloodletting. They also work gently as they stir stir-fries, retrieve broccoli and mushrooms, hold peppers over the fire, and toss salads.

Start with a pair of 12-inch-long stainless steel tongs that lock closed for storage. The tips should be scalloped, so they can grab slippery food without mangling it. A loop at the hinge allows for hanging near the oven or barbecue grill.

Any extra features or materials only add bulk and weight. Tongs don't conduct enough heat to need "insulating" plastic on their arms.

And they're too macho to wear those silly plastic mittens designed to protect nonstick pans (not necessary, as we've outlawed those altogether—see page 93). Ignore retractable or telescoping tongs, or any models that are anything but plain as can be.

Plain tongs are fancy enough, especially when you take their origins into account. They're the Western version of cooking chopsticks—the extra long wooden or bamboo sticks used in the Far East for millennia—a refinement of one of man's earliest inventions, the flint-sharpened spear used to hunt and roast animals over a fire.

What makes tongs so nifty? It's all in the metallurgy. Tong magic is made possible by a little coil of spring steel, also used in clothespins and clipboard clips. Spring steel is flexible, able to stretch out without snapping and bounce back to its original, coiled shape over and over again without wearing out. It may sound modest today, but it changed daily life when it was formulated late in the 1860s. (It begat the paper clip, too.)

Now that barbecuing has become a competitive consumer sport, megatongs have become the weapon of choice for men in aprons battling propane fires. Tongs have increased in size and weight to keep up with the massive scale of the new phenomenon of outdoor kitchens. The newest of supertongs are 20 inches long; beefed-up with wider, thicker arms of plastic-armored steel and equipped with large, cowhide hanging strips. Reject these monstrosities. Remember: The smaller the tongs, the braver the man—or woman.

Spatula

Lift, Flip, Scrape . . . and Again!

What do cookies, pancakes, omelets, burgers, and fish fillets have in common? All of these fried, baked, and broiled foods require the same utensil, and nothing else will do. Whether you call it a spatula, turner, or flapjack flipper—every kitchen should have a versatile device strong enough to lift burgers, wide enough to hold pancakes, and thin and flexible enough to coax even the most fragile fish fillets, cookies, or eggs off hot metal.

Before the arrival of nonstick cookware, the spatula was an attractive, one-piece tool of steel. Today, most turning tools are overengineered, using too many materials to form the sorts of squishy handles, hard shafts, and soft paddles that promise to go easy on hands and cookware.

Nylon, the commercial name for a polymer called polyamide, was the material that first replaced steel turners. Suddenly, consumer kitchen utensils turned a sinister matte black, promising to be soft on cooking metals and quiet in the drawer. Heat resistant to at least 400°F, a nylon turner could scoop burgers off nonstick pans without gouging the veneer. But the nylon still tended to melt a bit, giving off an unlovely and unappetizing smell.

Silicone was the next kitchen miracle material. Often brightly colored or translucent—anything *but* black!—it holds on to vivid dyes and has a higher melting point than nylon. Most silicone kitchen utensils are labeled heat resistant from 500°F to 600°F, some as high as 800°F.

But there's no longer a need to worry about which soft spatula will resist heat. Once you swear off nonstick cookware and switch to bare steel and naked cast iron (see page 93), you can return to the best spatula of all. It's all steel. Its thin edge is unsurpassed by those of its plastic imitators. And it will last as long as your pots and pans.

Vegetable Peeler
Ergonomics Hit the Kitchen

Don't peel it. Eat it. Keep the peel on that apple or cucumber. Scrub that new or Idaho potato, boil or bake it, and eat it up whole. If you've gone to the trouble of buying a genuine item of unprocessed food, you might as well keep it intact and ingest the peel's wonderful fiber and vitamins. (Even pesky carrot skins can be scraped clean with a paring knife.)

We're paranoid about skins. We think they're too bumpy, dirty, waxy, or soaked with deadly pesticides. Maybe we'd be healthier if we learned to enjoy natural textures, rinsing and scouring like the Japanese, or if we stopped waxing our cukes and apples altogether and started growing chemical-free, organic foods on a widely affordable scale.

Paradoxically, it's often the old-fashioned, homespun family dishes that are to blame. Holidays and family picnics call for apple pies and potato salads and the endless bouts of peeling they require; just in case, we keep vegetable peelers in the kitchen drawer, whether we use them or not. The task's legendary drudgery lives on; bulk peeling may be the most thankless kitchen task of all.

When the OXO company began selling its Good Grips brand Swivel Peeler in 1990, it caused a sensation among cooks. Here was an upscale kitchen gadget inspired by the chunky, ergonomic tools made for the elderly and handicapped. The ugly handle, of a soft, almost fleshlike substance, was meaty and strategically squishy, with rows of finger-massaging fins. The stainless steel blade was sharp, and could swivel to follow curves. The combination of the two surprising features—cushy handle and serious blade—turned a mundane, fatiguing task into a strangely pleasurable experience that required a lot less muscle.

OXO's peeler marked a historic moment in product design. A new range of materials was emerging, along with a new philosophy called Universal Design. Advocates insisted that daily life might be better for everyone if designers made utilitarian things more comfortable and pleasant to use for as many different types of humans as possible, regardless of age, size, or ability.

Grip became a big deal. Designers tried to figure out how to adapt products to the vast range of hand sizes and strengths, from the light grip of a small child to the beefy clutch of a stonemason.

OXO began making other household tools with soft, nonslip grips and fat diameters. Santoprene, a new "thermoplastic elastomer," made it all possible. The affordable material was the first moldable, soft plastic that was durable and heat resistant enough to live through many years of dishwasher steaming.

The success of OXO's intriguing grips ignited a consumer romance with empathetic tools and gadgets. OXO continued to reinterpret every conceivable kitchen tool with an enlarged grip, whether it really needed one or not.

Homespun dishes like apple pie and potato salad call for endless bouts of peeling.

Eventually the trademark grip became the sign of a well-engineered household tool—part of an ever-expanding market of gadgets overqualified to do what they needed to do.

Though new peelers compete to replace it, the Swivel Peeler lives on as an exemplary product and a souvenir of the 1990s.

And peeling truly is enough of a drag to necessitate a little extra comfort.

Grater

Would You Like Some Cheese with That?

Just looking at an old-fashioned box grater is enough to make your knuckles hurt. Each side of the metal tower was speckled with sharp burrs of different sizes. You strummed the tower with a piece of hard cheese, lost focus as you watched it disappear into the burrs, and ended up shredding your flesh. The grater also seemed to consume more than it harvested, and it wasn't any fun to clean.

Compared to its predecessor—a two-sided sheet of gouged metal—the freestanding box initially seemed like a nifty 3-D tool; but it turned out to offer more textures than anyone

> For a hundred years or so, box graters continued to work adequately . . .

could need and take up more space than it merited. After all, the grater has never been more than one of those intermittently indispensable tools. You don't need it very often, but sometimes nothing else will do. Substitute a knife or a vegetable peeler to shave, slice, peel, dice, or crush and the results are less than successful.

Parmesan cheese is reason enough to own a grater. A sprinkle imparts disproportionate depth to almost any dish that is not dessert, and some recipes can't work without it.

For a hundred years or so, the kitchen grater continued to work adequately, never supplying the deep pleasure of a sharp chef's knife or a guillotine egg-slicer.

The breakthrough came in 1994. Grater frustration forced Lorraine Lee, a Canadian housewife, to swipe her husband's new woodworking tool and misuse it to zest an orange. The slim, elegant file-shaped wood scraper with an ultrasharp rasp was a novelty at the couple's hardware store. The Lees were so amazed by the fast and exacting zesting that they began selling the rasps, repackaged as kitchen graters, through their mail-order tool catalog.

The manufacturers of those rasps had also discovered their use through accident and adaptation. For twenty years, Richard and Jeff Grace, two brothers from Russellville, Arkansas, had been making high-tech printer parts using a photochemical machining technique. (The process cuts metal using chemicals rather than conventional hand tooling.) The brothers had been fascinated by the accumulation of menacing, razor-edged scrap—sharper than the usual debris in machine shops; that hazard inspired them to create a series of very sharp woodworking tools, brand-named Microplane.

After Mrs. Lee's zest success, the Graces began making and marketing stainless steel food graters with hundreds of tiny razor-sharp teeth. The Microplane graters were not only efficient, but they also allowed cooks to reverse the grating process, passing the food over the grater—like a bow over a violin—in smooth, elegant gestures. With less pressure required, and no need to lean into the motions, there were fewer flesh wounds. (Focus is still crucial, though.)

The graters are available in several textures, from fine grating to wide shaving, but the "classic" Zester/Grater transforms the hardest of hard cheeses, citrus, or chocolates into fluffy ingredients indispensable to some of the world's most transporting recipes.

Wine Opener
Works Like Magic . . .

The sommelier opens your wine invisibly and instantly. With practiced speed, her classic waiter's corkscrew tears the foil and impales and extracts the cork, all while staying hidden in her hand. This is the professional way to liberate wine in a restaurant, a place that conceals the messy labors of meal preparation and makes food appear magically.

Home, however, is place to revel in the manual dynamics of food making. For this, nothing has surpassed the double-winged lever corkscrew. It performs a fascinating ballet on the theme of mechanical advantage. It also fits in a drawer, costs almost nothing, lasts forever, and requires minimal manual strength or skill.

Most perfect of all is the classic,

chromed brass and steel winged cork-screw with no frills—unchanged since 1930, when Italian designer Dominick Rosati patented the model. His creation quickly became a staple in every Italian household and was eventually exported all over the world. The wonderfully animated and anthropomorphic tool excitedly throws its arms overhead for drilling and slowly lowers them for extracting.

Taking wine too seriously will squeeze the bonhomie right out of any dinner.

It takes about a hundred pounds of pull to pop a cork from a bottle neck. So how does it work? The motion of the levers is transferred to a rotating motion in the gears, and from there into the vertical motion of the worm (the spiral drill shaft), multiplying your forces by those of mechanical advantage. (It's not that difficult—it just takes a bit of practice.)

If it's visual excitement you're after, Alessi, the Italian maker of artistic housewares, offers an even more iconic version of the simple tool. Designer Alessandro Mendini's 1994 creation turned the corkscrew's handle into a head, and its core into a dress. The witty Anna G costs about ten times more than a standard model, but the tool-turned-art-object has graced many a wedding registry.

Owners of expensive rabbit-shaped lever devices and other fancy openers will ask: What's wrong with opening a bottle of wine with a single, mistake-proof, exertion-free motion?

Answer? Overkill. At its core, wine is a sensory lubricant designed to help people become more convivial over the course of a long evening of eating and talking. In these frantic days, we're too antsy to relax that much, so we exploit wine as a medium for connoisseurship, technical expertise, and gear accumulation. Too bad. Taking wine so seriously brings out competition and judgment, squeezing the bonhomie right out of any dinner.

You've got to wonder when the overkill will stop. Is the technological dishing of ice creams the next frontier? Why not replace the generic spoon with a dedicated ice cream decanter: a heated, battery-powered Teflon dipper that carves a perfect sphere from the hardest ice cream? And what of cost?

To Europeans, the American custom of opening a bottle of wine with the latest precision gadget looks silly—just as European hamburger-eating, with utensils, seems to Americans. Why remove the nice, greasy hand contact with the warm burger, or the special skill required to clamp the stack of ingredients together while you lift it mouthward? Make the experience tidier, or safer, and you lose something.

Now it's time to face facts. Most wines don't need corks or bottles. It's just an aesthetic conceit. Boxed wine is the way of the future. (No glass, no cork, just a disposable container with a spout.) We usually buy a wine for an evening, or a season, not for it to spend posterity in a wine cellar. Thus, there's no reason the wine can't age (if necessary) at the winery, then travel like milk, from maker to dealer.

But it turns out not to be about the facts after all. Wine making is one of the few processes that has remained undisturbed by progress. Grapes still need the same old mysterious mix of natural elements in order to thrive. Friends still appreciate the magical way wine improves their chemistry. The opening of a wine bottle is a little ceremony full of expectation.

We hope to be surprised by the wine. We hope that each sip will offer lots of sensory attributes: a wonderful nose, lovely color, graceful legs . . .

Let's prolong the suspense. A humble corkscrew lets wine speak for itself, giving more impact to a bottle that turns out to be great. Surprise! A newfangled wine opener says, "This wine better be good." The fancier the tool, the higher the expectations, and the deeper the sorrow when an expensive bottle turns out to be common.

At the end of this era, while wine is still being bottled in glass bottles, with corks made of cork, the appropriate opener is one that conveys a sense of tradition, and a notion that time can stand still. It can—until those inevitable juice boxes of personal wine portions finally arrive, complete with straws.

Meat Thermometer

Roast It to Perfection

Hate meat thermometers? You can scare yourself into buying one by reading the USDA's consumer websites, where the list of pathogens that can potentially poison undercooked meat is long and horrific: salmonella, e coli

0157:H7; campylobacter, mad cow disease, and more. It's enough to scare you into vegetarianism.

Good thing all the bad stuff can be killed off with a magical dose of heat. And the yummy, juicy revelation, delivered by a precise cooking thermometer, is that that dose is actually much smaller than you think it is.

In other words, the meat thermometer will show you how much you've been overcooking your meat all these years as you judged doneness by eyeballing, pressing, poking, or checking the color as your mom or grandma instructed.

S afely cooked meat is actually much pinker, softer, and juicier than anything you would have dared serve your family or guests. Well, that applies to poultry and pork, anyway. Extra-rare hamburgers and steaks may not reach safe temperatures, and the USDA is working to make them obsolete via huge food safety education campaigns.

A bona fide lab device, impressively responsive and accurate . . .

Which thermometer will tell the truth? There's a confusing array out there, with many different mechanisms and techniques: disposable plastic pieces that pop up or change color, two-piece wireless devices, and talking gadgets that tell you when your roast is done.

The most useful of the lot are the tried-and-true, the popular, and the wonderful-but-expensive.

The big, old-fashioned dial version is now called an "oven-safe bi-metallic thermometer." It's the durable, leave-in apparatus your mother grew up with—way before turkeys had pop-up sensors—and it needs a big hunk of meat to hold it upright. Inside the probe, coils of two different metals expand at varying rates, corresponding to how the metals react to heat; the coils move an arrow on the large analog dial. Since the whole is leave-in, there's less hopping around.

The tool of the moment is the popular "instant-read" digital pocket thermometer, able to measure thin foods with no more than the small tip of its probe. Its interior thermistor works like a little microprocessor: Temperature changes create electrical resistance on a piece of ceramic semiconductor material. Instant-read it is not, however: A thermistor takes about ten to twenty seconds to deliver a final reading. Because nervous cooks tend to test food several times, the lag sometimes leads to an overventilated oven and a perforated roast.

And then there's the Thermapen. (Science geeks, hold on to your pocket protectors—heat surveillance just got a lot more fun.) The Thermapen is not a kitchen gadget, but a bona fide lab device that comes with its own signed and dated certificate of calibration. (Really, does it get any nerdier than that?) It works through a thermocouple: two wires made of different metals and joined at one end; when they sense a temperature change, they create a voltage.

Although it's not much to look at (a plastic case with a retractable probe), its responsiveness feels like magic to veteran cooks. A thermocouple is the only device able to take an instant reading within a very wide temperature range—in one to three seconds, between –58°F and 572°F, using no more than an eighth of an inch of immersion.

The Thermapen's speed and design, with its large digital readout and small probe tip, allow you to perform exploratory measuring impossible with big, slow thermometers. Food becomes more intriguing as you watch ingredients, anatomy, and oven temperament influence the cooking process unevenly and unpredictably. Who knew there was so much going on? The Thermapen lets you defy the odds by rescuing your roast or bird when it reaches your idea of perfection. That idea will change, by the way, once you realize what a precisely cooked roast can be. Better.

Downside? Sticker shock. At $90, its price will raise some eyebrows, though it is considered a bargain in lab circles. But it all depends on your level of devotion to the cause. Calculate the price of the frail digital thermometers you've trashed plus the emotional cost of the roasts you've ruined with feckless monitoring, and the Thermapen might seem more like a Bic than a Montblanc.

~~~~~~~~~

Fry Pan
The Original Non-Stick

From a design standpoint, the cast-iron pan is one of the world's coolest products. It starts out ugly as sin and heavy as hell, with its witchy, dull blackness, thick proportions, and bad reputation for turning to rust

unless treated with ritual care. Then, presto, once you start using it, it performs all kinds of magic that fancy tripli pans cannot manage. Before long, that fry pan looks beautiful. (Even its heft will begin to feel lovable.)

The design lesson is simple: Material matters.

Heat some oil, way hot, on that cast-iron pan, and watch nothing happen. The bottom doesn't ripple or blacken. No mystery fumes.

Slap on a steak, and watch the meat brown deeply and evenly. No sticking! Move steak-in-pan under a hot broiler for a few minutes, and the pan returns unharmed, with the steak having undergone a remarkable transformation—all part of the pan's magic: the thick bottom holds on to heat, sealing the juices inside the meat.

No one-trick ponies, cast-iron pans can improve upon a variety of foods: pancakes, popovers, French toast, omelets, stir-fries, frittatas, upside-down cakes, and, of course, corn bread. In some cases, the metal even manages to boost nutritional value by leaching digestible traces of iron into the food.

In the larger scheme of things, a cast-iron pan is among the greenest of all man-made products. It lasts forever. But in a pinch, it can be melted down to make something still more useful. (Although what could that possibly be?)

No other pans can reach such high temperatures safely (no off-gassing or contorting), maintain that heat evenly, and travel between direct flame, broiler, and oven unharmed. Cast-iron pans have two other features unknown to young cooks drawn to shiny modern cookware: They're the most dependably nonstick pans around, capable of outperforming any version of Teflon, and they cost nearly nothing. Iron is cheap, and the cast-iron manufacturing process is basic, unchanged for thousands of years: Molten iron is poured into a sand or clay mold.

There *is* one recent, useful improvement: Tennessee-based Lodge Manufacturing, which has been in the business since 1896, now makes a "preseasoned" line with a foundry-baked, soy-based finish.

Truth be told, rust prevention was never that arduous, though cast-iron acolytes pride themselves on their personal techniques. Basically, just oil an empty vessel and bake it. But factory seasoning reassures skeptics for a few extra dollars. And its advent provides the final, decisive argument in the long debate over the real and imagined dangers of nonstick pans.

Convert to iron. Ban nonstick pans from your house. Clear out all those rubbery, nonstick utensils. You'll no longer have to worry if Teflon flakes will make you sick (they won't); if perfluorooctanoic acid, or PFOA, gives Teflon factory workers cancer (it might, says the EPA); or if the fumes from overheated Teflon, misused, will kill pet birds (they have).

Choose a 10-inch cast-iron pan with two handholds—one long handle and one loop. Keep it parked on the cooktop. And prepare to initiate your friends and family into the ancient cult of cast iron.

Dutch Oven

The Self-Cooking Phenom

It won't be love at first sight. But affection comes with the first meal and deepens over time. Yes, it's only a pot, and a homely one at that. More primitive than anything else in the kitchen, the Dutch oven is a heavy, squat hulk—but one that will endear itself to anyone willing to give it a try. Unlike a trendy gadget that performs one task quickly, the Dutch oven can cook an amazing range of foods and does so as languorously as possible.

It was one of the earliest of America's bare necessities, shipped to the New World from Europe, then transported across the plains by pioneers and cowboys who used it to cook up mass meals over the campfire. Tight-lidded cast-iron pots had been used for centuries all over the world, but Dutch craftsmen showed a particular talent for sand casting very smooth pots, and during the seventeenth century English entrepreneurs took to casting and exporting Dutch-inspired pots across their growing colonies.

In the late nineteenth century, French craftsmen produced a fancier sort of Dutch oven, cast in iron then coated with colorful layers of glass; baked on at high temperatures; recoated; and baked again. The smooth, enameled cast iron resists rust, is easier to clean, and leaches no minerals. And it tends to be about ten times pricier than the plain stuff, due to the artisanal glazing and firing steps required.

Traditionally made of bare cast iron, the D.O. is big, or very big, usually with a 5- or 8-quart capacity. It's walled by thick sides, with a thick bottom, big handles on both sides, and a heavy lid that sits tight even as foods roil and burble below. Its density allows for searing without risk of distortion or scorching, and the pot holds heat evenly on the stovetop, in the oven, or on an open fire outdoors.

The genius of the Dutch oven lies in its uncanny ability to cook many things without harming the ingredients or itself. The thing is indestructible. (In the unlikely event that it does crack under extreme conditions, it can be welded back together.)

Braising is the technique that

allows the D.O. to transform just about anything, animal or vegetable, into a transporting meal. There's nothing complex about it.

Technically, braising means cooking browned ingredients slowly, at low temperatures, in a closed pot with some quantity of liquid. While it is possible to braise in other vessels, the Dutch oven is the only one that can travel from direct flame to the oven, maintain a good seal, and radiate even heat from all sides like an oven within an oven.

The D.O. mellows its contents into a dependably wonderful fusion of flavors. It works every time. The skill of the cook and the precision of the oven, or lack thereof, cannot prevent the

... shipped to the New World from Europe, transported across the plains by pioneers and cowboys ...

alchemy from happening (given some rough proportions of good ingredients, and a couple of hours).

Recipes are not really necessary. Throw in a chicken, brown it over the stove, toss in random raw vegetables and some liquid, slip the lidded pot into the oven, and bake under moderate heat for a spell.

Some classic recipes actually require the D.O. It gives a deeper dimension to lowly cuts of meat, but

it also justifies the costly ones in osso buco, for example. Brown some floured veal shanks and vegetables, pour in broth and wine, and exit to watch a long movie. When the credits roll, you open the lid to find a finished meal. The melt-in-your-mouth shanks have produced their own sauce, and the whole gives off an intoxicating aroma.

Devoted fans of the D.O. insist it is much more than a pot, more akin to a mobile cooking appliance—able to perform like an oven, a cooktop, or a grill and capable of cooking *anything* indoors or out, while continuing an unbroken tradition.

Dutch oven fans convene all over the world. The Lone Star Dutch Oven Society seeks to "preserve the art of black pot cooking" and its cowboy heritage. The Japan Dutch Oven Society seeks to do the same while wearing more festive, if less authentic, cowboy outfits. The International Dutch Oven Society entertains all forms of Dutch oven cooking, including novelty acts. (Campers can bake pizza in a D.O. by spreading hot charcoal under the pot and on top of the lid.)

Tricks aside, the Dutch oven does a whole lot with very little, and that's the beauty of it. (Cowboy hat sold separately.)

Stockpot

The Big One

A stockpot is a big vessel that helps you live larger. It flash boils all the squirmy, ungainly foods of summer (lobsters, corn, clams) and makes enough pasta for everyone, invited or not, who shows up for the party. Unofficially, it works as an ad hoc ice bucket and wine cooler when space is tight.

The stockpot also makes stock, the foundation of all cuisine. Not to be confused with soup, stock is the liquid made by simmering a serious quantity of rough ingredients: vegetables flavored by some combination of meats or seafood and fish, seasoned with herbs and/or spices, and submerged in lots of water. The idea is to simmer the brew slowly, strain out the solids, and continue cooking the juice gently until it's "reduced" down to the right intensity.

As grandmas love to remind you, homemade stock has no peer, in either flavor or virtues. It cures all that ails you, warms your soul, freezes for months, and makes most dinner recipes better. (When in doubt, use stock instead of water.)

Another way of putting it: The stockpot boils water and lots of it. And for that it needs to be large, lightweight, and noncorrosive.

The biggest model is much too bulky for most. The costliest one is heavily detailed; layered with durable but overly weighty materials; and emblazoned with a brand name that gets you no mileage.

What you need is a pot that is small enough to store but big enough to make pasta for ten, made of one strong, light material and equipped with big, well-attached, insulating handles.

The vessel of choice is an eight-quart, all–stainless steel pot with big (not huge) riveted loop handles on the sides and lid.

Why stainless? The sketchiest stockpots are plain, bare aluminum. Reject all of them. Aluminum leaches into acidic foods and can alter their taste and color.

The cheapest stainless pots tend to be made of a thin gauge of steel, the kind that warps and burns on the bottom. A thicker gauge holds heat better and cooks more evenly, should you decide to melt or sauté. But thin or thick, stainless tunnels heat directly into cooking fluids or substances with little finesse. When you're boiling water, that's a virtue.

Consider auxiliary materials as well. Resin handles may stay cool longer but won't withstand oven heat. Welded handles (melted to the pan at high temperatures) are streamlined and easier to clean, but riveted handles (fastened on with metal pins) are more durable. A tempered glass lid lets you watch the pot boil, but it's much heavier to lift than plain old stainless.

You can diversify your stockpot by choosing a model with an aluminum disc encased in the stainless steel base. *Or* use a heat diffuser, an **O**-shaped, trivetlike wafer of heat-holding cast iron that you insert underneath the pan, over the burner. It keeps your food from burning and prevents the pot bottom from blackening on the outside. Off the flame, it works as a trivet.

Why not just buy a stockpot that does everything well? Weight is one reason. Cost is another. The most versatile pot is one made of three layers of bonded metals. The exterior may be stainless steel, aluminum alloy, anodized aluminum, or copper. The middle layer may be a heat-conducting material such as aluminum or copper. And the inside surface may be stainless steel, the most nonreactive metal for cooking.

One of these serious pots—called *tri-ply, triple-layer,* or *clad*—may not be three times as heavy as an all-stainless steel model, but it's bound to be a heck of a lot more expensive. Should such a pot arrive as a gift, don't reject it. No, indeed, embrace it. Just remember that a $400 stockpot is a luxury that won't (necessarily) change your life.

How big is big enough? Fervent stock makers, who use lamb femurs and grouper heads, scoff at anything below 16 quarts. And an absurdly huge stockpot is a bare necessity in Maine, where lobsters are practically given away for free. But farther south, domestic stockpots range from about 6 to 20 quarts. Eight quarts, the most useful size, is the one included in the standard newlyweds' starter kit of 6 to 7 key pots and pans.

Saucepan
The Everyday Pot

A humble, medium-size saucepan will perform a miscellany of simple tasks that other vessels can't handle with the same finesse. It will steam rice and other grains, blanch vegetables, warm soup, steam oatmeal, and cook tricky sauces and desserts. A lidded, 2-quart saucepan works well for a small household; 3 or 4 quarts works better for a larger brood. Choose a stainless steel model with an aluminum disc embedded in the base to hold and spread heat. (Unless the label or box specifically mentions aluminum in the base, it's not there.) The steel should not be coated with anything. No Teflon or nonstick surface by another name. No plastic on the handle or lid.

Construction details matter, not only because they make the pot prettier, but also because they influence its handling and cleaning. The easiest pot to clean will be the one with the smoothest, simplest joints. A glass lid is heavier than a metal one but offers a nice view. A flared rim makes for easy pouring. Riveted handles will stay attached indefinitely, while welded and screwed attachments may loosen over time. Most handles are designed to dissipate heat, but not all will feel comfortable in your palm. Visit a selection of pots in person; pick them up to feel their weight and balance.

Finding the right retailer is the rub. The pots in foodie stores can be costly; big-box stores, with exceptions, tend to favor low-end varieties. Department stores carry a good, middle range of cookware and often put saucepans on sale. But the easiest option is going straight to a kitchen supply store and asking for a lidded, two-quart stainless steel pot with an aluminum disc on the bottom. The choices will be limited, but the salespeople will save you the four grand you might have blown on that matched set of fantasyware.

Broiling/ Roasting Pan

A Better Burger

The typical broiling pan has gone from very bad to just plain dangerous. It started out as a nesting pair of heavy, uncleanable trays, then became a featherweight pair of nonstick pans that start buckling and off-gassing as soon as you defy the chemical maker's warning: Don't heat over 500°F. (Above 660°F, the coating starts to decompose.) Translation: A nonstick broiler pan is inane!

How did broiling pans manage to escape the design revolution that improved, or at least reshaped, every other consumer widget? Alas, the evolution of the lowly broiler pan illustrates the way tenacious misconceptions about how things work can actually inhibit real progress.

In 1975, a new kind of broiling pan was quietly launched by Lee Drannan Smithson, a chemist now living in Dayton, Ohio. He trademarked his invention, a deceptively simple device, as the WaterBroiler–WaterRoaster, and has been selling it to consumers, one by one, via direct mail and website ever since. That his innovation has not become a mainstream commercial product, ubiquitous as the colander, explains a lot about design. Unless the product can sell itself, by looking like what it's supposed to look like, it can't compete in the big marketplace. A product that needs explaining, like his, is a hard sell. More on that later.

First: Why broil? And what is broiling anyway?

Where our ancestors roasted animals over wood fires, we broil or grill. Outdoors, we cook burgers over propane-heated faux coals. Indoors, we slide the meat under the broiler, which reaches a temperature of about 500°F. The electric version is a wavy tube of radiant metal; the gas version is a series of flaming jets.

Essentially, broiling uses direct heat to cook food quickly. (Baking uses indirect heat, the warmed air, for more patient cookery.) The intense direct heat can brown and sear, creating flavors other cooking techniques can't replicate. But the act demands an alert cook. A few seconds of neglect can change a meal from golden perfection to a fireball of smoking, alarm-tripping loss.

Success or failure, the disadvantage of broiling has always been its messiness. A traditional broiling pan is a shallow perforated tray sitting an inch or so atop a deeper pan. In theory, the tray holds the food, and the grease and liquids drain into the pan below. But often, the broiling pan traps grease and liquids in the upper tray, where they spatter and smoke—or they're left in the bottom tray to become a baked-on finish. No surprise, then, that broiler-pan cleaning requires its own set of industrial-style gloves, in thick rubber, to protect against the gritty cleansers and steel pads involved.

The trays' clunky design harkens to the broiler's origins. When modern electric- and gas-heated kitchen stoves replaced coal-fired models, the broiler elements were not built into the ceiling of the oven cavity as they are in better models today; instead, they were contained in a separate broiling chamber underneath the oven. The pan matched the oven in shape (rectangular), and material. Presumably, that early broiling pan was designed by a person who did not cook. He designed stoves. And stoves, like locomotives, autos, or anything else powered by ignitable fuel, were overengineered in heavy carbon steel coated with rust-resistant finish.

Fortunately, the broiling pan of the future is here, its design informed by Lee Drannan Smithson's conviction: The broiling process is not inherently brutal, but is, in fact, a peaceful cooking technique made violent and disgusting by "ill-conceived" pans.

The WaterBroiler–WaterRoaster is unrecognizable as a broiling pan. Smithson's lightweight device is round, not rectangular. It's silver, not black, and likely to remain bright and shiny over the years, trumping the familiar sight of those grease-blackened steel pans. At 12 inches in diameter, it looks small compared to standard pans but manages to fit a surprising amount. The upper tray resembles the round grill of an old-fashioned barbecue stand; the drip pan looks like a pie plate with big loop handles. Nothing fancy.

Its simplicity only dramatizes its success, which comes from *not* doing what other pans have done. After a

Cleaning a broiler pan once required industrial-style gloves, gritty cleansers, steel pads.

pan full of burgers or chicken legs has been broiling for a while, the first surprise is silence. No splashing, no burbling, no sizzling, no screeching of the smoke alarm. When the meat is done, it tastes the way it looks, neither desiccated nor raw, but just like ad copy always says: moist on the inside, crisp on the outside. Afterward, the pan needs no scouring, just a trip through the dishwasher's regular cycle.

The pan's only flaw is a commercial one. It needs a personal introduction to explain why it costs the same as a much beefier one that looks more expensive. Smithson says the pan has "three secrets." First of all, the rack

> When the meat is done, it tastes the way it looks — not desiccated or raw, but moist on the inside, crisp on the outside.

is a wire grill (not perforated sheet metal) with minimal surface area, so it sends dripping fats right into the pan below. Metallurgy is the second secret: Both the grill and drip pan are made of stainless steel, which enables heat to travel quickly and directly to the food—and that's the whole point

of broiling. Third, the stainless is polished smooth, so it resists sticking.

Smithson's technique explains the rest. Pour 1½ cups of cold water into the pan before broiling, he recommends, and the water will catch the pan drippings and keep the metal ungunked. It will also humidify the oven without steaming the food.

To turn that broiling pan into a roasting pan, you just press a different button on the oven—*bake* instead of *broil*—and wait longer.

Unless a big chain or manufacturer decides to license his product, Smithson will go on making the pans (in India) and collecting grateful testimonials from happy broilers all over the land. ("[WaterBroiler Pan] works wonderfully."—Pierre Franey, *The New York Times.*)

And that's part of its charm. It reminds you that the big companies don't have all the answers after all. The inventor/entrepreneur is still alive and well, cooking silent burgers in Ohio.

Microwave Oven

A Greener Way to Cook?

Much as the Raytheon Corporation, one of America's largest defense contractors, likes to sell itself as a titan of stealth technology, its major gift to humanity is the microwave oven: the metal box that cooks food superfast with spooky radio waves, the electromagnetic frequencies also called microwaves.

While working on radar sets in 1945, Raytheon engineer Percy Spencer was testing magnetrons, the machines that make radio waves, when the melted candy bar in his shirt pocket inspired him to use radiation to cook food on purpose.

Two years later, Raytheon introduced the world's first microwave oven: the Radarange, a six-foot-tall, 750-pound behemoth. It took another twenty years to shrink the machine into a countertop consumer appliance.

Over the past forty years we've had a love-hate relationship with the miraculous machine. Its price has continued to fall, and the selection of microwavable food products in every possible niche (juvenile, diet, heart healthy, vegan, junk) has kept expanding.

Love-hating the ovens began as soon as they appeared. They were fascinating, but expensive; fast, but not intuitively simple. Free microwave cookbooks showed awestruck homemakers how to prepare the most ambitious of recipes in the new

> Free microwave cookbooks showed homemakers how to prepare ambitious recipes in the new machines.

machines—big hunks of meat, fragile desserts, fancy French cuisine—in an effort to prove that those boxes could outperform any thermal appliance in the kitchen. Cooks failed miserably, however, producing raw roasts or eerie lumps of carbon. And consumers feared the radiation. Was it as unhealthy as X rays? If the oven leaked rays, how could you know? If you were absorbing leaked rays, what was the worst-case scenario?

In retrospect, it was a marketing fiasco. What could the machines really do, and how did they do it? Product literature and advertising tried to prove that the ovens could cook anything but neglected to explain the novelty of the thing: a heat source that was invisible and strangely cool to the touch. Manufacturers recommended special techniques and containers. They listed taboos: metal, eggs, etc. But they did not, and still don't, explain the basic science that clarifies all the warnings. Are they worried about scaring the public with talk of sci-fi rays and atomic particles?

Here, once and for all, is what actually happens. The oven's "magnetron" produces electromagnetic waves that make the water molecules inside food rotate. The rotation causes friction. The friction creates heat. The more water contained in the food, the faster the molecular action, and the shorter the cooking time. The oven box seals in the radiation while the oven is operat-

Without knowing how the oven works, it's impossible to love it for its virtues, which happen to be increasing. To begin with, the fuel crisis has promoted the microwave to a new level of dignity as the greenest cooking device in the kitchen. Because it is able to cook food quickly and directly without obstacle—a metal pot and burner (cooktop) or a large cavity (standard thermal oven)—a microwave uses significantly less energy than other appliances.

Its health profile has improved lately as well. Nutritionists have been weighing in, praising the machine as the safest and fastest way to defrost frozen food, especially meats. It's also touted as an ideal way to heat fresh vegetables: Cooking them gently in their own moisture helps seal in the vitamins and minerals often dumped out with the cooking liquids left over from boiling and steaming.

An energy-efficient water boiler, veggie zapper, leftover reheater, meat defroster, snack processor, and cooker of "emergency" meals like frozen pizza, the microwave becomes a modern necessity

> An invisible heat source that was strangely cool to the touch . . . What could the machines really do, and how did they do it?

ing, and the door is designed to open only when it stops. Scientists vouch for the safety of the ovens because the "nonionizing wave radiation" they use is not the radioactive kind; because the doors work; and because low exposure levels are considered to be safe. (Cell phones use microwaves too.)

by virtue of its wide range of tasks.

Sadly, now that so many of us have finally come to peace with the machines, manufacturers are trying to up the ante. They claim the newest microwave can do everything. Brown! Toast! Grill! The oven boxes are being outfitted with fans and hot halogen lightbulbs to simulate the work of convection ovens and broilers. The extra functions require extra buttons, which make the controls ridiculously intricate and unreadable.

A microwave that microwaves is all you need. Leave the other functions to the toaster oven and wall oven. Relax with the knowledge that all microwaves are pretty much the same. One delivers the same quality of rays as the next. What's crucial is the mass of the machine and the cavity; the insides of two similar-looking machines can vary greatly in size. The most minimal controls work best. And the envelope should be in an easy-to-clean color and texture.

The goal here is to acquire the smallest machine possible for your specific desires, in a tone (dark or light) that disappears against its matching background. There's nothing pretty about the prettiest of microwaves, so there's no reason to flaunt that box. A medium oven, of 1 to 1.5 cubic feet with 1000 to 1500 watts, cooks plenty.

Choose a manufacturer that stakes its reputation on its own brand of microwaves, one it actually makes in its own factories. The warranty process is simpler, and you know whom to call if something goes wrong—no middlemen. Right now, Sharp, proud inventor of the revolving carousel tray, makes more microwaves than anyone else. And since the company also makes solar cells, maybe someday its two divisions will create a green offspring: the first solar-powered microwave. (Let's hope it's a bit smaller than its giant ancestor, the first Radarange.)

Toaster Oven

The Little Toy that Could . . .

Toasters and toaster ovens are two different animals. It's easy to love a toaster. It's a one-trick appliance, but it does what it's told quite dependably, year after year. The first, the Toastmaster, appeared in 1926, designed to join its owners right at the breakfast table. An adjustable timer and spring-loaded bread holder—both patented by Charles Strite in 1919—allowed the shiny, streamlined appliance to grill bread on both sides simultaneously, and then to automatically launch it into view as toast.

When Wonder Bread introduced machine-sliced, machine-packaged bread in 1930, domestic toasting machines became more than a sign of wealth—they symbolized faith in the future of industry, and all the good things it was about to deliver.

The toaster was at the forefront of the era of "convenience foods," hybrid creations packaged to look like edible toys. In 1964, Kellogg's launched the Pop-Tart, a "toaster pastry" and one-handed breakfast that required neither refrigerator nor oven. Named after Pop Art, the product's packaging mimicked a new dog food product sold in a foil pouch. Fascinatingly unappetizing in taste and appearance, Pop-Tarts parodied food.

Over the next three decades, toasters endured, getting sleeker and more affordable all the time. But in 1956, GE introduced a curious machine called the Toast-R-Oven. The hybrid metal box could toast or bake and held food horizontally, like a real oven.

It was a confusing convenience— welcomed, then cursed. Cute and petite as a little girl's very first toy oven, the lightbulb-warmed box actually baked and broiled at real oven heat. And it toasted, to boot, though only one side at a time. It replaced neither a regular oven nor a standard toaster but somehow seemed too magical to pass up. It was made for convenience foods, and vice versa.

But in some ways toaster ovens were the most maddening of all small appliances. They failed to make toast as fast as real toasters (flipping was required); food fused on their doors and inside their unwashable cavities, creating a baked-on patina of grime; those doors fell off their flimsy hinges; and the sheet metal-and-plastic exterior became dented and worn-looking in a matter of months.

And toaster ovens endured decades of bad restyling, acquiring more and more features at every turn. Today the standard model is a souped-up, multitasking machine that toasts (both sides), broils, and convection bakes (a fan circulates hot air for faster cooking). For big meals, the toaster oven acts as a tiny second oven. For small meals or snacks, it saves the energy and preheat time of using a big built-in oven.

Those extras may be appealing, but sometimes the tradeoff is an overly complex interface and mediocre performance. Only one manufacturer has treated the toaster oven with consistent dignity over the years, and that's Krups, the German company turned French. Their little ovens never stoop to the latest fads, and show the things for what they really are: simple boxes with heating elements. The glass doors are flush, the sides and top flat. Because Krups has kept the designs simple, the joints and hinges hold up well, and the thing disappears modestly into the countertop jumble. Made of substantial steel and plastic,

> For big meals, it's a tiny second oven; for small portions, it saves on energy and preheat time.

the box is rugged, yet its detailing and control graphics are refined.

In conclusion, on the turf of limited counter space, the battle between the two toasting machines—toaster and toaster oven—has been won. There's only room for one toasting machine, and that's the one that can make your breakfast as well as convection-bake or broil your dinner—the contemporary toaster oven.

Kettle

A Faster Boil

The first task of the morning is the boiling of water. Could anything be simpler? Not these days. We want our water to bubble up fast and magically in a big machine with lots of buttons, a machine that not only heats the water but also dribbles it over a mound of pulverized coffee beans suspended over a heated pot.

For most of the day, the big machine sits empty, hogging counter space and looking increasingly obsolete as newer, faster, smarter, larger models arrive on the market, promising to drip water more dramatically.

Meanwhile, the boiling of water for anything else—tea or other infusions, hot chocolate, oatmeal, miso, instant soup—requires different equipment: stovetop teakettles, saucepans, microwaves, and so on.

drinks or liquid meals they might fancy. And one machine is plenty.

The electric kettle is the answer. What it does is fast and simple. At the bottom of the kettle, a stainless steel heating element acts as a hot poker, using 1500 watts to boil water directly. What it won't do is take up lots of space, try to look important, and promise everything.

Though there are many electric kettles on the market, the best known is also the best performer: the Ibis by Bodum, a Dane-founded Swiss company. A tall and sleek oval form made of heat-reinforced polypropylene plastic, the Ibis's virtues are manifold. Once the water boils, the machine turns itself off automatically. The standard, 50-ounce body is cordless, so you can carry it anywhere. (The base plate holds the wall plug.) Kettle owners admire the speed of the boil—

> ## The British, the most experienced water boilers in the world, solved the problem long ago.

What to do? The British, the world's most experienced water boilers, solved the gear issue long ago. Hot water, they decided, should be available quickly and efficiently to all takers, whatever only four minutes for 50 ounces—and Bodum claims it uses less energy than any stovetop kettle.

But in a world full of pretentious water boilers, it is shape that makes the Ibis unique. While bulbous, bulging teakettles and coffee gadgets collect dust and stains just by sitting around, the vertical walls of the hardworking Ibis will stay clean and modern.

What will you do with the time, space, and fuel gained by not using your cooktop to boil water? Invite that new neighbor over for coffee.

~~~~~~~~~~~~~~~

Teapot
Personality Counts

R ub Aladdin's lamp—the vessel with the long spout and the tall handle—and a genie pops out. Everyone recognizes that symbol of instant gratification. The teapot, another spouted vessel with a handle, also tends to get people's hopes up.

Ever since the Ming dynasty, tea leaf infusions have promised remedies. To wake up, fall asleep, cure a cold, melt stress, bond with friends, negotiate with enemies or outlive them, you need only perform a simple ritual: Put the proper tea in the teapot; add hot water; let it steep just long enough; and drink the infusion leisurely.

The tea may not grant your wishes immediately, but drink it slowly and carefully and it somehow begins to feel beneficial.

A couple of decades ago, the American notion of tea went no fur-ther than a tea bag called Lipton. Real tea was the brown dust encased in a dunkable tissue bag, and herbal tea was something used by hippies and witches.

Tea bags eliminated the need for teapots. Now that the comeback of whole foods and organic produce has brought whole tea leaves back to the marketplace, tea bags have gone the way of instant coffee. Convenience has been replaced by flavor, and teapots are back.

Which pot is best? It's one with meaning, one you feel obligated to keep and protect whether you're a tea person or not. It might be the family heirloom pieced together with glue; the hip Swedish wedding gift from your best friend; or the kitschy Queen Elizabeth teapot you bought in London.

A pot with meaning, one you feel obligated to keep and protect, tea person or not . . .

The personality of the meaningful teapot is, frankly, more important than its performance. Its form is evocative to begin with, just anthropomorphic enough to make you think about human appendages and gestures (arms, noses, heads, bellies). But it's abstract enough to conjure up other living things too: animals, fruits, and vegetables like gourds and squash.

The teapot can evoke entire cultures. In one eyeful, it can reveal as much zeitgeist as a whole museum. To compare eighteenth-century France and Japan, just put a flamboyant Rococo porcelain teapot next to a plain black *tetsubin* (a flat, somber cast-iron teapot). Both nations might have been drinking the same beverage, but they were clearly approaching daily life in wildly different ways.

Before you choose your own evocative teapot, think about the emotions and sensations you want to unleash with it. In other words, choose a purpose for the pot and its contents.

A pot of tea can be a timing device for mild social encounters at any moment of the day. Its arrival signals the start of a quiet pause during which those gathered agree to do nothing but relax and chat. Leisure, uncomplicated by meals, is the purpose. The larger the teapot, the longer the break. The teapot-as-timer is also a tool for business, especially in Asian nations, where fraternizing over beverages is part of every negotiation; an austere pot would better suit that purpose.

In traditional Japanese homes, the teapot has also worked as a space heater. All day long, a cast-iron teapot would simmer over a stove of hot coals; water was always ready for tea, and the dry winter air benefited from the steam. Today, any teapot can work as a tiny radiator-humidifier and as an excellent hand warmer as well.

The tea-making ritual isn't complex. You dump a measure of dried leaves into a pot of hot water, let it steep, and pour it into a cup. The role of the teapot is open to question, however. Should the pot insulate the tea? Protect the pouring hand? Contain an integral strainer? Press the tea or let it float? Last forever? Withstand direct heat? Prove easy to pour and easy to clean? Display the contents? The more devoted the tea drinker, the more fervent the answers.

In the absence of an existing heirloom, nothing can match the teapot that makes a spectacle out of the tea itself. An all-glass teapot—of strong, heat-resistant borosilicate—allows you to watch the dried tea as it tints the water and unfurls into floating leaves. Don't worry about straining or pressing devices; just let the leaves settle to the bottom, monitor the color, then pour into an insulating cup (see page 149).

It almost makes winter seem like a good idea.

~~~~~~~~~~~~

Dish Drainer

Say Good-bye to Mildew

The dishwasher is full. The dishwasher is broken. There's too little for a load. The lasagna pan won't fit. Everyone has to do a little manual dishwashing now and then. It's actually a good thing: Dishwashers are designed for overkill—sanitizing the dirtiest dishes by using piping hot water in long cycles of washing and rinsing. People, on the other hand, wash dishes with shorter sessions of much cooler hot water. Both methods work, but human dishwashing can save water and power on small loads. So put on some good kitchen gloves and put that sink to use.

Aside from the knuckle power, draining is the ugly part of "doing the dishes." No matter which method you choose—immediate towel drying or leisurely air-drying—the rinsed tableware customarily spends some dripping time in a sink, over a sink, or in a countertop draining device.

The classic plastic dish drainer is so annoying to clean that it tends to end up growing a variety of molds; it's the dirtiest of kitchen secrets.

Designers have tried to invent the perfect dish drainers, and their efforts are fascinatingly architectural: chromed steel scaffolding, swooping plastic pans, intricate wooden ladders. But all tend to be difficult to wash and impossible to hide away, just like their rubbery precursors.

There is, however, a simple solution that won't be appearing in the housewares section anytime soon. It's a swim towel.

If you've used Speedo's superabsorbent sports towel on your skin, you've felt the miracle of PVA foam—the letters stand for "polyvinyl alcohol." Okay, it's a bit weird, but that's part of its charm.

The solution won't be appearing in the housewares section anytime soon . . .

The towel starts out rigid as cardboard, softening as it absorbs water. (It can absorb about twelve times its dry weight in water before becoming saturated.)

PVA foam is a synthetic sponge with an open cell structure similar to that of a natural sea sponge. It wicks lots of water immediately and dries out fast, without encouraging mold and bacteria. The same kind of PVA towel is also sold as a car-drying towel—online, and in the auto section of big-box stores—replacing the classic suede cloth called the "shammy," or chamois.

How do you use it? Like a yoga mat. Just lay it flat on the counter—it's about the size of a hand towel—and pile on a layer of dishes. The towel provides some friction, and rather than dripping or pooling, the water is wicked into the cells. When the dishes are drained, let the towel dry flat, then stack it with your cutting boards. If you have more than a counter's worth of dishes, just recruit the stainless serving platter described on page 152. Line it with the swim towel and park it somewhere convenient. Air-dry the towel once the dishes are dry, and machine wash to refresh.

It's also great for wiping down counters, cleaning up spills, and towel-drying sopping wet hair (hopefully not all in one go).

~~~~~~~~~~~~~~~~~~~~~

Dish Towel

Permanence is Back

A t its worst, the dish towel is the most disgusting thing in the kitchen: a limp, mangy rag always too wet to do its job. If we buy dish towels at all, we expect them to be slightly more permanent versions of paper towels: cheap, short-lived, and ill made in the lowest grade cottons available. And our addiction to paper products has made its mark: It is in fact nearly impossible to find decent everyday dish towels.

We're accustomed to the crisp, hygienic touch of the paper stuff, advertised by strong lumbermen in flannel shirts. They are always new, always dry, ever disposable, and thus antimicrobial—the ultimate marketing hook. Given the choice between protecting our families' health and preserving the purity of Canada from the mess of industrial paper making, Canada loses.

Germ fear is the same emotion that launched household paper products at the start of the twentieth century. In 1907, Arthur Scott invented the paper towel when a factory error stuck him with a large quantity of toilet tissue rolled too thick. Scott had the rolls perforated into sheets and sold them to the city of Philadelphia as a replacement for the germ-spreading, rolling cloth towels in school lavatories. "Sani-Towels" didn't emerge as a household product until 1931, and they didn't replace cloth towels as a kitchen necessity until much later.

Such hygienic overload was never actually necessary in the home, and now that we're faced with a state of environmental emergency, it's time to regress. The proper dish towel is not a throwaway, but a well-woven rectangle of good-quality linen formerly known as a tea towel.

Flax, the plant fiber that makes up linen, is the ideal source for several reasons. The production of cotton is extremely resource intensive, using up loads of water, herbicides, and pesticides; not so with flax, which is simply easier to grow.

Textile experts say linen is remarkable in that it's actually stronger wet than dry and able to absorb more

113

than twice the amount of water as cotton. It also dries faster and takes up less space.

As for longevity, ancient Egyptians expected it to last well into the afterlife—as proved by their linen-wrapped mummies. And archeologists' findings confirm that it's the oldest fabric around.

At the very least, you need linen dish towels to dry wineglasses after a hand washing in hot soapy water. According to glassmakers, that's the only way to give glass the kind of crystalline transparency wine deserves. The material is incomparably lint free, and its thinness allows for better reach into the bowl of the wineglass.

Eventually, you learn that linen has a life. Crisp and stiff right after washing, it relaxes as you use it and renews itself with each laundering. Over the years, it may change character, becoming softer without losing its strength. Linen towels should never be thrown away, only passed down to future generations and finally retired to less public service as polishing cloths.

Choose a dish towel as you would a scarf, that useful swath of fabric that feels nice on the skin but also decorates the closet in between wearings. Search for a towel that makes you happy to look at. Since wet dish towels need to languish around the kitchen, they might as well look good as they dry.

The more you like it, the more you'll use it. The more you use it, the less you'll use the things you've been using to avoid your former dish towel. That's fewer trips to the grim bulk stores for twelve-packs of paper towels and more pantry space to reclaim.

If anyone asks you where you got your exquisite towels, however, they may not like the complex answer. Wonderful but affordable linen dish towels come from tag sales and thrift shops, from street markets in countries like France and Italy, and from foreign websites.

Perhaps someday, fine tea towels will return as the coveted wedding present they used to be, and happy newlyweds will finally be able to properly dry all their newly acquired champagne flutes.

> Ancient Egyptians expected linen to last well into the afterlife. . . .

Coffeemaker

Take the Plunge

The automatic coffeemaker is the SUV of small appliances. Like the sport utility vehicle, it is big, often black, and humorless if not menacing. It promises more protection than it can deliver. And it takes the thrill out of a potentially sensory adventure by making it all about the machine. No human finesse required.

In Italy, where the cars are tiny and fast, petite stovetop coffeemakers (Mokas) make an intense brew. That paradise has helped many a convert find the real thrill in driving *and* coffeemaking. Neither needs a lot of metal and plastic. In fact, the intensity of the adventure increases in direct disproportion to the size of the gear.

The automatic drip coffeemaker hogs more than its share of counter space. It seems to use mysterious, invisible forces, powered by electricity and controlled by electronic sensors, to complete its important mission— hence the claim on all that counter. The coffeemaker projects authority, especially in the morning, when it comes alive, pulsating with hisses and gurgles. Its attitude, along with its indecipherable buttons, assures you that it knows how to make coffee better and faster than you do.

In reality, the machine's work is mundane. It heats water, drips it slowly over coffee grounds, and acts as a hot plate to keep the brew warm. The owner must do the rest: fill the water tank, pour the ground beans into the filter, and clean the residue.

Ever since the gadget's appearance, beginning with Mr. Coffee in the 1970s, American consumers have expected it to keep advancing, as all small appliances do, in both features and styling. But what more could a coffee machine do?

Create time. That dream became a sort of collusion between the manufacturer and the consumer. Consumers bought into the myth that paying for fancier machines could buy them some minutes during the morning rush, along with a higher standard of living. Eventually the machines grew bigger, even as microprocessors got smaller, so they could be programmed to make better coffee more rapidly. The ultimate machine can be expected to boil water, grind beans, transfer ground beans, and brew coffee before its owner is even awake.

S ome rethinking is in order. Such a device is much too big for a one-note breakfast appliance, and it won't budge to create room for making *real* meals. Like that SUV, it starts to look outdated as soon as it gets home, and it needs frequent cleaning. You have to read the pamphlet to figure it out, then explain it all to parents and other visitors. And when the grinder stops working for no reason at all, right after its warranty expires, you have to replace the whole thing or buy a backup appliance!

During this frantic search for extra time, the truth about coffee has escaped us completely. Yes, the temperamental bean is grown in a laborious process and prepared for roasting in an elaborate series of steps. But the theory behind coffee *brewing* is idiotically simple: Like tea, coffee is an infusion; you put the stuff in hot water and drink it before it gets cold.

It turns out one can brew excellent coffee as easily as one prepares tea. Switch to a French press, or *cafetière,* a tool that's been around since the 1850s. (The term "French press" came later, after the French company Melior perfected and eventually licensed the tool.)

The concept? You pour ground coffee into a cylinder, pour hot water over the grounds, then plunge a mesh filter through the mush, so the sludge remains below and the filtered coffee sits on top.

What does it actually taste like? Stronger than drip coffee, weaker than espresso. Coffee buffs explain that French press coffee offers up more of the bean's essential oils.

As for the tool itself, it's easy to understand and to clean. In the event that a part breaks or is lost, you won't have very much trouble replacing it. The warranty on the frame is long. And perhaps best of all, it won't clutter your kitchen. Because it's portable, it can hide away after breakfast and reemerge during dinner parties, when you move it to the table and perform the pressing with a flourish. (Or have guests serve themselves from multiple small presses.)

The best presses come from Bodum, which sells sturdy, modern designs, reasonably priced for everyday use. The best of Bodum's models is the Melior. The frame is stainless steel; the beaker is borosilicate glass; and the handle is Santoprene, a plastic that can mimic Bakelite.

(But wait, there are more options. The beaker comes in nonbreakable polycarbonate. The frame comes in chromed brass. The handle . . . this is where retail stores come in handy.)

Coffee hobbyists will describe a dozen steps necessary for preparing this coffee, but the series can be reduced to this:

1. Boil water.
2. Spoon some coarsely ground coffee into the glass beaker.
3. Pour in the hot water. Stir.
4. Wait a few minutes.
5. Press the plunger down.
6. Drink the coffee while it's warm.
7. Gift your automatic drip coffee machine to anyone who will take it.

Pot Holders

Not So Complicated After All . . .

Two suede pot holders. That's all you need. Suede. What you *don't* need is far more interesting, though, and that's the baroque kitchen body armor you see everywhere now. Where did it all come from? How did cooking get so dangerous all of a sudden? What happened to all the puppet-shaped mitts in cute ginghamy fabrics?

Now "pot holders" are Nomex and Kevlar arm guards that go all the way to the elbow. They are giant pairs of rubbery-but-stiff, dolphinlike silicone oven mitts that seem to have a life of their own.

Sure it's fun gearing up like firefighters and Hazmat technicians, but that insulation weighs you down, reducing your fine motor control and actually adding potential danger to the process.

You don't need to wear anything that feels weird on your skin or makes your forearms sweat. And you don't have to buy whole-arm protection that's too huge to fit in a drawer and too gruesome to hang in plain view.

Here's another case where the indoor kitchen has been influenced by the outdoor kitchen aesthetic—the craze for grilling outside on a stainless steel, propane-fired megagadget as big as the cart of a New York hot dog vendor. As kitchens and backyards have gotten hotter—with the installation of cooking appliances with more BTUs, more burners, more grills, higher flames, and bigger ovens—mitt makers have tried to convince us that we need heavier protection and better coverage for all that heat.

But when you look at the actual heat-adjacent labor being done at home, quite infrequently, in or on those devices, it's not all that scary—a pan of brownies exiting a 325-degree oven, a few burgers being flipped, a pan of eggs moving four inches from stove to counter. With a tiny bit of dexterity, a little practice, and some concentration, an adult can ace most cooking gestures without serious insulation. (Dodge that steam, avoid that broiler.)

This is where those suede pot holders come in. If you watch what you're doing, they give you just enough coverage to avoid burns. A thin, malleable swatch of leather makes a surprisingly good heat insulator. And both sides work well: one's rougher, for better gripping, while the other is smooth on the palms.

The standard models are sewn like a pocket (you slip your hand inside) and equipped with a hanging loop. They can be rinsed off or machine washed, but unlike fabrics, the leather will take on a nice, rugged patina with use.

If you don't believe that leather can take the heat and possible flames, just look at welders' gloves—still made of trusty old cowhide.

Trash Can

Refuse Gets Some Dignity

Trash is the last frontier of household innovation. (Perhaps because we hate to think about garbage as much as we hate to handle it.) We're a nation of prodigious trash makers, yet we have no idea where to park the garbage inside a house, where to store it outside a house, or where it goes once we've paid the trash haulers to disappear it, preferably to a distant state during the wee hours.

We fit ugly plastic bags inside our trash cans, wrestling with them on the way in and on the way out. We hate the plastic bags, and the way the trash cans flaunt them and the mess inside, instead of making it all invisible and odorless.

Unwilling to throw good money at bad trash, we buy plastic bins that are unpleasant to look at and unwieldy to handle. Why glorify the contents? On any list of household chores, garbage duties rank the lowest in popularity: tossing garbage into the kitchen trash can (gross); changing liner bags (annoying); dumping full bags in the outside trash bins (offensive); walking trash bins to the curb and back (awkward).

The only citizens who learn to love garbage logistics live in environmentally hip communities where recycling is a municipal art form, a ballet of coordinated collection services separating one genre of refuse from another. Residents of those sensitive places don't really trash their trash, they collect and package it. Mindfully, they rinse their bottles and bundle and bow tie their newspapers. They take pride in their artisanry and expect others to feel the same way.

If you live in a place where trash isn't a political or aesthetic issue and peer pressure doesn't motivate, you may be inspired to live a green life for selfish reasons. One of the perks of curating trash, beyond creating smaller landfills and cleaner everything, is a more meaningful, playful relationship with the garbage you once despised.

To do this, you must find a virtuous trash can, one that is handsomely proportioned and mechanically smart. This sounds like a ridiculous mission, of course, especially when you start comparing the prices of good cans with those of look-alike bad cans; but the big-box stores' twenty-dollar versions are in no way comparable to the hundred-dollar stainless cans. And the rewards can actually change the way you live in big ways and small, altruistic and not.

Okay, there *is* a caveat. Before you buy the trash can that's going to transform your life, you're going to have to rearrange that life a bit. You'll need to follow a five-step plan.

The first step is one you've heard before. Buy fresh, perishable food. Commodities, not commercial products. Live apples, not applesauce snacks. That eliminates tons of packaging right there: frozen food boxes, aluminum cans, glass bottles, and so on. Think of it this way: The slimmer your kitchen garbage, the slimmer your body will become.

The second step is also nutritional. Drink water: filtered tap water, or bulk spring water, but not value-added, flavored, or vitamined water in two-sip bottles. More health, less packaging.

The third chore is gruesome until you get into it. Toss all vegetable scraps into a compost pile, pail, gadget, or heap. Use the finished compost to feed plants. (Own plants. They freshen the air while looking alive and perky.)

The fourth directive is easy. Sequester clean paper and plastic. Reading, writing, and packaging material take up more space and weigh more than any other household debris. Pile them separately, away from kitchen trash, and you'll make fewer trips to the curb. Newspapers can collect in cardboard boxes or fancy containers. If your town's recyclers do not pick them up now, they will in the very near future.

The fifth step, alas, is a lot more radical. Decide to stop buying cheap merchandise and replacing it with new junk all the time. Endeavor to buy stuff with a long life, including the kitchen trash can itself.

A trash can designed for a long life will not only outlast most household appliances, but will also deliver a surprising amount of daily pleasure in the way it looks and works.

Actually, a good trash can is a sort of appliance: a metal machine with moving parts. The better the parts, the smoother and quieter the device will be.

Buy fresh.
Drink water.
Start a compost.
Sort.

Look for a round or squared tubular shape, with a hinged, nonsqueaking lid operated by a foot pedal or finger pressure. The can should have a lightweight, pull-out liner bucket that enables the bag to disappear from view while remaining fixed to the rim. The outside body of the can should not chip, rust, or dent easily. And it should outlast one generation. (If you bought the can while your kids were infants, you may not have to replace it until they graduate from college.)

The Dutch company Brabantia is currently making trash cans with a ten-year warranty, in line with its corporate mission to develop household products that will last up to twenty years. This contrarian approach is pretty remarkable at a time when the best appliance makers are hell-bent on outmoding their own products and reducing their warranty limits.

How does all this affect the experience of tossing trash? Suddenly, it becomes an interaction. You push something, the lid opens smoothly to accept your offering; it closes quietly. The device turns a mindless act, performed hundreds of times per week, into a pleasant exchange of action and reaction. Because its mechanics must be solid enough to last, the can is tactile and noticeably nonflimsy.

Try the pleasingly svelte, cylindrical Brabantia thirty-liter/eight-gallon "Touch Bin" in matte stainless steel, textured to hide fingerprints. The size is spacious but not overwhelming. And the design is quite elegant. A plastic liner bin fits loosely into the can's steel shell, concealing the trash bag's rolled-over edges. The lid's touch-top, operated by a plastic hinge, eases open in response to a gentle touch and stays open until you flip it down. The patented system makes a good seal but feels quite effortless.

How does such a loveable bin change your life? It commands respect. It doesn't exactly reprimand you when you toss stuff away, but somehow it ends up being treated better and getting filled with less junk than your former trash cans—which you will be happy to ditch in return for a long-term relationship.

The trash can is also a reminder that whatever you bring into your house—even a vessel for things leaving it—ought to be something solid enough to enjoy.

COOKING

W HEN IT COMES TO KITCHENWARE, it's important to touch and handle before you buy; you don't want to end up with a prohibitively heavy stockpot or a knife handle that just doesn't feel right. In many cases, I've based my sourcing recommendations on whether you can visit the products in person, handle them, and purchase them without the additional costs of packaging and shipping.

Another thing to keep in mind: Just about anything made of cast iron, stainless steel, or glass can be bought very old, old, or slightly used at very low prices via online listings, thrift stores, or yard sales.

CHEF'S KNIFE

- Try: The 8"-stamped stainless steel version with plastic handle from Sanelli's Premana Professional line
- Find it: Kitchen and restaurant supply stores

Cost: $38 to $47

PARING KNIFE

- Try: The 4"-stamped stainless steel version with plastic handle from Sanelli's Premana Professional line
- Find it: Kitchen and restaurant supply stores

Cost: $9 to $12

BREAD KNIFE

- 9" to 9½", with scalloped teeth, a stainless steel blade, and a handle in wood or other material
- Find it: Interesting kitchen supply stores; online

Cost: $20 to $30

CUTTING BOARD

- 10" x 17" Richlite board by Epicurean
- Find it: High-end kitchen supply stores; online

Cost: $20 to $25

MEASURING SPOON

- The "Nuscup"
- Find it: Some big-box stores; kitchen supply stores

Cost: $10 to $15

MEASURING CUP

- Good Grips Angled Measuring Cup by OXO, 2-cup model
- Find It: Any purveyor of kitchen supplies

Cost: $8 to $10

MIXING BOWL

- 5-quart stainless steel mixing bowl
- Plain, shallow, and lightweight
- Find it: Any purveyor of kitchen supplies

Cost: $15 to $50, depending on the thickness of the steel and detailing

SALAD SPINNER

- Easy Spin Salad Spinner by Zyliss
- Find it: High-end kitchen supply stores; some big-box stores

Cost: $20 to $30

MESH STRAINER

- Stainless-steel, fine mesh
- 6" basket diameter
- Find it: Any purveyor of kitchen supplies

Cost: $8 to $15

SALTCELLAR

- No shakers. A dispenser for pinching and sprinkling, suitable for both table and kitchen counter
- Try: A polished stainless-steel sugar cube dispenser with a pivoting hood
- Find it: Some kitchen and restaurant supply stores

Cost: $15 to $20

PEPPER MILL

- Peugeot's small Bistro pepper mill, in dark-stained beech wood
- Find it: Kitchen and restaurant supply stores

Cost: $25 to $35

CAN OPENER

- Swing-A-Way portable can opener, model No. 407
- Find it: Corner stores; big-box stores; department stores ... anywhere

Cost: $10 to $13

SCISSORS

- Fiskars No. 8
- Find it: Any purveyor of stationery, hardware, or sewing supplies

Cost: $10 to $15

COOKING SPOON

- 12" to 14" stainless steel
- Find it: Kitchen and restaurant supply stores

Cost: $10 to $15

TONGS

- 12"-long stainless steel, with locking mechanism
- Find it: Kitchen and restaurant supply stores

Cost: $10 to $15

SPATULA

- Stainless steel
- Find it: Kitchen and restaurant supply stores

Cost: $10 to $15

VEGETABLE PEELER

- OXO Good Grips Swivel Peeler
- Try: For simplicity the Kuhn Rikon vegetable peeler (plastic handle and Y-shaped carbon steel blade) is as tiny as can be and goes for about $4.
- Find it: Any purveyor of kitchen supplies

Cost: About $10

GRATER

- 8"-long Microplane Zester/Grater
- Find it: Any purveyor of kitchen supplies

Cost: About $15

WINE OPENER

- Stainless-steel double-winged lever corkscrew
- Find it: Any purveyor of kitchen supplies

Cost: Under $10

MEAT THERMOMETER

- The "Thermapen" thermocouple
- Find it: Online, at www.thermoworks.com

Cost: Under $90

FRY PAN

- Lodge Manufacturing's 10" cast-iron "Pro-Logic" skillet
- Factory seasoned with a proprietary soy-based, rust-preventive finish
- Eco-rating: This fry pan will far outlast your kitchen, or any appliance in it!
- Find it: Any purveyor of kitchen supplies

Cost: About $20

DUTCH OVEN

- Lodge Manufacturing's 7-quart, 12" cast-iron "Pro-Logic" Dutch oven
- Factory seasoned with a proprietary soy-based, rust-preventive finish
- Eco-rating: This Dutch oven will far outlast your kitchen, or any appliance in it!
- Find it: Any purveyor of kitchen supplies

Cost: About $80

STOCKPOT

- 8-quart, stainless steel
- Aluminum disc in the pot's bottom, stainless-steel lid, riveted handles
- Find it: Try restaurant supply stores first.

Cost: $40 to $60

SAUCEPAN

- 2-quart, stainless steel
- Aluminum disc in the pan's bottom, stainless-steel lid, riveted handles
- Find it: Try restaurant supply stores first.

Cost: $30 to $50

BROILING/
ROASTING PAN

- The WaterBroiler–WaterRoaster Pan
- Designed, manufactured, and sold by
  Lee Drannan Smithson
- Find it: Online, at www.waterbroiler.com
  (Drannan Cookware Company)

*Cost: About $50; features a one-year
money-back guarantee*

MICROWAVE OVEN

- Midsize model made by Sharp
  or other reputable company
- 1 to 1.2 cubic foot capacity,
  about 1200 watts
- Find it: Purveyors of small appliances

Cost: Under $90

TOASTER OVEN

- Six-slice, digital convection toaster oven
  made by Krups (simplest model available)
- Eco-rating: For small quantities of food, uses
  far less power than a built-in oven/broiler.
- Find it: www.krups.com features
  a list of retailers.

*Cost: $160 or less;
look for sale models for better pricing.*

KETTLE

- Bodum's Ibis electric water kettle
- Eco-rating: Uses less energy than a
  traditional stovetop kettle.
- Find it: Department stores; online; big-box
  stores; some kitchen supply stores

Cost: About $35 to $45

TEAPOT

- Borosilicate glass teapot
  (with or without strainer)
- Find it: Tea and coffee supply stores;
  kitchen supply stores

Cost: $35 to $45

DISH DRAINER

- PVA foam towel, aka "superabsorbent swim
  towel," aka "auto shammy"
- Approximately 18" x 24"
- Find it: Auto supply section of big-box
  stores or purveyors of outdoor gear

Cost: $10 to $15

DISH TOWEL

- 100% linen
- Eco-rating: Comes from flax,
  a sustainable crop; lightweight and
  compact in the wash and quick to line or
  machine dry; long-lasting and durable
- Find it: High-end kitchen supply stores;
  purveyors of European linen

Cost: $10

COFFEEMAKER

- Bodum's 8-cup, 32-oz. French press (Chambord); stainless steel frame and borosilicate glass beaker
- Eco-note: In case of damage, no need to replace the whole apparatus— Bodum sells spare parts.
- Find it: Department stores; online; big-box stores; coffee and tea supply stores; some kitchen supply stores

Cost: About $40

POT HOLDERS

- Suede with pouch for grip
- Find it: High-end kitchen supply stores, online

Cost: $10 to $15

TRASH CAN

- Brabantia's 8-gallon, matte stainless steel "Touch Bin"

Note: *The bin comes with a ten-year warranty.*

- Find it: High-end kitchen and home supply stores

Cost: $130 to $140

CHAPTER FOUR

DINING

INVENTORY

- Dining Table
- Dining Chair
- Dinner Plate
- Small Plate
- Soup Plate
- Fork

- Table Knife
- Teaspoon
- Soupspoon
- Water Glass
- Wineglass
- Mug

- Napkin
- Serving Platter
- Serving Bowl
- Sugar Bowl
- Creamer

The rise of suburban Tudor mansionettes, with their overblown dimensions, has created a fashion for formal rooms and furniture too prim to enjoy.

The dining room has become the loneliest place in the house, a repository for the formal "dining room set"—a large period reproduction table surrounded by matching chairs. Those chairs remain empty most of the year as owners continue to eat in the kitchen, den, or great room (a high-ceilinged kitchen-den fusion), on laps, counters, bars, or informal tables.

Before you acquire a dining table, or a mansionette, for that matter, visit the formal dining room and consider turning it into a place where you'll be unafraid to serve family and friends real dinners as well as make messes (helping with homework assignments, scrapbooking, gambling, and so on) after dinner has been cleared. Be honest. If the room is just too fancy or austere for your weekday lasagna—and so many of them are—transform it into a space that's worth heating and cooling: a library, an office, or a music room.

Wherever you set up your dining space, consider streamlining. Traditionally, no household is considered complete without two sets of tableware: one lovely, expensive set for special occasions and one affordably clunky set for normal days, the idea being to impress guests with immaculately polished silver and uncracked china. But entertaining is—and should be—a lot more casual these days. Why buy an expensive space-hogging collection "just for company"? You're not running a hotel or restaurant, after all.

To take it a step further: There's no rulebook dictating that a set of china or flatware be a *matched* set. It's just an arbitrary custom. If you're buying for quality, a spoon and knife might be made of unlike materials and handles. Why not, when they perform such different functions? Just like cookware, dining gear chosen separately, over time, proves far more satisfying than a set of identical pieces.

Take both a practical and artistic approach. Essentially, what you're looking for is dinnerware and glassware that feels good, is long-lasting, can stand up to a dishwasher, and— the most elusive quality of all—appeals to you.

Add some good food and a couple bottles of wine, surround it all with a group of decent folks, and enjoy one of the greatest things in life: the pleasure of company.

~~~~~~~~~~~~~~~~~

Dining Table
The Gathering Spot

P repare to abuse your dining table. It ought to be the sturdiest, most indestructible piece of furniture in the house, with legs able to support the largest turkey, a surface able to absorb the plate banging and spoon gouging of toddlers, and joints hardy enough to withstand moves from one home to another. The dining table has been mollycoddled for too long.

How many people should it seat? Depends on the size of your ideal or average dinner party. Everyone has a magic number. Ace hostesses claim that four guests are too quiet; that ten demand serious prep work; and that six are just right. (For these purposes, let's go with that, though you should follow your preferences.)

A rectangular table sized for eight diners is a good choice, as it can hold six people in two comfortable configurations, with room for surprises. (Round tables are more compact but less handy as occasional work surfaces.) Unless you can't imagine seating more than four souls or fewer than ten, figure on 36 inches for the width and 72 inches for the length.

Of course, you'll need to make sure that the size suits your dining area.

Lay out the table dimensions right on the floor. Using a tape measure and some newspaper, piece together a 36-by-72-inch rectangle or oblong. Place some real or imaginary chairs around the table and try walking around the arrangement. Is there enough room to circulate, to fit in a beloved hutch or buffet? If space is tight, shrink the footprint down a little (34 inches by 68 inches), or a lot, to a table for six (34 inches by 60 inches).

Then you'll be ready to begin the search for a serious piece of furniture, one so attractive you'll want to keep it forever. (Steel yourself: Such a piece is likely to be expensive, and finding it will demand serious legwork.)

Narrow down the options by eliminating anything made of overly hard materials that will be cold on the forearms, harsh to the ears, or unsightly when scratched or chipped. That means no glass, metal, or stone.

That leaves tables made from plants: familiar hardwoods (ash, beech, maple, cherry, walnut, oak) and managed or salvaged tropical woods (teak, mahogany, mango, rubber wood, and bamboo). Conventional hardwoods are lightweight enough to

---

A serious piece of furniture, it should be attractive enough to keep forever.

---

move around, and blond enough to stain, or restain, light to dark. Heavier tropical woods start out dark and can be stained darker. (Keep wood in its natural color, however, and it will be less likely to show scratches and dents.)

In general, environmentalists favor local hardwoods from well-managed forests over exotic woods shipped from distant lands. Though in recent years bamboo lumber has been espoused as a responsible choice, it brings up some complex issues. The best move of all is to avoid the whole debate by using local recycled wood, in the form of a preowned table in any solid wood.

Beware, though, that the visual difference between good wooden tables and bad wooden tables is slight—at the beginning, anyway.

Seek out a table with solid legs and a top covered by nothing but a thin coat of clear protective sealer, preferably one that's nonhazardous—free of solvents or VOCs (volatile organic compounds). Water-based sealants or sealants made of natural oils like

linseed, soy bean, or safflower would fit the bill.

The best tables are put together with real wood joinery; their tops are not single pieces of wood, but rather a series of solid planks lined up or interlocked to form a continuous surface.

Actually, many modern dining tables don't have solid hardwood tops. Furniture salespeople will assure you that this is par for the course: Most fine pieces of furniture and prized antiques are "wood veneered"—constructed of imperfect hardwoods and covered with a beautiful layer of show-wood. True enough. But salespeople also vouch for laminates as a modern equivalent, and that's where it gets tricky.

A laminate is generally a thin sheet of fused paper and metal foil, often containing a photograph of the natural material it's imitating, and sometimes embossed with an imitative texture as well. The problem is that laminates are glued to the surface of "engineered wood"—plywood (thin wood sheets glued into panels) or particleboard (glued sawdust and wood chips pressed into panels)—rather than real, solid hardwood. Once the laminate surface is harmed, it can't be properly repaired. And laminate continues to degrade and lose value over time.

A solid, planked table gains character as it ages and may hold its value, or gain some over the long run. If it gains the wrong kind of character, it can be periodically restored, or completely revamped in a new finish.

As for form, the equation is simple: The legs of a rectangular table create its personality. The simplest structure—one leg per corner—provides the most flexible seating plan.

But it's the shape of the legs, tapering down to the floor or curving in rococo swirls, that gives the table true presence, which will last long after diners take their leave.

Dining Chair
Comfort and Presence

With so many designers and architects out there struggling to craft iconic pieces of furniture, it won't be long before another remarkable dining chair appears on the market—just as one did a mere 150 years ago (see box, page 132). Maybe it will make us feel weightlessly suspended as it performs some kind of ultrasonic leg therapy yet to be invented! Or maybe it will be made of svelte, resilient bio-plastics molded from the same organic ingredients as dinner itself.

For the moment, here are the nine basic traits of a good dining chair:

1. Personality, not just prettiness. The curves of legs and back animate the chair. Empty or occupied, it should enliven a room but never overwhelm.

2. A comfortable back, angled gently to support the sitter's spine in a slightly relaxed—not bolt upright—position. A backrest with a bit of flex provides nice support for a backward lean.

3. A forgiving seat, slightly concave, in wood or a breathable material that's easy to clean. Neither too hard nor too soft, the seat pan should cradle the buttocks evenly—no pressure points.

4. Lightness. There's no excuse for a heavy chair. Lightweight chairs, well constructed, are just as strong and handsome as hefty ones, and they move easily for parties and housecleaning.

5. Grippability. Some chairs are easier to lift than others. Consider center of gravity, bulk, and available handholds. A grippable chair feels lighter.

6. A friendly material that ages well. Solid wood is the best; beech wood is the lightest. Solid, sealed, unpainted wood takes on more character when it's dented and gouged, while disguised woods (painted or veneered), metals, and plastics look better in pristine condition. Wood feels hospitable, since it's warm to the touch, and dining chairs touch much of the anatomy: back, arms, thighs, calves, and hands. Wooden chairs also soften the acoustics of a dining room by absorbing sound rather than bouncing it back.

7. Good proportions. In order for the sitter to fit under the standard dining table, the top of the seat should be 18 inches above the floor; the seat itself should be about 15 inches deep, long enough to support the thighs but short enough to allow

THE CHAIR OF CHAIRS

Perhaps no chair has seated happier sitters than the so-called Vienna café chair of 1859, produced by Michael Thonet in his factory in Moravia, part of the current Czech Republic. The Kaffeehausstuhl Nr. 14, or coffeehouse chair number 14 (aka "the chair of chairs," aka "the world's most successful commercial product") was designed for inexpensive mass production. Thonet's efficient process bent local beech wood into durable "bentwood" shapes that were joined by just a few wooden parts and screws.

The chair was economical in several ways. Café owners liked that its compact profile could fit many patrons into tight quarters. It was lightweight, and its open back formed a handle that made for easy lifting—good for regrouping or floor cleaning. And patrons liked the way its curved seat and back supported their buttocks and spine; they sat longer and spent more money.

Modernists began loving the curvaceous chair in the 1920s. Its biggest fan was the French architect Le Corbusier—"Never has anything been created more elegant and better in its conception, more precise in its execution, and more excellently functional." The chair would inspire modern classics like the bent plywood Eames chair, Breuer's Ceska (a tubular steel curve holding a wicker caned seat), and Frank Gehry's basketlike concoctions of bent and glued beech strip.

The most official offshoots of the Vienna café chair are currently made by Gebrüder Thonet Vienna in Austria. But bentwood chairs of all kinds, high end and low, will keep on multiplying all over the world. And why not? The simple truth is that no better chair has been invented in the past 150 years.

contact between sitter and backrest. The width of the seat is less critical for posture, but it is important for body size; heavier sitters may choose seats wider than a svelte chair's 15 inches.

8. A streamlined profile. A good dining chair ought to be narrow, shallow, and lean: more skeletal than voluptuous, taking up no more room, or materials, than it needs. No arms, no high backs, no upholstery. The best dining chair is a structural miracle that feels far more commodious than it looks. The smaller its profile, the better it crowds guests around a holiday table, and the less it crowds the room when guests are gone.

9. Great joints. There's no way to fake them. Cheap chairs, glued and screwed, will soon fall apart. Chairs with good mortise-and-tenon joints may last for centuries.

How many dining chairs do you need? Singles need at least four; couples need six, in order to be able to seat two more couples; and a family of four needs at least eight, in order to seat its mirror image, another set of parents with two kids.

~~~~~~~~~~~~

Dinner Plate

Serve It Up

This is an argument for consuming a real dinner, on a real dinner plate, every day of the week. What is a real dinner? Fancy or plain, it's the product of a sincere, affectionate effort to organize a variety of nutritious ingredients on one surface—hopefully a durable, attractive disc made of a handsome, nondisposable substance.

Americans are not big on plates. Aside from aboriginal tribes of hunter-gatherers, we may be the most anti-plate culture in the world.

That has a lot to do with what we eat—many forces conspire against the plated family dinner these days. The mobile pizza trade delivers hot meals requiring neither dining surfaces nor utensils. Frozen food conglomerates package fast, rectangular meals on plastic freeze-and-zap trays doubling as dinnerware. The starch industry produces taco shells, wraps, sub rolls, hamburger buns, bagels, and other enticing forms of edible packing. A prominent televised presence reminds citizens to wolf down all those fast meals in front of yet more TV.

True, preparing a real dinner is not a particularly easy feat, especially if you've already convinced yourself that you have better things to do. You don't. Get over it. Nothing is more important than spending soothing digestive time with family and friends or pets and plants.

For one thing, it makes you healthier: Nutritionists insist that the plating of meals forces diners to confront the amount of food they intend to eat and to eat it at a slower pace than they would with casual grab-and-graze methods. Plates can also shame you into eating better food: McNuggets scarfed over the sink may be filling enough, but decant the things onto a decent plate and you may think twice.

Plates might even make you smarter! (Okay, there's no scientific basis for that, but still: A slower dining pace does allow more time for conversation, which builds vocabulary and boosts curiosity.)

That said, a group of forward-thinking dinner-plate contrarians is currently struggling with questions like these: If we're so advanced, why are we still washing dishes? Why are most dishes breakable, made of the same old clays used for a thousand years? What of cheap, degradable bioplastic dinnerware we can sweep right off the table and into the bio-trash?

At MIT, the Media Lab's Counter Intelligence Group answered these questions with the Dishmaker, a prototype that creates nontoxic acrylic dinnerware on demand. Dirty dishes go into an undercounter machine, where they are melted down, sterilized, and reformed into fresh plates. Why bother? Inventor Leonardo Bonanni thinks it takes less energy, over the long run, to keep recycling one of his plastic dishes than to create a single ceramic dish in a hot kiln.

Outside of MIT, the traditional plate still reigns, and it's made of ceramics: clay and minerals, baked and sealed using a great variety of formulas and levels and styles of craftsmanship. It all looks pretty similar to most of us, and we call it the same thing: china. But some of it is lovely and durable, and some of it is a waste of money and materials.

Earthenware and stoneware, the most popular and economical kinds of ceramic dinnerware, are what we typically use for our "everyday" dishes. Fired at low temperatures, earthenware is made of a soft, porous clay and requires glazing in order to become impermeable enough to hold food safely. (Once the glaze is cracked, the pottery loses its hygienic seal, and its minerals can leach out into food and liquid—a health hazard if that piece of ceramic happens to contain lead.) Because the clay is not very strong, earthenware plates need to be thick.

Fired at high temperatures, stoneware is harder, denser, and much heavier than earthenware. Although it's usually glazed, it's much less absorbent than earthenware. Considered the most rustic of common ceramics, it's opaque, grainy, and often dark in color.

Then there's porcelain, a tenth-century Chinese invention. It's made of two key ingredients: a white clay called kaolin (aluminum silicate), and a mineral called petuntse (aluminum and potassium silicate). When mixed together, the clay and minerals react like flour and butter, forming a porcelain paste that can be molded into shapes. Fired at temperatures well over 2000°F, the ingredients fuse into a very

> We call it the same thing: china. But some of it is lovely and durable and some is not.

dense, hard, and vitreous (glasslike) substance. Although the unglazed porcelain is waterproof, it is usually finished with a clear glaze for a smoother sheen.

A note on terminology: Bone china is a type of ceramic that incorporates real or synthetic bone ash in the mix (Real bone ash actually comes from animal bones.) A European invention modeled after Chinese porcelain, bone china is lighter, whiter, and stronger due to its chemical composition, but it's expensive and labor intensive to make.

While bone china is considered a luxury, porcelain need not be. It's pricier than all other ceramics (save bone china), but using it with practicality can justify its cost.

For years porcelain was considered indispensable for holidays and parties but too costly for daily use. That's why middle-class households stored two sets of dinnerware: the good dishes and the family dishes. During the last decade, however, China (the place) widened its distribution of china (the ceramic). Porcelain left the fancy confines of bridal registries to line the shelves of big-box stores.

That means there's no longer cause for housing two sets of dinnerware. Stocking twice as many identical plates allows for longer intervals between dishwashering and a streamlined table-setting process.

Thin and sleek in profile, a porcelain plate is easier to handle and stack than bulkier dinnerware. The plate is not only lightweight but also remarkably resistant to breaking, cracking, chipping, scratching, and staining. And it's beautiful. Food looks good on a porcelain plate, and the tapping of a fork sounds musical. So buy the best porcelain you can, and use it proudly, for macaroni and cheese as well as for steamed bass.

How to choose your plates? A well-established company selling classic designs is more likely to be able to replenish your stock as needed; similarly, a company offering open stock (à la carte purchases) will prove more useful than one favoring full sets of matching china. (A reminder: Never buy anything in sets. Choose each item on its own merits.)

A dinner plate should be about 11 inches in diameter, with a 1½- to 2-inch rim. Hold it at eye level to examine its gradient—it should slope gently toward the center, as sauces will slosh over the rim of a flat plate and pool on a plate that's too deep. This subtle detail actually makes quite a difference in serving and clearing.

The final step of the shopping process is the most pleasant of all. Invite a group of compatible people over to check out the new plates and give them a spin. Serving dinner would be nice too.

~~~~~~~~~

Small Plate

More than a Companion Piece . . .

There's something magical about a small plate with the right diameter. Nine inches is too large, 7 too small. But a small plate measuring 8 inches across is perfect for doing whatever the dinner plate is too big to do. During a full dinner, the small disc may become a bread plate, a salad plate, or a dessert plate; in between dinners, it can hold anything you eat on the fly—a bagel, a sandwich, or any kind of microwaved minimeal.

The ideal small plate is round, lightweight, and resistant to chipping, cracking, or breaking. Not paper. Not plastic. Not cheap china. Just as with the dinner plate, real porcelain is the way to go.

Because the small plate often appears on the table alongside the dinner plate, the two should match or look compatible (or clash convincingly enough for it to look intentional). Unlike the dinner plate, the small plate should be rimless, to allow for more usable surface. Though the small plate won't need as much of a gradient as a dinner plate (it's unlikely you'll be serving appetizers or eating snacks that are dripping in sauce), it shouldn't be too flat. Examine the side of the plate to see if it has enough gently sloped concavity to keep juices and dressings from sloshing over.

And when scarfing down pizza, use small plates to make slices look bigger—you double the guilt and cut the consumption by half.

~~~~~~~~~~~~~~~~

Soup Plate
A Little Bit of Flourish

The soup plate provides a very good argument against matched sets of china, mainly because most don't include soup plates at all. And those are too important to be left aside—they're deserving of singling out and tracking down. A soup *plate* should not be confused with a soup *bowl*. A soup *bowl* is shaped simply, like a half coconut with a flat base; it takes up very little storage or table space. A soup *plate* is a shallow bowl with a wide rim; its diameter is no smaller than that of a dinner plate.

That may sound unnecessarily cumbersome, but a rimmed bowl has versatility on its side. It supplies enough space for topping cereals with fruit, and salads with tomatoes. It allows room for stews and braised dishes bristling with bones or shells. It lets you see what you're eating and gives you room to maneuver.

It's also the proper way to serve a drippy course to dinner guests—its wide rim catches drips and keeps table and guests dry. Since the wall of the soup plate is lower than that of a soup bowl, it allows for shallow dips of the spoon, away from diners and their laps.

Finally, a shallow, rimmed bowl is simply more elegant. Serving

> Rimmed bowls allow room for stews and braised dishes bristling with bones or shells.

and clearing are more graceful, as the plate can be held by its rim. (A rimless soup bowl forces handlers to cradle hot sides when serving, and to grab slimy interiors when clearing.)

137

While a soup bowl tends to make all soups look like they were poured from cans, a soup plate turns even the most humble creation into a colorful composition. The wide rim acts as a frame, turning even alarming soup colors (algae greens and Pepto pinks) into little "color field" paintings—those one-hue canvases from the 1960s. Served in a deep soup bowl, risotto has the grim look of porridge; presented in a soup plate with a bit of garnish, the same dish can transport you to Tuscany.

Fork

The Gastronomical Spear

Forks may seem indispensable for civilized dining, but they came to the table late in history, long after spoons and knives. Even the haughtiest of ancient Romans, lavish party-givers who stocked some of the fanciest silverware around, ate with their fingers; they simply served meals in bite-size pieces, using spoons and knives when necessary.

Matched sets of eating utensils didn't really catch on in Europe and North America until the eighteenth century. Then, they were rare and prized as valuable items of household chattel. Poorer families would own a few pieces of pewter, a toxic tin-and-lead alloy, while wealthier families ate with silver, which left food untainted.

In those days, when real "silverware" was always made of solid, hand-wrought silver, dinner guests could surmise much about their hosts from the first forkful of food. The greater its weight, the richer the family, or the higher its aspirations.

The Industrial Revolution saw the rise of plated silverware, or EPNS (electroplated nickel silver)—a base metal of nickel, zinc, and copper plated with real silver. The trickery brought affordable, mass-produced "silver" to many tables.

But it was the 1916 invention of corrosion-resistant stainless steel that transformed the dining landscape for good. Durable, affordable, and tarnish- and stain-resistant flatware was too convenient to bypass, even by those who already owned silver.

S tainless steel is just what it appears to be: solid steel, plus chromium to prevent corrosion and nickel to add shine and plasticity. Different types of stainless are described by an AISI (American Iron and Steel Institute) number; the type of stainless most commonly used for flatware is 304.

Today, real silver is best left in the vault; one silver fork costs as much as five place settings (about twenty pieces) of good stainless flatware, and silverware (even plated) requires the kind of polishing, hand washing, hand drying, and careful storage that few people care to perform.

True, for some, the emotional pull of real silver, with its notions of heritage, quality, and elegance, will be too powerful to overcome; if that's the case for you, I challenge you to go all the way—use that silver every day. Or at least once a month. Sound feasible? If not, consider your motives. Are you just buying into the silver game because you think you have to? You don't.

Just as with plates, streamlining is key. No need to stock two sets of flatware, plain and fancy. Invest in a handsome stainless set and allow your family to use the best "silverware" every day. Likewise, reject the notion of fork types: salad, fish, and main course. Life is too short. Just use a fork.

What should it look like? Slightly anthropomorphic, with a slender body supporting head and tail, it's likely to have a personality of its own—pompous, friendly, rarefied, perky, or even a bit sinister.

How many tines should a fork have? Some historians insist that forks improved as they morphed from primitive, single-bladed "eating knives" into two- and three-pronged models, culminating in the civilized four-tined fork. But this is a bogus theory of evolution. Four tines trap too much food; three perform better and are more graceful, as proved most convincingly by Danish Modern designers and occasionally by traditional flatware (reproduction "William and Mary" designs from the late 1600s, for example).

The best fork will help keep food off clothing and table. It might even make you look better-informed when you use it as conversational punctuation.

W hat to look for? Test a fork's balance by playing around with it in the store; shamelessly pretend to lift peas and skewer brussels sprouts, secure in the knowledge that you're investing in a lifetime of more enjoyable meals.

Some forks seem lively, some feel leaden. A featherlight fork feels especially good to people with young, small, tired, or mature hands. Old-fashioned holdouts may prefer implements with the stiffer, heftier feel of carpentry tools.

Distrust excessively artistic flatware. The more sculptural the fork, the higher the expectations for the meal, and upstaging food with hardware is never a good idea.

Since you can't really tell how a fork works until you've eaten with it, try out one set of flatware from a place that will let you return it intact. (The hassle of your return is built into the retail price, so take advantage of the policy.) Choose a finish that will still look good after being boiled in acidic dishwasher soaps and tumbled around in drawers: stainless that has a bit of grit—whether it's matte, brushed, or textured—rather than a mirrorlike shine.

Spend time searching for a fork that you love. When you find it—and you will know right away—buy eight, at the very least.

Table Knife

With Which Your Bread Is Buttered

T hough we love to shell out for expensive, super-sharp kitchen knives, high-performance table knives have gone out of fashion. A "set of steak knives"—with rustic handles, daggerlike points, and toothy serrations—was a very suave wedding gift in the 1960s, the dawn of the backyard grilling rage.

Dangerous table knives were also fashionable in medieval Europe. During the toniest banquets, diners would wield one very sharp, pointed knife in each hand: one sawed at the communal hunk of meat while the other speared chunks, nailed them to the plate, and lifted them to the mouth. These were not simply utensils but valuable personal weapons of status that men carried everywhere. Women could ask knife-owning men to slice their meat as needed.

Knives became more domesticated during the early seventeenth century, when forks arrived on the scene and replaced knife-spearing. (Later, Louis XIV reputedly sought to reduce dinnertime violence by barring pointy knives from the palace dining rooms.)

Those knives were made of two pieces: hard blades of rust-able carbon steel and softer handles of silver, ivory, wood, or inexpensive "base metal" alloys. Both handle and blade required special care.

During the next centuries, table knives would join the refined lineup of matching utensils called the place setting. The widespread adoption of stainless steel in the 1920s furthered the cause, merging handle and blade into a continuous surface, easily dishwasherable and far more sociable.

These days, the table knife may be milder than ever before, but it's still indispensable. Shape matters. The better the design, the more effective the slicing will be. (And there's no need for a specialized set of meat knives; why not shell out for sets of apple knives, sandwich knives, pork knives, and tofu knives, while you're at it?)

In hand, the knife should feel nicely balanced, substantial but not too heavy. A knife handle comes in two configurations: solid and flat or hollow and bulbous. The fatter handle may look more ergonomic, but only field-testing can measure its real comfort; a handle shouldn't be so excessively curlicued that it would impede a nine-year-old from cutting her own chicken breast.

The length of the handle—neither too long nor too short—should allow the pad of the extended forefinger to rest at the point where the blade meets the handle. That zone should also be comfortably flat.

The blade comes in a variety of profiles—from threateningly jagged to playfully wavy—with equally variable cutting abilities. A slightly serrated blade is preferable to a smooth edge. Though a sharp point does come in handy for tough cuts of meat, the table knife needs to be equally amenable to buttering or peanut buttering delicate slices of toast; a comfortably rounded point is a better choice for a generalist's household.

One more thing to be aware of: Table knives may be brandished by emotional guests gesticulating during discussions of hot topics.

If you don't stick to age-old dinner-party etiquette banning talk of religion and politics, be prepared for some dueling.

Teaspoon

Dainty or Utilitarian?

Where would recipes be without the teaspoon? Every recipe calls for a teaspoon or a fractional teaspoon of this or maybe that. But a child's first cooking lesson includes a clarification: A teaspoon is not a "measuring teaspoon." The first is shallow and imprecise; the latter is deep and precisely .167 of a fluid ounce.

Among the members of the standard five-piece place setting, the teaspoon does the least amount of work. It cannot cut, saw, spear, shovel, or lift much weight. In fact, it seldom needs to show up until the very end of dinner. But lightweight as it is, its role can't be taken over by any other utensil.

The teaspoon need not cut, saw, spear, or lift much weight.

A teaspoon is a good dessert dispenser, perfect for delivering small bites of food too sugary, or too cold, to be eaten in larger heaps. (Try slurping ice cream from a soup spoon.) Chiefly, though, the teaspoon is a stirring tool, good for transferring sugar, honey, or other additives into coffee or tea and swirling the mix.

While the soupspoon is a tricky utensil that may drip, scald, and embarrass if ill designed, the teaspoon, it seems, need not be ergonomically smart. And so there are scads of fanciful teaspoons out there, with swirled handles that cannot be grasped and must be daintily poised between thumb and finger, tiny tips useful only for stirring, or huge bowls mainly designed to match a flatware set's soupspoons. Once dinner is over and the mess cleared away, why not introduce spoons that are just as frivolous as the dessert?

The answer is melon. A sturdy, grippable stainless steel teaspoon with a not-too-blunt plow tip is the only way to scoop juicy slabs of cantaloupe, honeydew, and watermelon. Or baked apples, hearty pies, and crusty profiteroles . . . Need I say more?

Soupspoon

Where Etiquette and Utensil Meet

Like the poker player's tell, the tilt of the soupspoon is a conspicuous cue. When shoveling liquid meals, the educated diner never scoops toward the body, but always away from it. Although eating soup properly is purely optinal these days, defenders of etiquette point out that a shallow scoop away from the body is actually the cleanest method, as it controls dripping.

It's well worth finding a soup-eating tool that not only allows correct spooning but actually promotes it.

The spoon's handle should be wide and flat enough to give the thumb a firm, no-slip grip. A slick cylindrical handle won't do; it's too easy for the spoon to roll out of control, and you're stuck with a grabbing and shoveling motion.

The spoon's bowl matters too. Shallow skimming is easiest with an oval that narrows at the tip—such a spoon can also double as a serving utensil or cereal spoon, unlike the old-fashioned circular spoon.

Hold a spoon sideways to examine the angle of its shaft, or handle, and the curve of the narrow neck connecting shaft and bowl. Those proportions, which vary from spoon to spoon, come to bear on scooping style. A neck that's too flat encourages accidental scooping and dumping, while a neck that's not flat enough requires a high level of dexterity. As with all flatware, only pantomime will tell you which spoon feels right.

The finish of stainless steel, the best material for all table utensils, will be most noticeable on the bowl of the spoon. A nonreflective texture will hide the fine scratches that all stainless accumulates over time.

Dead weight is not an advantage for a soupspoon, but weight distribution, or balance, is key. Light foods like broths feel better with a lightweight spoon, but some amount of heft is necessary for control—think of the way a good car handles on the road.

Of course, handling isn't everything in soup-eating etiquette. In the words of humorist Bennett Cerf, "Good manners is the sound you don't make when eating soup."

Water Glass

Sturdy and Dependable

How is a good water glass different from a good wineglass? A good wineglass makes you drink less wine. A good water glass makes you drink more water. The wineglass is the loveliest, most delicate drinking vessel in the house. Its fragility makes you consider your grip. Your heightened attention helps you savor the wine, and the savoring slows down your rate of drinking.

A good water glass should be just the opposite: a durable, easily washable container that helps you down lots of water (70 ounces and up!) all day long.

We've always known water to be a more urgent necessity than food. But lately, it's become an American obsession with a name: hydration.

Technically, hydration is the process of getting enough fluids into the body via any means: drinking liquids, eating food, hooking up to an IV. Recently, however, hydration has become a form of personal expression. Fit people flaunt their personal choice of portable water as a fashion accessory. Every hip gym has a see-through fridge full of brightly colored hydration products with wild graphics and sculptural shapes. Often the water is not even water, per se, but a goal-oriented "wellness beverage" (as the Coca-Cola Company, seller of four hundred bottled drink brands in two hundred countries, calls its wares). Meanwhile, water is also being molecularly reengineered, "super-oxygenated" to boost athletic performance by delivering a bigger dose of O_2 per ounce.

The water craze is quite an ironic one. How can so many health-minded people throw away so many millions of little plastic bottles? Isn't the health of our planet essential to the health of our bodies?

The outdoorsiest of exercisers prefer reuseable hydration solutions—backpacks holding plastic bladders attached to long sipping hoses, or durable plastic "water bottles" with built in "bite and sip" valves. Sold by purveyors of outdoor equipment, the costly water holders are updated and reengineered often, and they're fetishized by their owners, as all techy gear tends to be.

Unfortunately, both kinds of hydration tools—single-use and reuseable—are made of plastics whose safety researchers continue to question. Lab experiments suggest that these plastics leach chemicals into the body. Polycarbonate resin, the unbreakable clear material of upscale water bottles, leaches a hormone disruptor called bisphenol-A, especially as it ages, heats up, or comes in contact with acidic liquids.

There's no question about it: The healthiest (and greenest) hydration comes from the proverbial long, tall glass of water. A glass made out of glass leaches no toxins, resists microbes, is easily washed by machine, and won't scratch or cloud.

Something you use so often should be companionable, an object you can enjoy using with meals and taking to bed with a book; it should feel nice on the mouth and hands and travel in and out of the dishwasher intact. Neither too heavy, nor too light, it shouldn't be easily crushed or chipped. (Water is heavy, so the glass shouldn't add to the load.) Should it break, it need not be missed; there should be plenty of cheap replacements—matching or not.

Look for a glass that can hold 8 to 10 ounces of water, just enough to be lifted effortlessly by an average-size person. An overall diameter of 2½ to 2¾ inches feels good in the palm and looks well proportioned for a height of 5 inches or so.

Among the legions of identical glasses out there, which one do you choose? One designed for water and nothing else; one aimed at the food service industry, not the lone consumer. (In a market overcrowded with options, that's always a good indicator of quality and value.)

Libbey Inc., an American company that's been making glasses since 1818, still manufactures the iconic commercial water glass best known as the "diner glass"—the one with the mysterious midglass bulge around its circumference. That bulge is really a bumper, designed to absorb blows as waiters gang up glasses when busing tables. (It protects the rim, the most fragile part of the glass.)

Libbey's 10-ounce No Nik heat-treated Collins glass is a taller version of their original diner glass; it holds plenty of water with grace and brawn. Unless you care to order a box of six

The healthiest hydration comes from the proverbial long, tall glass of water.

dozen from your local restaurant supply store, though, Libbey recommends you call one of their two outlet stores and order a small quantity by phone. (See page 160.)

The company offers other curvaceous-but-tough, diner-style water glasses, each more evocative than the next. They look like America, and they're even made in it: Ninety percent of Libbey's food service glasses are still produced in sand-rich Ohio and Louisiana.

GLASS AND CRYSTAL

Glass: an ancient material we use every day. It starts out as sand, or silica. Melted, or molten, it becomes glass, changing character and shape when combined with other raw materials and mouth blown, machine blown, molded, or pressed. Soda-lime glass (made of sodium carbonate and the mineral lime) is the most common type of glass, the stuff of windows, bottles, jars, and drinking glasses. Borosilicate glass is a lab and industrial material developed in Germany in the late nineteenth century; made with about 5 percent boric oxide, it resists chemical corrosion and can withstand fairly extreme and sudden changes in temperature.

An old-school leaded crystal goblet

Crystal is trickier. Basically, crystal is completely clear glass. Though it's treated with the same reverence as real silver (a different animal than faux or stainless steel), in fact, compositionally it doesn't differ that much from regular glass—it's all in the craftsmanship.

Not so for lead crystal, patented in 1674 by George Ravenscroft, an English glassmaker commissioned by the royals to compete with Venetian glass (known for its elaborate shapes and colors). By adding lead oxide to the silica mix, he produced a colorless, heavy material with flawless transparency. The greater the lead content, the better its ability to refract light, bending it into a spectrum of colors. The lead gave crystal its sparkling quality and also softened the mix, which allowed the kind of deep cutting and engraving that dramatized refraction.

"Lead crystal" is now a trade designation that uses lead content to determine crystal's quality. It varies by region; the EU requires a different percentage than the United States. Everyone seems to agree, however, that the highest quality "full lead crystal" must contain at least 24 percent lead oxide.

The cult of crystal is deeply entwined with that of wine connoisseurship. Sipping a precious wine from a hefty goblet that's etched within an inch of its life . . . it's enough to make you feel like a king.

But times change, and now that we're aware of the link between lead and a myriad of possible health problems, that luxury doesn't sound quite so luxurious. Occasional wine drinking in leaded glasses won't kill you, but some crystal makers have been hard at work replacing lead oxide with other metals, including titanium; lead-free crystal wineglasses promise all the clarity of leaded glass, together with a longer lifespan.

Wineglass
Fuss-Free Elegance

The perfect wineglass is the one that just broke in the dishwasher. You remember it well. The crystal-clear bowl twinkled in candlelight, the rim was thin and elegant, its balance divine. It was a memorable purchase or gift, and now it's gone. If you measured the brief pang of losing that glass against the long-lived pleasure of using it, which emotion would be stronger? That answer determines the kind of wineglass you really need. But first, let's face your deep-seated insecurities about wine. Admit it: You don't know what you're doing. You assume that everyone else knows more or has a more sensitive palate than you do.

Okay, some of them might, but so what? Because wine is so many things—inebriant, health food, connoisseurship toy, expression of wealth, token of friendship—its enjoyment is complicated by lots of voodoo, fads, and blowhard convictions. The smartest thing you can do with a bottle of wine is uncork it without fuss, let it breathe, and then let *it* do the talking.

A good wineglass is one that helps you enjoy the pleasant rhythm of sipping wine, freed of distractions. If the glass is too awesome in stature or in style, it outshines mediocre wine; a homely glass dulls the pleasure.

On the other hand, grown-ups know that *nice* wine, savored over the course of an evening in *nice* glasses, can mellow a mixture of strangers and inspire a group of friends. Serving bad wine in pink plastic vessels is funny only to illegal, underage drinkers.

The wine tumbler—no stem— presents an elegant compromise. Should wine enthusiasts turn up their noses, they might like to know that the tumbler has been endorsed by the big guns: In 2004, Maximilian Riedel, the eleventh-generation scion of the famous Austrian glass-making family, debuted the "O" series, a collection of tulip-shaped crystal tumblers. Riedel's grandfather Claus invented the notion of unadorned, "functional" wineglasses. Each shape was designed to enhance the flavors of a specific varietal, oxidizing the wine to the proper degree, then directing the flow to the part of the palate most sensitive to its particular bouquet. Before Claus Riedel, there were no red and white wineglasses—just fussy goblets. Point being, these people know their wineglasses.

Wine tumblers are made in a range of materials, but lead-free crystal is best and borosilicate glass is a

> Serving bad wine in pink plastic tumblers is only funny to illegal, underage drinkers.

less expensive alternative. A well-made tumbler should fit comfortably in the palm and feel just like a stemmed wineglass to the lips. It will stack more easily in the dishwasher (if you must), save room in the cupboard, and work well at parties, where its low center of gravity will enable it to travel smoothly on roving trays.

Though tumblers, like stemmed glasses, are tailored for reds and whites, and even for specific varietals, for the average wine drinker it's perfectly fine to buy one type of tumbler—in whatever shape you like best—and use it for every wine.

That said, for some, the tumbler will be unthinkable: the fingerprints too messy, the transfer of the hand's warmth a high treason. If that's the case, an old-fashioned stemmed glass it shall be. (Better for toasting, it's true.)

Does real crystal make wine taste better? Some claim its porous texture opens the fragrance. Hmm. But certainly crystal alerts all the senses. First, you're surprised by its weight, then confused by its invisibility (the wine seems to float); then amazed by the immaterial feel of the glass lip (so thin). Then there's the decadent thrill of keeping a preciously fragile mouth-blown crystal glass intact during the course of a meal. (Okay, it's not really all that hard, but somehow it does make one feel nicely grown up.)

Mug

Cozy Up to It

"**D**uring the early twenty-first century, North Americans freely admitted their addiction to infusions of roasted coffee bean powder. Strangely, the beverages were consumed in clunky pottery—tall, heavy ceramic cylinders called mugs—more primitive in shape and substance than the most ancient of drinking vessels."

That's what future anthropologists might write about us. They will wonder why we drank coffee with cups we could barely lift, and why those cups continued to grow in size and weight from the mid-twentieth century to the start of the twenty-first. The coffee cup has morphed from a modified teacup on a saucer to a thick-walled, saucer-less cylinder best lifted with two hands.

Office life might explain the expansion. Desk workers sharing a distant coffeemaker need a large vessel to reduce the number of refill trips. A heavy, wide-based mug not only keeps the coffee warm, but it also prevents any spills on paperwork. Big mugs hold the promise of alertness for modern citizens, all notoriously underrested. But the more you drink the addictive brews, the more you need to drink to sustain your high, and to offset the subsequent crash.

While a daily cup or two of joe isn't a problem, and may in fact be a boon to your health, overly enthusiastic caffeine intake can be hazardous and increases the likelihood of insomnia.

The good news is that perception and intake are closely related; it's no secret that enormous restaurant portion sizes have had something to do with the rise of obesity. Serve yourself

The elegant bit of trickery has to be experienced firsthand.

less food, on a reasonably sized plate, and you're likely to eat less. Fill a smaller cup, and you're likely to drink less coffee—it's as simple as that.

Finding a wonderful, liftable replacement for the outdated mug is an important task. After all, for coffee drinkers, the coffee holder is the most intimate tool in the kitchen. You press your lips to its warm surface, wrap both hands around it, down its hot contents, and feel the caffeine urging your senses back to life. For this relationship, you need a loveable vessel.

Consider the anti-mug, Bodum's beautiful glass tumbler, featherlight, yet insulated. From the start, the impossibly thin, double-walled glass won design prizes for its sculptural engineering. Not always a sign of utility, but part of its design charm is an elegant bit of trickery that has to be experienced to be admired. The fragile-looking tumbler can suspend any liquid—steaming hot or iced cold—within an inner layer of paper-thin glass. The outer layer insulates.

The first surprise comes when you pick up the glass—it doesn't break; the second when you look at the coffee—it's floating! (The double walls lend the liquid an eerie suspended quality.) The next and slightly dangerous sensation comes with a sip of the liquid: It's much colder or hotter on your palate than it was on your hand. Furthermore, the insulation prevents cold drinks from sweating (condensing), and the glass chemistry keeps the tumblers from becoming etched and clouded in the dishwasher.

Like lab beakers, the tumbler is made of borosilicate glass (see page 146). The magically thin material can withstand heat, temperature shifts, scratching, microwaving, and bumping around.

Nor is the tumbler a standard industrial product made by machines on a production line. It is individually made, with artisanal techniques, on a grand scale. Each glass is mouth-blown by a glass worker in China; another worker tests the glass walls for consistency.

For consumers, this is confusing, but puzzlement only serves to enhance the appeal. A surprisingly reasonable price suggests that it's just another mass-produced widget ready to take abuse. But its beauty implies that it must be a touchy, arty *objet* that needs babying. The reality lies in between. Simply observe a couple of no-nos: Do not forcefully chuck ice or spoons in the bottom of the glass.

Bodum's double-walled glasses are made in collections of different profiles and shapes, but the rounded, Pavina-style tumbler's 9 ounces are ample enough for a good dose of morning coffee. No handle, which only increases the joy of being able to grasp the cup with your bare hands. And it's a lot more appealing than a big, opaque, freebie mug called VIOXX or VILLAGE IDIOT.

If you don't think glass coffee cups look macho enough, visit Istanbul to watch tough-looking guys sip tea from little tulip-shaped glasses—the standard vessels for their standard beverage (Turkish black tea). Those lovely glasses, gracefully lifted, somehow enhance the toughness of the tea drinkers.

As for Far Western tea drinkers, who prefer the tradition of porcelain cups and teabag–holding saucers, borosilicate glass offers a new spectacle:

Brew loose tea in a glass teapot; watch the leaves unfurl; then pour the strained tea into a double-walled glass cup to complete the aquarium effect.

Because it's new, and not identified with one drink or another, the Pavina shape works with inebriants as well as stimulants. A Pavina can dole out whiskey, beer, and cognac, or even soda, juice, tea, or water for that matter. Websites selling wine paraphernalia have recommended the Pavina-style double-walled glasses as wine tumblers too.

If these designs have a downside, it's purely semantic. "Pass me the insulated, double-walled borosilicate glassware, please."

~~~~~~~~~~~~~~~~~~~~~~

Napkin
Out with Paper

Every home ought to have guests, and grown-up guests ought to have real napkins. Your mother already told you that. Mothers don't sanction meals without napkins, because an absence of napkins defies civility. Let's work backward. Even if you "entertain" (translation: cook self-consciously) only once a year—Thanksgiving?—you'll want to use food and props to convince everyone that you are a good host, and they are esteemed guests. This is what civilization is all about: theater.

Civilization is also about textiles. We dress up both our bodies and our dining tables for special occasions, because it's not just the grub that makes an impression. It's also the things we touch: the nicely balanced fork, the smooth wineglass, the warm table covering. And the linen napkin.

The impeccably spotless and starched linen napkin disappeared from households for a number of reasons that no longer prevail: As cotton overtook all other fibers, linens became expensive to buy; with weak detergents and heavy steam irons, they were impossible to clean and press; and as women went out into the workplace, convenience won the war over aesthetics—women no longer had time to iron their own clothes, let alone fancy table accessories.

But now that wrinkling has become a statement of fashion and enlightenment, napkin care is simple, and prices are low, once you factor in ecological goodness. One linen napkin costs the same as five to ten paper towel rolls, but replaces hundreds of rolls over its life span—and how can you calculate the cost of a tree?

You can easily find linen napkins online. Spray stains with one of those amazing hydrogen peroxide (chlorine-free) spot removers; machine wash; skip the dryer; smooth them out; and hang or stack them to dry.

Good thing you still get to use your beloved paper towels when it's just you and your family, right? When you're chowing down in front of the TV, there's nothing like a nice, thick, heavily textured paper towel or two to swab your greasy kisser.

Wrong. The only way to amortize the cost of your linen napkins, and to truly make a difference to the environment, is to get into the habit of using them all the time. (Okay, almost all the time.) When it's just you and yours, use them three times before washing, and save water and time as well.

Serving Platter
For the Moveable Feast

A serving platter works like a big dish. Unfortunately, nothing is harder to wash, dry, and store than a big, fragile dish. The solution is a big dish that's really not a dish, but a tray. (Though it shouldn't look like one.) What you're looking for is a versatile shape with dimensions neither too huge nor too modest. That would be a sharp or rounded rectangle with a flat surface, no smaller than 8 by 16 inches, framed by a low rim. Ovals and circles are lovely, but only a rectangle can be stacked vertically without rolling around. The rectangle tends to be able to hold more too.

The bigger the platter, the more important the material. Ceramics, including everything from earthenware to porcelain, are out: too chippable and breakable during washing, drying, and storing. Wood and bamboo are out as well; too hard to wash and sanitize.

What remains is stainless steel. A reflective finish looks loveliest, but a brushed, or "satin," finish will cover the inevitable scratches stainless surfaces collect. Because you can toss around a lightweight, breakproof platter without fear, you're more likely to use it more often.

A good stainless platter helps you cater your own parties and holidays. It holds big hunks of food like nothing else. It can display a giant roast while containing the juice and providing room enough for slicing. It can frame a whole fish, freshly caught or shipped from Alaska. It turns a random bunch of appetizers into a slick antipasto and serves as a handsome cheese board for an array of moldy shapes. For dessert, it arranges piles of sweets—cookies, pastries, brownies—into a buffet. And a platter can work like a busing tray, moving food from kitchen to patio or from barbecue to table.

In between events, a rectangular platter may be stored out in the open, on a counter or table, and used to corral kitchen equipment or clutter. When it's time to clean the work surface, you whisk off the tray without having to reassemble the objects each time.

A platter is yet another thing that ought to be purchased in person. Is it light enough to carry? Big, but not too big? Practical but not industrial-

> It turns a random bunch of appetizers into a slick antipasto platter.

looking? Handling it is the only way to find out. Dealers of commercial kitchen and bakery supplies are a good source.

Once you finally find the ideal platter, the best way to break it in is by serving breakfast in bed to someone you love. (Or getting that someone to serve it to you.)

Serving Bowl
The Multitasking Implement

A good serving bowl is the presentable basin that brings food from kitchen to dining table. It's not a fragile crystal antique, or a temperamental wooden set you dare not use. It's a big, indestructible bowl that will perform ten different tasks and replace a pile of redundant vessels and wedding gifts clogging the cabinets.

The big bowl encourages you to make fresh food more often. It simplifies the logistics of food preparation and presentation by answering a few questions: Where will I mix it? How can I keep it warm or cold? How can I serve it? How can I store it? And what can I use to reheat it?

The right bowl is shallow enough to show off salads, with their miscellany of bright ingredients, and wide enough to fit wide serving utensils. It's moisture-proof enough to store leftovers in the refrigerator after dinner, and microwavable for ease in reheating. It's also durable enough to work as a baking dish for casseroles or stews. And, of course, it should be able to withstand the dishwasher.

For years, real cooks have been using Pyrex mixing/storage bowls to work as ad hoc serving and salad bowls. Pyrex is the company that launched amazing borosilicate bakeware in 1915. Presentable enough, its current line—made of tempered soda-lime glass—has the ability to withstand the heat of the oven, microwave, or dishwasher and the cold of the refrigerator or freezer. (What it

> Pare down that pile of redundant vessels clogging the kitchen cabinets.

can't survive is direct proximity to the heating elements in toaster ovens, broilers, or stovetops.) Porosity, or lack thereof, is another benefit: Glass can't absorb flavors, odors, or stains, and it dries very fast. To top it all off, the Pyrex mixing bowls come with fitted plastic storage lids.

Eventually Pyrex decided to introduce a line of fancier "serveware" bowls called Simple Elegance—

shallower, rimmed shapes "sculptured" with texture. Unfortunately, not all models sport the excellent plastic storage lids, and availability is spotty.

No matter: The mixing bowls have no competition in terms of low-price usefulness. Plus, they are still made near Pittsburgh, Pennsylvania, using good old-fashioned American sand.

Sugar Bowl
A Touch of Hospitality

Back in the day, nonsmokers always kept ashtrays on hand for visiting smokers. The trays accessorized coffee tables and were a standard part of household decor until laws and manners changed. Guest ashtrays disappeared when it became both legal, and polite, for hosts to ban smokers and the public health hazard they created.

But what about sugar eaters?

If sugar is such a bane, shouldn't you hide your stash rather than flaunt it? Will serving sugar became a liability someday, like serving alcohol to minors—or will biochemists pronounce it the surprise health tonic of the future?

Furthermore, what passes for sugar these days, anyway? Should it be a plant or a chemical? Real or fake? Should it be powdery, sandy, grainy, or rocky? A squeezable liquid, or a pourable syrup?

Today's sugar bowl is yesterday's ashtray. It's an old-fashioned mark of hospitality. Here in the Western world, we have two ritual beverages—coffee and tea—and guests are entitled to expect one or the other, especially at the end of a meal. When the drink arrives, they can still count on the host or hostess to ask: cream and sugar?

It's a vintage question. Back in the days when tea and coffee sets were standard entertaining equipment, the sugar bowl and creamer formed a matching duo standing ready to adulterate thin drinks (made with weak beans or tea bags) with thick flavorings.

Now, no one really demands cream that is cream. It must be quasi cream or milk.

And no one requires the sugar to be regular sugar, the sparkly white stuff that fits into sugar bowls. But everyone does expect to find a representative of one of three categories of sweetening product that may

---

The sugar bowl and creamer formed a matching duo, always at the ready.

---

or may not lead to obesity, tooth decay, or cell mutation, depending on which lab tests and lobbyists you believe. That choice of sugar, or lack thereof, reveals a great deal about the politics and nutritional hopes of the household.

Real sugar comes from sugarcane or sugar beets. Standard household sugar—also called regular sugar, white sugar, or granulated sugar—is the fine or extra-fine, snow-white product of thorough processing.

Turbinado sugar is the amber-colored stuff, with larger crystals and a deeper flavor than white sugar. Although it's often called "raw sugar," it's actually a specially processed product, made in much smaller quantities, at a higher price, than table sugar. Genuine raw sugar goes to a special plant to be washed, under sanitary conditions, in a way that retains some of the molasses and its nutrients. (Okay, not many nutrients, but more than are present

in white sugar, which is 100 percent sucrose.) Turbinado isn't a health food, although health food stores were once its only vendors. It's really just a funkier version of sugar, but for some the aesthetics are a good enough argument: Wholesome is better than pretty, chunky is better than flawless, brown is better than white, because food should look like real food—imperfect.

Honey is another amber-colored version of sugar that feels like health food, even though the body treats it just about the same as it does refined sugar. The more local and less processed the honey, the stronger its message.

Then there are the nonsugar products called nonnutritive sweeteners, no-calorie sweeteners, or artificial sweeteners. Those are the nonfood chemicals known by their brand names and the bright colors of their paper packets. Blue is aspartame, sold as Equal. Yellow is sucralose, sold as Splenda. Pink is saccharin, sold as Sweet'N Low. These are the subject of great debate among chemical manufacturers, competing sugar plant growers, soda companies, lawyers, politicians, scientists, citizens' groups, and the FDA.

In the battle of sugars, real and fake, the next contender is neither genuine sugar nor chemical sweetener. It's a South American plant called stevia, used by the Japanese since the 1960s as an alternative to the chemical sweeteners. You can grow stevia plants in the backyard and make your own hyperpotent, calorie-free organic sweetener by drying and crushing the leaves. You can also buy it prepared, at health food stores or online. But if you happen to own a bottling plant or candy factory, you can't put stevia in your products. (The FDA has not approved stevia as a food additive due to insufficient evidence of its safety.)

Whatever your personal sweetener choices, when guests come over for coffee, you should present them with a small, all-glass container with a tight top to keep out humidity and critters. Stock it with a tiny quantity of turbinado sugar, a compromise that will neither scare the traditionalist nor offend the New Ager. Sugar is one of the prettiest of kitchen supplies, and a glass container helps to show it off.

Note to discerning readers: Yes, it's a recurring theme—in design terms, clarity is as simple as it gets. And simplicity is beautiful.

Creamer
"Nonfat Half-Caff with a Splash of Cream?"

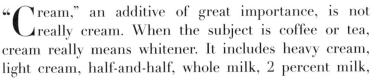

"Cream," an additive of great importance, is not really cream. When the subject is coffee or tea, cream really means whitener. It includes heavy cream, light cream, half-and-half, whole milk, 2 percent milk, 1 percent milk, nonfat milk, nondairy liquid creamer, diet nondairy creamer, and mystery powder.

The choice is not arbitrary. Allegiance to one of these drink diluters reveals more about a person than his choice of beverage. It may signal class, age, and origin, along with the drinker's neuroses about body fat, sex, and self-esteem. Put the wrong whitener in anyone's coffee, and you not only render his drink undrinkable, but you may well insult him with an unintended presumption. ("Diet creamer?")

A young Seattleite may insist on genuine cream as a birthright. His city roasts great coffee, which electrifies its citizens and stimulates their opinions on culinary matters, whiteners included. The civic agreement—great coffee deserves nothing but cream!—is so widespread that many cafés and delis proudly offer the real stuff or nothing at all.

In New York, etiquette goes to the other extreme. Instead of getting what is "best," you get whatever you want. The bigger the buffet of milks, creams, and noncream creamers, the more convincing the welcome.

Why does everyone get so worked up about the subject of whiteners?

Coffee is important. As an addictive stimulant, it makes the brain think harder than usual, and thinking makes you feel animated, smart, opinionated. In the morning, even a whiff of the stuff gets you out of bed and into action, prepping you for a day of decision making.

What is your first decision? The coffee itself may evade your control. (Certainly there's a better quality of coffee out there, beyond your kitchen or corner barista.) But the morning selection of whitener, poured in a careful proportion, is the first triumph of the day, a little act of free will expressing a deeper philosophy about life—anything from carpe diem to Just Say No.

The ultracustomized, superpersonal coffee experience is new. Vintage tableware proves that there used to be a national agreement about coffee additives. The coffee/tea set, a traditional wedding gift circa 1950, paired two matching vessels: typically, a sugar bowl with symmetrical handles and a cream pourer shaped like a rounded gravy boat. Midcentury sugar was finely granulated and snow-white. The companion whitener of choice was pasteurized, milkman-delivered cream. "Coffee" was a light social occasion that let new suburbanites meet one another and affirm their decisions to seek order, ownership, and modernity outside chaotic cities. Drinking the same stuff, gently altered, was more than polite. It was progressive.

Why does everyone get so worked up on the subject of whiteners?

Today, the thoughtful host honors guests' dietary idiosyncrasies, pretensions, and sensitivities, no matter how ridiculous. One old-fashioned creamer won't do. You need two at the very least, depending on where you live and who you are. (Hauling out several plastic cartons of white stuff, directly from the refrigerator, is too informal.)

The most efficient vessels are not creamers at all but the smallest spouted vessels available. Creative choices abound. Cutest of all are Japanese soya sauce dispensers: petite, versatile vessels with small spouts and lids designed to pour precise streams of liquid. Vertically shaped, they take up little space in the refrigerator, in the pantry, or on the table, where they will amuse your guests—which is your job, geisha or not.

THE SMART LIST

DINING

B EAUTIFUL, WELL-MADE TABLE SETTINGS are the most accessible of all household goods. But in this realm quality is hard to judge. Some respected brands are worth the premium, others not so much.

So shop in the same way you want to eat—with slow, sensual deliberation. Touch and hold glassware and silverware up to the light. Notice how some forks and glasses jingle and clink better than others, how some pieces make you feel elegant and others brand you a klutz. Consider bypassing retailers and assembling your own à la carte collection of vintage, heirloom, and purchased items. Enjoy the search!

DINING TABLE

• Real hardwood treated with a clear coat of protective sealer; top may be planked or solid
• Real wooden joinery
• Rectangular in shape; sized for 8 diners
• Find it: Home design stores, or buy used/antique

Cost: $700 and up new; much less used

DINING CHAIR

• Lightweight wood with a slim, attractive profile
• Solid mortise-and-tenon joints
• Try: A simple café chair like Design Within Reach's Kyoto (about $110); if that's out of reach, restaurant supply stores sell similar versions at half the price.

Cost: $50 to $200

DINNER PLATE

• Porcelain, 11" across, with a gentle slope and a 1½" to 2" rim
• Try: Porcelain by Revol, a French company that's been family-owned since 1789 and still makes its own compound; the plates can withstand temperature extremes, from a freezer to a hot oven.
• Find it: Department stores, home design stores, kitchenware stores

Cost: $10 to $30

SMALL PLATE

• Porcelain, 8" across
• No rim and only a very slight gradient
• Find it: Department stores, home design stores, kitchenware stores

Cost: $8 and up

SOUP PLATE

- Porcelain, with a rim of ample width
- The plate's bowl should be deep enough to handle robust meals, but not so deep that it makes a hefty serving look meager.
- Find it: Department stores, home design stores, kitchenware stores

Cost: $10 and up

FORK

- Stainless steel dinner fork
- Three tines rather than four
- Shopping tip: Test it out in the store to see how it feels in the hand.
- Find it: Department stores, home design stores, kitchenware stores

Cost: $6 to $10

TABLE KNIFE

- Stainless steel
- Slightly serrated edge
- Shopping tip: Test it out in the store to see how it feels in the hand.
- Find it: Department stores, home design stores, kitchenware stores

Cost: $6 to $10

TEASPOON

- Stainless steel
- Not-too-blunt plow tip
- Shopping tip: Test it out in the store to see how it feels in the hand.
- Find it: Department stores, home design stores, kitchenware stores

Cost: $6 to $10

SOUPSPOON

- Stainless steel
- An oval bowl that narrows at the tip, a slightly curved neck, and a comfortably wide, flat handle
- Shopping tip: Test it out in the store to see how it feels in the hand.
- Find it: Department stores, home design stores, kitchenware stores

Cost: $6 to $10

WATER GLASS

- Durable 5-ounce water glass with an overall diameter of $2\frac{1}{2}$" to $2\frac{3}{4}$"
- Try: A 5-ounce No Nik water glass from Libbey
- Find it: Call Libbey's factory outlet to order directly (318-621-0265).

Cost: $1 to $5

WINEGLASS

- Stem-free wine tumbler in lead-free crystal or borosilicate glass
- Try: A tumbler from Riedel's crystal "O" series, or Bodum's Pavina double-walled tumbler; for lead-free crystal stemware, try titanium tempered glass in Schott Zwiesel's Tritan line
- Care: Proper hand washing gives wine glasses the clarity they need. Soak the glasses in very hot water, wash gently, and dry them with a linen towel while they're still wet.
- Find it: Department stores and high-end kitchen stores; online

Cost: Two for $20 to $25

MUG

- Bodum's Pavina double-walled tumbler
- Find it: Department stores; online; big-box stores; coffee and tea supply stores; kitchen supply stores

Cost: About $10

NAPKIN

- 100% linen napkin
- Eco-note: Linen comes from flax, a sustainable fiber source; it's lightweight and compact in the wash and line-dries quickly, saving on energy; it's also long-lasting and durable.
- Care: Spray stains with a chlorine-free hydrogen peroxide spot remover; machine wash; smooth out; and hang or stack to dry.
- Find it: Online, in eco-conscious housewares stores, or in stores selling European linens

Cost: $5 and up

SERVING PLATTER

- Rectangular stainless steel tray
- 8" x 16" or larger, with a slight rim
- Find it: Commercial kitchen/bakery supply stores

Cost: $20 to $30

SERVING BOWL

- Pyrex glass mixing bowl with lid
- Find it: Kitchen supply stores; big-box stores; department stores

Cost: $12 to $15

SUGAR BOWL

- All-glass sugar bowl with lid
- Find it: Kitchen supply stores; department stores; restaurant supply stores

Cost: $10 and up

CREAMER

- Several small, spouted creamers or creamer substitutes
- Try: Japanese soya sauce dispensers
- Find it: Online; department stores; Asian housewares stores

Cost: $5 and up

CHAPTER FIVE

CLEANING
&
FIXING

INVENTORY

- Mop
- Cleaning Cloth
- Toilet Brush

- Broom
- Dustpan and Brush
- Feather Duster

- Vacuum Cleaner
- Screwdriver
- Hammer

W hy clean house?
Behold the typical college dormitory, a laboratory of deferred household care and its consequences. Airborne dust impedes breathing and triggers allergies. Dust in bedding, laundry, and upholstered furniture breeds dust mites. Bathroom fixtures become petri dishes for mold, mildew, and bacteria. Unwashed laundry exudes odors caused by invisible microorganisms. And pet-

rified pizza invites mice, ants, cockroaches, and other scavengers to a floor-level buffet.

To put it in more general terms: Living spaces accumulate debris (sloughed skin, human and pet hair, food particles, fabric fibers), which becomes food or shelter for unwanted life-forms—which, in turn, contribute their own waste products, creating food for a lengthening food chain . . . and so on and so on and so on.

The point of housecleaning should be to remove that food, not necessarily to kill everything in sight. There's a big difference between cleaning and disinfecting or sanitizing. Cleaning removes the debris we call dirt; disinfecting kills most of the bacteria within the dirt. By EPA standards, a disinfectant must kill 99.999 percent of microorganisms in thirty seconds—and that's just not necessary. Confusing for those of us taught to sanitize everything we could soak or spray. . . .

We're trained from a young age to see and smell household chemicals as wholesome and virtuous. Happy TV commercials for self-activating, antibacterial, whitening, scouring, mildew-defying cleaning products convince us that we need to protect our families from dangerous scourges. We hum their jingles with pride as we uphold America's famous standards of spotlessness.

Fear is the dark underside of all that scouring. The ads keep announcing newly discovered biological menaces that can only be obliterated with the new, improved products they tout. (Remember the antibacterial soap craze?) For moms, failure to engage in the fight against germs is tantamount to child neglect.

Turns out, we've been hoodwinked—time to wake up and smell the fumes. The chemicals may be far scarier than the scourges they target. Researchers say we're creating a new kind of unhealthiness: Inside our tightly sealed buildings, the chemicals combine, creating unsavory compounds of unknown safety. More worrisome analysis predicts the rise of superbugs: Overdisinfecting threatens to create invincible, mutated strains of bacteria and viruses. Then there's the problem we already know about: Chemicals may sanitize our interior world, but once flushed away, they pollute the one outside our doors.

Our habits may be hard to break, but natural cleaning is definitely on the rise. Testing all over the world has concluded that 95 percent of the chemicals we use at home—and even in hospitals—can be safely eliminated by cleaning with water alone. It sounds impossible, but it's true. (More on that later.)

The transition to this new era of cleaning won't be easy. But it will catch on. And when it does, what will become of those corporations, with their disposable gadgets and the chemicals they swish around? Will their iconic jingles fade away?

Let's find out.

Mop
Goodbye, Bucket

The remarkable thing about floor cleaning is that it has resisted innovation for so many millennia. There have been no whiz-bang solutions, no amazing inventions beyond the squeeze mop. You can ponder this mystery firsthand by visiting most any hospital room. No matter how many supersophisticated, phenomenally costly machines surround the patient being treated with hypersanitary products and advanced pharmaceuticals, the nightly floor-cleaning ritual remains archaic: Equipped with a heavy mop made of cotton yarns and two large buckets of soapy water, a janitor enters the room, dips his mop into the first bucket, swirls the solution over the floor, rinses and wrings out his mop in the second and repeats.

Those strong cleaning chemicals (quaternary ammonium chlorides and butoxyethanol) are safe for neither humans nor the environment. But in order to prevent one room's germs from spreading to the next, janitors need to change the mopping solution often and use lots of the bad chemicals. All the mopping, wringing, and solution changing is backbreaking, unhealthy work: bad for the janitors, the patients, and the hospitals too.

Turns out there is a better way. In 1999, the University of California Davis Medical Center began to look for an alternative to conventional "wet loop" mopping, launching a case study with a cost-benefit analysis.

The study turned up a solution: the microfiber mop. It looked lightweight to the wary staff, unlike serious industrial cleaning equipment. And it was. The mop head was a thin metal rectangle, the traditional sponge replaced by a thin, Velcroed on microfiber pad. The head was attached to a light aluminum pole. The idea was to use one or two pads per room; in between uses, the pads could be chucked into washing machines.

What was the big deal? Turns out those flimsy things actually cleaned better than the old mops, using almost no chemicals. (The janitors used 0.5 ounces per room as opposed to the traditional 10.5 ounces.) The mops' higher initial cost was offset by the savings: 95 percent on chemicals, 60 percent on lifetime mop costs, 20 percent on labor, and less water too. Those savings obviously reached deeper than the wallet—to whit, the U.S. Environmental Protection Agency began ranking the hospital's microfiber program as a "best practice" in 2002.

With recommendations like that, you'd think the microfiber mop would have moved from hospitals to homes and become America's favorite floor cleaner by now. Not so. In big-box stores and supermarkets, the places where consumers buy most of their cleaning gadgets, microfiber mops are outnumbered by old-fangled mops—but they're gaining ground.

Price and education are the factors keeping the new mops off the retail market—you have to know what you're buying before you're willing to pay three times the price of something tried-and-true. Some mops with washable mop pads pretend to be microfiber when they are really made of terry cloth or other cheap polyester textiles not manufactured as true, split-fiber microfiber (see box, page 167). And if the costly thing in question promises nothing but invisible, implausible-sounding scientific results, retailers dare not stock it until it catches on. (It can dust, wash, and polish floors more thoroughly, and antibacterially, than any mop ever made, using nothing but water! One mop pad lasts for hundreds of machine washings!)

But there's another issue too. Microfiber mops are a bit like hybrid cars. Many cleaning chemicals contain petroleum, and makers of petroleum products don't necessarily want you to know about microfiber. If it catches on and millions of households stop buying all those New! Improved! cleaning agents advertised on TV, plenty of corporations will suffer.

If this sounds like a conspiracy theory, just look beyond our borders, where environmentalists have promoted microfiber cleaning for a decade or two. The stuff only became visible in the United States within the last few years. Chemical companies can count on the fact that the microfiber mop pad, thin as a bad bath towel, cannot sell itself to an unprepared consumer.

The savings: 95 percent on chemicals, 60 percent on cost, and 20 percent on labor . . .

To believe in this mop you either have to read nonbiased institutional test results or give it a trial run. How do you use it? Lightly dampen the mop pad, slap it on the floor, and press the Velcro-ed mop head onto the pad. Note how quickly you can mop a whole room. When the pad looks dirty, either rinse it or change to a clean pad. Let the floor air-dry or give it a glossing over with a dry pad. After cleaning, toss the pads in the washing machine or hand wash, then let air dry.

Mopping goes so fast it's actually fun. (For an extra dose of fun, try the new cleaning slippers with detachable microfiber soles and skate your way to a cleaner home.)

~~~~~~~~~~~~~~~~~

Cleaning Cloth
What Can't *It Do?*

The microfiber revolution need not be confined to the floor. Try cleaning your windows with two microfiber cloths and plain water: Wet one cloth, clean one pane of glass, and polish with a dry cloth. Keep rinsing the wet cloth and keep going. The sparkling, unlinted, unstreaked glass will disprove all the contradictory advice you've gleaned about proper window washing. Branded blue chemicals, precise vinegar recipes, professional squeegees, rags, newsprint, and paper towels all become ancient history.

What else can you clean with a microfiber cloth? Just about anything. One cloth cleans all, though certain weaves suit some tasks better than others; a thin, smooth cloth polishes slick surfaces well, while a thick, fuzzy cloth can wash and rinse rougher surfaces.

Dry-dust electronic screens and other fragile equipment, along with mirrors, tabletops, and countertops.

Clean those surfaces that the strongest chemicals just seem to smear: fingerprinted stainless steel appliances, sinks, and greasy glass cooktops, for example.

Remove water spots, soap scum, and tub rings. No endless scrubbing, no scary foams.

Polish accessories like eyeglasses, jewelry, purses, and shoes.

Spot wash and dry carpet spills.

Clean an entire car—from upholstery to control panel, washing, drying, polishing, and buffing—with nothing but water.

Get the picture?

INSIDE A MICROFIBER

A microfiber is a very thin, synthetic fiber finer than one denier; that's about one hundred times thinner than a human hair. Invented in Japan in the 1970s with a very early incarnation as Ultrasuede; transmuted into a highly absorbent hairdresser's towel; "discovered" by a Swedish entrepreneur; transformed into a Swedish hospital cleaning cloth; and rediscovered by another Swedish entrepreneur who started the first microfiber cleaning product company in 1992, the microfiber has always been a shape shifter. It's been used in everything from clothing and towels to upholstery fabrics and industrial mops, all in a wide range of yarn grades.

How does it work? High-quality microfiber starts with Grade A yarn or better. When it's the real thing, it absorbs about seven times its weight in water; dries out two or three times faster than cotton; refuses to grow mold and mildew; sheds no lint or other allergens; holds its shape; and can be machine-washed hundreds of times.

Cross-section of a microfiber cloth

Microfiber is made of two familiar polymers: polyester, the most common man-made fiber, and polyamide, also known as nylon. Each fiber is composed of a star-shaped polyester core, with wedge-shaped polyamide filaments fitting into its grooves; its microscopic thinness is achieved via a dousing of chemicals during the dye-bath stage.

This complex, porous geometry helps the resulting textile collect dirt and hold water. A dense concentration of fibers—90,000 to 200,000 per square inch—creates a large surface area, essential for absorption and release. The material has abrasion on its side as well: Its sharp filaments scrape surfaces clean; used dry, they gather up static electricity to attract dust.

How to account for all of microfiber's different iterations? It has to do with the ratio of polyester to polyamide. (Polyester is the scrubber; polyamide the absorber.) A 70/30 ratio is good for bath mats, for example, while an 80/20 ratio is best for cleaning.

Quite a mouthful, indeed. There's no getting around it, and that's part of microfiber's uphill battle. The product is so remarkable, and so multitasking, that it takes a good deal of explaining. Best just to try it and become a convert!

One more thing: Microfiber is a 100 percent synthetic, noncompostable material made with petroleum products. That may be hard to swallow, but it will behoove us to admit that sometimes synthetic products act greener, in the long run, than natural ones.

HOW TO CLEAN

Between overcleaning and under-cleaning lies a happy medium that keeps a house fragrant, soothing, and healthy to live in. The cleaning-averse should know that cleanliness is not the same as orderliness, an aesthetic that's purely subjective and highly emotional. Compared to order, clean is easy. In fact, cleaning can be a healthy sport, meditative and athletic, when performed in the right frame of mind and with the right gear.

Some homeowners are notorious overcleaners. On the assumption that cleaner is better, they buy expensive, overachieving cleaning equipment designed for allergy sufferers and other sensitive people: superfiltering vacuum cleaners, sanitizing dishwashers, mite-proof mattress covers, ionic air cleaners. Weekly or biweekly cleaning with normal tools—combined with some nice ventilation—will do a perfectly good job of making a house pleasant for most residents.

Most cleaning tasks should be performed with man-powered tools that work as extensions of the hands. (One exception is the vacuum, one of the costlier pieces of cleaning equipment.) Choose each as though you were buying a tennis racket: It should feel good, look friendly, and be sort of fun to handle. The better you like your gear, the more frequently you'll use it. And that's a boon, because when it comes to housework, there is no substitute for getting it done, over and over.

Another rule of thumb: Household fabrics generate lint and hold on to dust. The cleanest house has the smallest yardage of drapes, carpeting, bed coverings, and towels—most of which should be washable by hand or machine at home, and, ideally, line dried outdoors or in. It also has the best ventilation, since air movement discourages unwelcome textile inhabitants of the microscopic sort.

Otherwise, the art of housecleaning has a few basic steps.

First, sweep, starting at the far corners of each room and working toward the center. Gather dust and debris into one or several heaps. (Everyone has a slightly different technique for gathering their dust piles; some like the piles large and central, while others prefer to create several small piles.) Sweep up the piles with your small dustpan and brush (see page 171).

Next, dust each room, starting at the ceiling and moving down, using a combination of dry dusting (with feathers) and wet cleaning (with a microfiber cloth). (Wear a dust mask if you are sensitive; if you suffer from dust allergies, by all means, delegate.) Wait for the dust to settle.

Then, vacuum your rugs and mop hard surfaces with damp microfiber pads.

And put on some good music while you're at it.

Toilet Brush

Buy Cheap and Hide . . .

There's nothing glamorous about a toilet brush—nor should there be. There's actually good reason to go with a cheap model (a plastic wand, with plastic bristles, on a plastic stand). A very basic brush and base design doesn't try to hide the tool but holds it upright, out in the open, where it can dry quickly. Encasing the brush wand in a sleek designer canister is a recipe for mold. (However, one shouldn't fear mold, or the brush itself, to the point of succumbing to the disposable-brush craze—it's just too wasteful.)

A good toilet brush and base combo should be as small, short, humble, and undistinguished as possible. Both serious-looking brushes (stainless steel *objets*) and funny-looking brushes (pink plastic flamingos) draw too much attention to themselves. The idea is to hide the thing: Tuck it behind the toilet, away from view, where its color disappears into the background.

No innovation here—the *real* innovation is in how you use the thing.

Television commercials have taught us that we need to gear up like Hazmat agents while pouring toxic potions into the dreaded bowl. Unnecessary, even in that gnarliest of places. The toilet brush is a tool, not a weapon. And there's absolutely no need to use aggressively-branded, pricey products that are bad for your body and your watershed.

Instead, buy a gallon of distilled (white) vinegar and a spray bottle.

Vinegar has an amazing ability to kill germs and dissolve stains, including mild calcium deposits. For light cleaning, just spray in the bowl and around the rim, and scour lightly with the toilet brush. For heavier cleaning, add a couple cups of vinegar to the bowl and close the lid. Walk away for a couple hours, then brush the insides of the bowl as usual.

Vinegar also makes the toilet brush last longer (though it should be replaced every couple of years).

Broom

Because You Can't Vacuum a Sidewalk

When our shaggy forefathers were hunkering in caves, they were probably sweeping with bunches of weeds; attaching those weeds to a stick for a more erect sweeping posture may have been the first ergonomic feat.

Today, handmade natural-fiber brooms can be found in every household store, anywhere in the world. And at a time when you see the same cars, sneakers, and TVs in Arkansas and Ibiza, natural-fiber brooms are among the diminishing number of products that reflect their regions. In Southeast Asia, the traditional broom sports wide curves of colorfully dyed palm bristles twisted into braided handles; the standard North American broom (invented in 1797) is made of stiff bunches of sorghum stalks called "broom corn" and attached to a pine pole.

No matter the advances in technology, the humble corn broom is still considered irreplaceable as a serious tool of commercial cleaning. It has an uncanny ability to sweep rough surfaces as well as smooth ones, indoors or out. It doesn't just move dirt around; the fine hairs at the end of its bristles grab onto particles and move them farther up into the broom. It doesn't require much manpower; a gentle sweeping action is surprisingly efficient. As with all the best stuff, the tool improves with age: Its bristles soften, and when they finally wear out, the whole tool can be composted.

Ancient as it is, sweeping often beats lugging out the big vacuum, especially for quick kitchen-floor duty. Light sweeping in between major cleaning can actually help to maintain floor coverings, as small dirt particles tend to scratch hardwood finishes and wear down rug fibers. And the more often that broom comes out, the less onerous that weekly or biweekly vacuuming and mopping session will be.

Seek out the best quality "household"-style corn broom at a janitorial or contractor supply store (where everything else will be plastic or steel). And whistle while you work—to the distinctive whisking sound of 100 percent sorghum.

Dustpan and Brush

They Belong Together

"In great design, form follows function." The adage is so tired that our ears have become immune to it. In this case, though, it happens to apply. What with cleaning being so unglamorous, the household cleaning industry remained largely design-free until the 1990s, when the OXO company introduced its Good Grips Dust Pan and Brush and turned a homely task into a pleasant surprise—or at least into a less severe form of punishment, depending on whom you ask.

Small brushes were made for minor household tragedies: a shattered vase, a dropped bulb, spilled beans—things too skittish or potentially dangerous to maneuver with a long-poled broom. The pans themselves need to be sturdy enough to hold a straight, sealed edge to the floor. But cheap plastic models proved useless; they were seldom precise or sturdy enough to catch all the detritus. Good dustpans had an edge but were often made of heavy, rustable steel. And though pans and brushes were meant to work together, they were sold separately.

A light plastic pan with an exacting edge—intelligently backed with a nonslip substance for precision—was only the tip of OXO's iceberg. New, durable plastics offered a ground-breaking combination of quality and lightness. Pan and brush were brought together, nestled into one very convenient and vaguely maternal unit; the brush's egg-shaped handle snapped smartly into the pan, and the whole could be hung proudly from a hook. The brush was no longer mangy but soft and well shaped, with just the right amount of nylon bristles for a fast, light sweep. The duo's bright colors and biomorphic curves were cheering, and the feel of its warm egg in the palm proved strangely rewarding.

And still is. The design went on to inspire a rash of highly designed, faux-OXO dustpan sets, but the original model still reigns supreme.

Feather Duster

Flounce Your Way to Spic-and-Span

A feather duster is a funny thing—you don't know it's indispensable until you use one. Maligned as it is by television commercials selling new and supposedly better-performing gadgets, the classic feather duster is the only tool able to flounce dust off bumpy or fragile surfaces.

Why bother? Dust removal is a cultural mandate. In modern life, the presence of dust suggests the absence of something important: money for hiring help, time for doing your own cleaning, concern for domestic tidiness. A dusty home portends domestic mismanagement. (For college students, of course, dustiness simply celebrates freedom from Mom and all her compulsions.)

Dust is the benign but constant accumulation of laundry lint, food particles, clothing fibers, ashes, sloughed-off skin and hair, pet dander, pollen, and soil blown or tracked in from the outdoors. It collects most visibly on dark, horizontal surfaces.

Only recently has dust become synonymous with danger. Among Americans, the increased occurrence of asthma and assorted allergies has boosted the invention of all kinds of products—pharmaceuticals, sleep apparatus, and dust-removing, air-purifying machines and services. The dust mite, a dust-loving microscopic critter scary only when photographically enlarged, has become the villainous mascot of dust commerce. The harmless mite, which resembles a harmful tick, has been exploited by allergy entrepreneurs—professional duct cleaning, anyone?—to suggest that mites are a monstrous kind of flesh-eating scourge.

With so much chemical and mechanical engineering devoted to dust proofing and dust removal, one would expect the most ancient piece of dusting equipment to have disappeared long ago. But the old-fashioned ostrich feather duster is ubiquitous and still widely praised as the most effective dust-removal device ever invented.

The feather duster also has a place in feminist history. The first duster, made frugally with surplus turkey feathers, was invented by ace home-maker Susan Hibbard, who challenged her husband for inventor's rights in patent court. (He claimed *he* had invented it.) She won, and her patent was granted in 1876.

B y the early 1900s, ostrich plumes had replaced turkey feathers. The more flamboyant ostrich quills were also more durable, and the barbed fringe created enough static electricity to hold dust until it was shaken out. The plume's fringes were strong enough to sweep away big swaths of dust, but gentle enough to caress the most fragile of gewgaws without knocking them over. The new invention, with its expensive, imported plumage and its inexplicable efficiency, became a domestic status symbol.

But as new, higher-tech household products were introduced in the 1920s, the feather duster was dismissed as a vestige of Victoriana, with its mawkish, dust-attracting bric-a-brac. Lots of cheaper dusters appeared: wands of yellow-dyed turkey feathers, fuzzy sticks of lamb's wool, bright pink bouquets of synthetic feathers. American amateurs experimented with these gadgets, but professionals in the commercial cleaning industry stuck with the old-fashioned ostrich feathers.

In the 1960s, yet another form

of backlash took hold: Dusters were discredited as useless dust-agitators by chemical companies selling multitasking aerosol waxing agents that applied shine as they removed dust. The ads told housewives they would never have to inhale dust again. (Instead, they would be breathing a noxious chemical mist described on the can in the finest print.)

With the recent revival of household arts and homeopathic methods, the feather duster is back (again) and available everywhere from discount stores to ostrich farming websites. The best dusters are found at industrial cleaning stores. Feather merchants grade the feathers for shape and size, which sometimes explains the difference in duster prices. Look for good, fluffy ostrich feathers glued and wired to a wooden handle (with a convenient hole for hanging); the wired end of the feathers will be covered with a cap, or ferrule.

Although ostrich ranching, like llama husbandry, is catching on

The dust mite, scary only when photographically enlarged, has become a villain.

in the United States, South Africa remains the world capital of ostrich farming and feather-duster making. In response to animal activists who want to know where those big feathers come from, ranchers reply that the birds are well raised (the better they're nurtured, the faster the feathers grow); and that their outer feathers are collected while birds are molting or gently plucked before the animals are harvested for meat and hides, the real source of income.

If you accept the ranchers' practices, agree to pay the price, and like the Belle Epoque look of the feather duster, only one question remains: How do you actually use it?

Simple. Dust first. Vacuum up any dust that has fallen to the ground. Shake the feather duster outdoors so the cycle can begin anew.

~~~~~~~~~~

Vacuum Cleaner

Ticket to Ride

What do you do when your vacuum cleaner stops working? You open it up, replace the bag, inspect the hoses, and check the electrical outlet. Still doesn't work? That's not surprising. Vacuum cleaners are designed for work that harms them. Banged and bounced all over the house, their motors are strained by clogged filters, overheated by misuse, and destined to one of two fates: repair or replacement.

A dead machine forces you to face the reality about vacuum cleaners. Unlike other small appliances—bought cheaply and anonymously at big-box stores, then junked and replaced cheaply upon sudden death—a vac should be a longtime companion, chosen carefully, and repaired lovingly by a trusted aficionado.

Think of a vacuum as a car, not a coffeemaker. You buy a new car from a big, respectable company, hoping said company will stay in business for a long time, doing well enough to support a wide network of repairmen and parts. The company sells its products through local dealers who maintain a close relationship with the manufacturer and offer up a close relationship with you, the buyer—during the buying process and over the car's lifetime. The salesmen explain the confusing mechanical and stylistic features of their cars and let you drive them around. The dealer upholds a car's warranties, repairing and replacing whatever is covered in the fine print. Once the warranties expire, you can continue your relationship with the dealer, or seek out an independent auto mechanic who becomes your new indispensable friend, at lower labor charges.

When looking for a vacuum cleaner, find the relationship first. Seek out the well-respected local guy who sells and repairs a variety of vacuum cleaner brands from his showroom. Ask the vac man what kind of vacuum cleaner you need, and answer all his personal questions: bare floors or carpet; how high is the carpet pile; how many kids and pets do you have; are you tidy or messy; got lots of drapes, stairs, or allergies? He will help you fit the vacuum cleaner to your house and its inhabitants. He will explain the warranties and later uphold them by fixing the vac when it breaks.

It's not really the best vac you're seeking, but the least vac for your living conditions. The more streamlined the machine, the more often you'll be motivated to push it around.

To qualify for the least expensive vac, you'll need a ranch house with bare floors, windows, and furniture, and a small household of clean-living, nonallergic, noncompulsive people. In fact, you can sweep and damp-microfiber-mop those bare floors and get away with owning no vacuuming machine at all. Vacuum cleaners really only have one purpose, and that's rugs.

Kids or pets? Tidy or messy? Fit the vacuum cleaner to your house and needs.

The vacuum man should keep you from buying more features than you need (power, filtering systems, agitators, "on-board tools" like stair nozzles), and he should also steer you away from bogus bargains. The latest craze is cheap vacuums featuring expensive HEPA (high-efficiency particulate air) filters. Sounds techy, but those HEPAs are installed in loose, flimsy units that leak dust ("blowback") before it's filtered. It turns out those pollen-catching wonders need not only well-sealed bodies, but also motors powerful enough to push exhaust air through their fiberglass gauntlets. And allergy-free people don't need HEPA filters anyway. Unfortuately, it's a misunderstood buzzword that's come to suggest quality.

The vacuum man will also keep you away from all those newfangled machines you so desire.

The search will eventually lead you to one of Miele's canister vacuum cleaners. The canister model (a rolling armadillo shape connected by a hose to a vacuuming "wand") is more powerful and adaptable to different terrain than an upright model. Miele's lightweight, compact, agile body, with a quiet but powerful motor, is famous for its cleanliness.

Miele offers a choice of filtering systems, from perfectly good to over-the-top. It's the first company to make HEPA-certified vacuum cleaners with tightly sealed HEPA-rated bodies, but Miele refuses to pander to confusion about that filter and offers perfectly good nonrated filters too.

You will balk at the price. But whether you buy a Miele or not, you should think about the mathematics of value. Miele, a German company making suave motorized products for a hundred years, speaks a language we no longer understand: longevity.

"We don't build these things for landfills," said one Miele salesman. "With a new part now and then, you should expect them to last for about twenty years, under normal use, in a home of two thousand square feet or more." The company has a refreshing policy of stocking parts for fifteen years after any model is discontinued; it warrants its canister motors for a long seven years and its other parts for one.

If your home needs a vacuum cleaner, obtain the simplest, most economical canister model your specs will allow, then designate a driver. Urge the man of the house to think of the vacuum as an expensive power tool, and you just might fill the position.

~~~~~~~~~~~~~~~~

Screwdriver
The Power of Torque

Don't think of the screwdriver as a hand tool. Think of it instead as a kitchen or writing tool, a skinny thing sharing drawer space with pencils and takeout menus, always close at hand and waiting to do or undo whatever little job is required by Mom, Dad, or kids over the age of seven.

A hand tool is a serious instrument tucked away in a toolbox and ensconced in a garage or basement, that male headquarters of procrastinated weekend chores. Take the screwdriver out of its element and into the open, where it can be unisexual *and* more likely to fix all the things on the "Honey-Do . . ." list that haunts every married man.

The screwdriver is unlike any other tool, anyway. It's the most used and most creatively abused of all hand tools. Misused, it can open paint cans and puncture, gouge, chisel, pry, or poke anything. The longer the shaft, the greater the leverage.

In its official capacity, the screwdriver is the lever that applies torque, the magical rotational force that increases in relation to the distance of the lever from its fulcrum. Guided by the slightest exertion, it can assemble/disassemble and tighten/loosen just about everything in the house, including major appliances and massive pieces of furniture like beds and bookshelves.

Turns out almost everything in the house is held together by a handful of tiny screws and one simple principle: righty tighty, lefty loosey. Here's a partial list of other screw-dependent chattel: kitchen cabinetry, small appliances, plumbing fittings and fixtures, sofas, chairs, tables, computers, printers, TVs, window treatments, light fixtures, gadgets, and toys.

Though the tool's design is simple, to screwdriver aficionados it's fraught with controversy. The controversy is about the *bit*, or tip, of the screwdriver. How many do you really need? And what shape and size should they be? The two most familiar shapes, slotted and Phillips, come in different sizes. Should each bit be attached to its own handle, or should it belong to a multitip screwdriver? If the latter, where should the interchangeable tips be housed? In a box, in the hollow handle, or in some newfangled configuration? Should the bits be single units, or reversible shafts? And how long should those shafts be? And what about racheting?

If that sounds interesting, pick up a copy of *One Good Turn: A Natural History of the Screwdriver and the Screw,* by Witold Rybczynski.

Otherwise, pick up a two-in-one screwdriver with a reversible shaft, with a $3/16$-inch slotted bit at one end and a no. 1 Phillips head at the other. If your local hardware store doesn't carry that model, opt for a four-in-one with two slotted bits ($3/16$ inch and $9/32$ inch) and two Phillips heads (no. 1 and no. 2).

The humble screwdriver is the most creatively abused of all hand tools.

Resist the urge to buy a power screwdriver. As a rule of thumb, anytime you go electric when not absolutely necessary, you run the risk of malfunction, technical confusion, and energetic wastefulness. (A human-powered tool is no guarantee against a clumsy hand, of course, but at least you won't have to call customer service to figure out what went wrong.)

Hammer

. . . All Over this Land

A household hammer ought to be more toy than tool. But send a man to the hardware megastore to buy a household hammer, and he will return with a professional-grade hand tool suitable for building a new house or tearing one down. And though when it comes to construction, it pays to buy the best you can afford, the same isn't true for household tools.

At, say, one-tenth the price of a carpenter's model, a household hammer is actually better suited to weekend chores—hanging pictures, mounting shelves, installing curtain hardware, and building science projects.

A genuine professional hammer is designed to do violent but exacting work, all day long, over the course of its wielder's skilled career. (Techy-looking as can be, with fiberglass shafts and Santoprene-covered handles, some even have tuning forks inside to dampen vibrations and reduce arm fatigue.) But even real carpenters don't use real hammers at home: Their heft makes them accelerate too fast when aimed at tiny picture hooks. A light "household nail hammer" with a hickory handle strikes the right balance.

Manufacturing a hammer does require some finesse, so it's best not to buy the cheapest no-brand model, which will cost less than a decent toothbrush. A good household hammer will have a forged tempered steel head, a steel claw, and a smooth, gently curved hardwood handle. The blunt end of the head is meant to tap small nails into wood or plaster; the claw is designed to extract nails. A well-shaped hammer head is slightly crowned at its center so that the force of its blow lands directly on the nail.

Classic steel-and-wood hammers are quaint American antiques in the making; they also happen to be some of the most inexpensive hunks of hand-worked hardwood around. Surely wooden hammers will become extinct long before yours stops working (an event you may never witness). Meanwhile they are just plain, cheap, handsome, and evocative of the peaceful days before nail guns.

THE SMART LIST

CLEANING
&
FIXING

C LEAN WITH WATER AND AIR. Stop buying all those expensive chemicals and disposable gadgets, and invest in a few long-lasting and reusable tools.

As microfiber catches on, big brands and stores are adding it to their home cleaning lineup. In general, janitorial and restaurant supply houses carry the best quality at the highest prices, but you can also order from websites selling discounted professional supplies, or, as always, directly from manufacturers.

Choose a vacuum cleaner—the costliest product in this realm—with live, expert consultation, based on your home and habits.

MOP

- Slim aluminum mop with a detachable microfiber pad
- Try: A Rubbermaid Commercial three-part microfiber mop "cleaning system," with a swiveling mop head and detachable, washable pads (also sold separately), and an aluminum mop head/pad holder; lighter-duty microfiber mops and pads designed for the consumer market are also available.
- Care: Machine-wash and air-dry pads after use.
- Eco-rating: You're eliminating all floor-cleaning chemicals, disposable wet wipes, short-lived sponge mops, and lots of water.
- Shopping tip: Buy microfiber pads and mops made by reputable manufacturers to ensure you're getting high-quality, split-fiber textiles (sometimes called "ultra microfiber").
- Find it: Janitorial suppliers or manufacturers' websites; increasingly, in big-box stores

Cost: Aluminum mop handle, about $10; aluminum mop head/pad holder, about $20; microfiber wet mop pads, about $10 each

CLEANING CLOTH

- Microfiber aka "ultra microfiber" cleaning cloths made for "general cleaning"
- Care: Machine-wash and air-dry cloths after use.
- Eco-rating: You're eliminating just about all household chemicals, as well as all paper towels, disposable wipes, and cellulose sponges. The cloths should outlast 300 machine launderings.
- Use it: Dedicate cloths for specialized cleaning tasks (i.e., bathroom, kitchen, and so on). Cut the cloths to a convenient size, and code them with an indelible marker.
- Find it: Janitorial suppliers, auto suppliers, the auto section of any big-box store, or manufacturers' websites

Cost: About $50 per dozen

TOILET BRUSH

· Plastic brush and holder
· Find it: Most any corner store, big-box store, or hardware store

Cost: $2 to $5

BROOM

· "Household corn broom" with wooden handle
· Care: Every few sweepings, clean the broom by combing it roughly with a brush or microfiber cloth, or, on rare occasions, by washing it in a detergent solution; to keep the broom's edge straight, hang it from a hook to air-dry and for general storage.

Note: *On very smooth surfaces like highly polished wooden floors, dry microfiber mopping may be more effective than sweeping.*

· Find it: Most any corner store or big-box store; for the best quality, look to janitorial suppliers.

Cost: About $10

DUSTPAN AND BRUSH

· OXO Good Grips Dust Pan and Brush
· Find it: In the cleaning aisle at big-box stores

Cost: About $10

FEATHER DUSTER

· 20"-long feather duster
· Ostrich feathers; wooden handle
· Find it: Janitorial suppliers or manufacturers' websites

Cost: About $15

VACUUM CLEANER

· Basic Miele canister vacuum cleaner with no HEPA filter; or the vacuum cleaner your local vacuum cleaner repairman/dealer recommends based on your household profile
· Find it: A Miele dealer or your local vacuum specialist

Cost: Miele, $500–$700; other known brands, $250–$500

SCREWDRIVER

· 2-in-1 screwdriver with reversible shaft and two bits—a $^3/_{16}$" slotted head and a no. 1 Phillips head; or, a 4-in-1 with 2 additional bits—a $^9/_{32}$" slotted head and no. 2 Phillips head
· Find it: Any hardware or big-box store

Cost: $3 to $5

HAMMER

· 8 oz. household claw hammer with wooden handle
· Find it: Any hardware store or big-box store

Cost: About $5

CHAPTER SIX

READING, WRITING, LIVING

INVENTORY

- Doormat
- Rug
- Sofa
- Coffee Table
- Floor Lamp

- Vase
- Music Device
- Desk
- Reading Chair
- Bookholder

- Phone
- Laptop
- Printer
- Picture Frame
- Archives

Most of the items in this book are designed to perform simple tasks over a remarkably long period of time. This chapter rounds up some of the household's most complex, productive, and perishable elements: laptop, printer, and cell phone. Their manufacturers hope you will chuck them in a year or less, once you're enticed by new features and models, and the machines have plenty of physical obsolescence built into them. And so we go on acquiring the next new thing, packed with surprises, hoping to stay ahead of the pack but knowing replacement is imminent. It's an awfully expensive game with no end in sight. And it's a silly one, too, because when you think about it, the most fascinating electronic products are those that bring people together. We talk and write to one another; we watch, film, and photograph one another with tiny machines. But what we don't have is enough time in the day to actually see the people we care about in the flesh. That's why all the equipment I've chosen is presented in the spirit of nostalgia. The fewer communication machines we own, and the simpler they are, the better we'll communicate in the most satisfying of all modes: machine free.

In the living room—the room that is specially set aside for familial and more formal entertainment—hosts try to tell the best version of their household stories. A century ago, that tale would have been an ancestral one. The drawing room upheld continuity by showcasing rickety antiques and inherited valuables, from silver-framed sepia photos to commemorative wedding gifts.

These days, the notion of preserving posterity has fallen by the wayside. Instead, the smart living room is supposed to be an expression of the owner's evolving personal style, as the shelter magazines call it. It's filled with fresh purchases, the favored, newish antiques of the moment, and fashionable paint colors inspired by the recklessness of DIY television. (Hurry! Transform your home in a day on a dime!) Talk about pressure. What if, heaven forbid, you find out you don't even have a personal style, let alone the energy to express it?

Why not design the living room for living, filling it with stuff you really use during downtime? Consider your actual activities. Your space should be able to contain anything from scotch-soused poker sessions to preschool crafts to Sunday morning crosswords.

Thinking of the contents of the living room in terms of their uses might sound complicated, but it actually simplifies things. Take the sofa, for instance. If you approach its purchase as the ultimate declaration of your class and taste, the painful choice will take forever. Think of the sofa as a vehicle with a purpose—casting couch for singles, oenophiles' club headquarters, or soccer mom central—and the thing practically chooses itself.

Doormat

Come On In!

The WELCOME mat was the dawning of an American tradition we now take for granted: lots of porch products trying to chat with passersby. A practical novelty, it symbolized early suburbanites' hopes about their neighborly futures. The message may have been muddy—a warm greeting woven into an abrasive surface for foot wiping—but the new suburbanites saw no irony.

The porch business has been flourishing ever since. The welcome mat ushered in decades of homeowner-personalized sentiment in the form of mailboxes, seasonal flags, and holiday inflatables.

Surrounded as we are by the influence of big business and media, isn't it high time we bucked the trend and stopped positioning ourselves as miniature corporations in need of banners, one-liners, and other hallmarks of the advertising trade?

By gripping snow, rain, leaves, grass, sand, and dust, a doormat prevents people from soiling floors. It actually prolongs the life of floor surfaces and rugs and reduces the need for cleaning (if you can't abide shedding your shoes at the door, as you would in Japan, or in hip households anywhere else). And that's all it should do.

Tires are well suited to doormatting. That may sound odd, but a geometric mat of sliced, recycled tires —actually quite an old-fashioned device—has become honorably green. Unfortunately, it's just as ugly as it sounds. At the opposite extreme are brightly colored carpets of woven polypropylene, tufted and sculpted for optimal shoe scraping and absorbency. You can buy them or have them custom etched with any old saying, poem, or even landscape, but an overly elaborate design is as foolish an oxymoron as a roll of Rembrandt-printed toilet paper.

In this noisy mat marketplace, the most elegant statement is also one of the least expensive: a no-nonsense doormat of natural coir, a rough, water- and salt-resistant fiber of coconut husks from fruit grown in Sri Lanka and India. It feels good to tread on a bristly patch of natural stuff. And when it begins to look worn out, you can compost it in the garden and get another.

Coir doormats are available from outdoor furniture suppliers and the usual retail sources, but an industrial flooring company can also custom cut you a half-inch-thick rectangle of coir matting at a length to fit your doorway.

Bottom line: The coir mat is handsome, but not too pretty to prevent your guests from doing what you dare not ask them to do: Wipe their feet.

Rug

Art for Your Floor

A removable rug promotes the kind of partying a permanent, absorbent surface scares off. Food can be slushier, wine redder, and hosts more confident in the knowledge that (almost) nothing is irreparable. When accidents happen, you just spot clean the wool, wash the whole rug outdoors, or whisk it to a skilled cleaner or repairer. If really raucous parties are your style, just roll up the rugs before the event.

The area rug also works like a picture frame: Just as a good frame glamorizes any piece of artwork, a good rug can pull together a group of mismatched pieces and turn them into a livable living room (or a cozy bedroom—see page 30).

Though not as enveloping as a sea of carpeting, area rugs can soften the acoustics of the room, offer warm, welcoming texture underfoot, and serve as brightly colored or patterned floor art—woe to the wall-to-wall carpeting that tries that.

A good rug actually *is* art. In medieval castles, huge wool tapestries predated decorative paintings (they also insulated the clammy stone walls). And in many parts of Asia and the Middle East, traditional handmade rugs, with their symbolic geometric imagery, may be the most important sources of meaning, beauty, and history, in a room—as well as the only pieces of "furniture" in many traditional homes and mosques. Rugs may work simultaneously as moveable art and furniture: adorning walls and tables, covering banquettes and floors, creating surfaces on which to sit, recline, dine, or pray.

In the West, rugs aren't prized for their versatility. Mainly, we just walk on them. Still, they represent a level of craft that's mysterious and compelling. The proof of their value comes in the liquidation: A good handwrought rug, new or antique, holds its value longer than anything else in a living room of freshly bought pieces. New furniture becomes used, but old rugs become interesting.

The best way to actually enjoy this investment is to buy the highest quality rug you can comfortably afford—be it $300 or $3,000—then use it with abandon. Go ahead and live on it. Rugs are extraordinarily resilient. They can be washed, repaired, even partially rewoven.

Rug neophytes can start with a flat "kilim" rug, woven and reversible (as opposed to a knotted rug, which is flat on one side, with a thick "pile" of cut yarns on the other). Because kilims require less time and wool than most Oriental handmade rugs, they're among the lightest and least expensive. Turkey is best known for its kilims, but the rugs are also produced in Iran, Pakistan, and various parts of the Middle East. The costs vary widely, depending on provenance, intricacy, age, and dyes; natural dyes are more desirable and more colorfast than synthetic; and older is better than newer, since semi-antique and antique rugs are deemed more authentic, folkloric, and less influenced by the generic preferences of Western markets.

How do you turn all this random information into adventure? Find a Turkish rug the Turkish way. Eliminate the middleman and get personal: Locate a direct importer/wholesaler of kilims, preferably one praised by word of mouth (ask a local interior designer). Bring your desired rug dimensions and color preferences, and be prepared to spend a couple of hours in a showroom.

It takes five people to choose a rug this way: one salesman, two rug wranglers, you, and preferably a pal who knows more than you do. The rug guys will flip the carpets while you comment. When you find one you love, give the dealer a chance to perform his sales pitch, including exhaustive specs and a bogus price.

At some point you must bargain.

> A good rug represents a level of craft that's mysterious and compelling.

Should bargain. Give it a try. Price tags are created by overindustrialized societies. Creative bargaining suits the artisanal nature of the product. If you refuse to dicker, simply go to a retailer, pay more, and learn less.

To decide on your dimensions, think of your theoretical rug as an island, and build a cozy settlement on top of it and around it, using a coffee table and upholstered seating. (New rugs come in standard sizes, seldom bigger than 8 by 10 feet.)

Color is trickier. A rug reflects light, as well as the color of the walls and ceiling. When you get it home, it's liable to look muddier or goofier than what you saw in the showroom. If you know what color your walls are, bring a paint swatch with you to look at alongside the rug.

(Note: This move won't help you become an interior designer, but it may fool neighboring shoppers.)

Sofa

Avoiding the Couch Complex

The heaviest, costliest piece of furniture in the home, the sofa says more about you than your home itself (unless you custom designed the abode of your dreams). But a sofa is the unmortgagable structure you choose, all alone, from a sea of options. On some level, whatever that thing looks like, you really mean it.

Unsurprisingly, it tends to be the most haunting domestic purchase of all—who hasn't fallen victim to the abyss of sofa remorse? Even if you put off the ultimate decision by buying an inexpensive "temporary" sofa, you'll probably still end up lugging it with you from home to home, just to avoid the torture of choosing another. For that reason alone, you'll do well to buck the trend of disposable couches and buy a long-lasting sofa you love as much as your favorite car.

These days Americans tend to buy their sofas without knowing anything about a sofa's anatomy, construction, or longevity. Retailers, well aware of this blissful ignorance, fulfill shoppers' fantasies, offering low prices on pretty packages.

Alas, getting the right sofa takes some work. Set style aside for a moment—stay out of those showrooms—and start off with size and function. Think about the amount of space you want to fill up with seating, rather than the size of your ideal sofa. Lay sheets of newspaper on the floor where you think the sofa should stand. To figure out height, pile some furniture, pillows, or cardboard boxes until you reach a level that works (low in a small room with low ceilings, taller in larger rooms).

Now walk around that mountain of stuff, look at it from across the room, and decide if its bulk overwhelms the room or gets swallowed up. Keep adjusting the dimensions until you get the proportions right.

Next, use a tape measure to determine the length, width, and height of the pile. The length will tell you a lot about your future sofa. The longest sofa will need three seat cushions; the shortest, a single cushion. The greater the number of cushions, the smaller they will be. That's good—small cushions keep their shape better and stay cleaner. (If they get inked or splotched, just reverse them or take them to the dry cleaner.)

For ease in cleaning, the back of the sofa should be covered with loose throw pillows filled with fluffy material, or with two or three firm, fitted cushions, as opposed to a continuous surface of rigid foam (a "tight back").

Removable pillows are also versatile; you can use them to quickly change the shape of the sofa. Toss them on the floor when you want to take a nap, or pile them as needed for reading feet-up. Prop them up or punch them down to adjust your stance from a formal, 90-degree posture to a casual, 180-degree slouch.

The sofa's arms provide much of its personality. Rolled arms look voluptuous and welcoming and are more comfortable for lounging than

> Buck the trend of disposable couches. Buy one you'll be able to love like a favorite car.

straight arms or no arms. Legs are best covered with a skirt for hiding dust bunnies—unless the design is modern, with bare legs and a streamlined seat that allows for thorough under-couch sweeping.

Once you've decided on a rough shape that suits your room proportions and lounging postures, it's time to commit to a life span. How long do you want the sofa to last? The correct answer: almost forever.

Buying a long-lasting sofa is like building a kitchen. You construct a sturdy framework, fully wired and plumbed, knowing the cabinets will look shabby and outdated in a decade or two, and that the appliances will fail. Instead of demolishing the room, you remodel, saving as much as you can. You don't buy a disposable kitchen.

The best way to buy a sofa is the custom route. As in remodeling, you select every detail of style, carpentry, and upholstery techniques and materials. The custom sofa can be made new and ordered though a furniture retailer or designer, or you can work with a local upholsterer to renovate an old sofa—which means replacing just about everything but the wooden frame and some springs. Both of these options are potentially rewarding. A last chance to work with real craftsmen! A finished product that is everything you wished for! But they're also costly and time-consuming.

If that's not within your means or time frame, two simple options remain: Adopt someone else's custom-made sofa via the Internet; or find a retailer selling sofas made by reputable manufacturers. Such sofa makers sell consistent, quality pieces. No need to inspect each joint. The retailer will be able to recite every detail of their fabrication. If they can't, keep looking.

What makes a sofa durable and long-lasting? It starts with the skeleton: a frame of kiln-dried wood, hung together by the strongest joints you can afford—the best are double-doweled, with corner blocks (hunks of wood) glued and screwed at each juncture.

The couch's legs will be stronger if they're actually part of the wood frame, not screwed on.

The frame holds the "deck," or seat, and back of the sofa in tension. Just as with conventional mattresses, there are springs involved. Foam is the spongy stuff that gives a sofa its cushiness. In upholstery, the foam in question is polyurethane, also called poly-foam, made with petroleum. (Latex, the natural foam I recommend for mattresses, is deemed too expensive and heavy for use in sofas.)

Though materials are nominally the same across all sofas, their quality varies as widely as their density. Actually, *density* is too simple a word for it. Foam's personality is measured by an IFD (indentation forced deflection) number, which describes support quality—a combination of density and bounciness measured by a battery of tests. In practice, the foam should be soft enough so you're sitting *into* it, not on top of it, but hard enough so that you can extract yourself gracefully.

The best sofas are made with costlier high resilience (HR) foams, long-lived and extremely responsive. (Sounds strange, but they're just livelier than regular foams.) There's also "Preserve," a new HR poly-foam made of polyol, in which soybeans replace about 10 percent of the petroleum.

Fabric is the subject that keeps most sofa buyers in limbo. After they finally choose one, they often regret it. Here's why: Consumers believe that soft, 100 percent cotton fabrics are more virtuous than synthetics. In some cases, that may be true. But cotton actually makes a terrible upholstery fabric. It wears quickly, wrinkles, pills, holds stains, and resists cleaning—and consequently leads a very short, rather shabby life. No good. All upholstery fabrics should be made of synthetic fibers, or synthetics blended with natural fibers.

The most durable upholstery fabric is an all-synthetic microfiber.

Years ago, that would have meant one thing and one thing only: Ultrasuede, one of the early microfiber textiles. But these days, microfiber comes in a great range of prices and textures, from corduroy to wool-like weaves. All of it holds up, resists stains, and proves much easier to clean than the best quality cotton.

Other than all this, there are only three more things to remember when seeking out the most public piece of furniture in the house:

No sectionals. Too boring and institutional.

No sleep sofas. Inflatable mattresses are cheap, fast, and more comfortable. A pull-out sofa makes for an uncomfortable sofa *and* a lumpy bed.

No white cotton sofas unless you wear all-white, and live alone on an island of all-white sand.

Coffee Table

Sip, Graze, Lounge

Think of the coffee table as the Neanderthal campfire. It's all about hunkering down with fermented drinks and finger foods in a safe circle of friends. A coffee table is nothing more than a level surface, reachable from the sofa. Who and what you put around that surface, and on it, is much more important than what it looks like or how it works. Or doesn't work, for that matter: Though the coffee table is the epicenter of cozy downtime, no piece of household equipment is less effective.

Our expectations are high. For guests, we want the coffee table to be part buffet spread, part personal museum, with a faux casual smattering of expensive books, revealing magazines, and expressive curios. Or, having grown up with that, we want just the opposite: a defiant lack of bourgeois clutter.

Whatever our inclination, we all regress to our primitive selves once the guests go home. Watching TV with a slouched lapful of dinner, we want the coffee table to be a squishy ottoman, supporting our legs in a long sprawl.

Simultaneously, it should be able to hold lots of messy newspapers, junky books, and silly magazines—to be read, of course, while channel surfing —all layered over a laptop teetering on a pile of paperwork. That's multi-tasking—the improvisatory American custom of simultaneously conducting personal and professional business.

Given all these needs, you would think it would make sense to seek out a multitasking surface. Unfortunately, the "adjustable coffee tables" patented by earnest inventors and entrepreneurs are the funniest pieces of furniture around. Engineered with the unsightly aesthetic of hospital furniture, they invite their owners to work on laptops or watch TV while dining in bed, which means you clear the desk/dining surface in order to stretch out and snooze. Terribly useful. Equally homely.

How do ace designers handle the coffee table? Every segment of the design trade promotes its own cof-

The ideal coffee table would disappear into the floor at the touch of a button. . . .

fee table cliché. Interior designers adore the giant, custom-upholstered ottoman that behaves like a table when topped with a serving tray. Architects prefer any icon that is sculptural in form, too expensive to use, conceived by a famous—you guessed it—architect. Product designers love tables made of strange, witty materials.

The ideal coffee table would not be a table but a system inspired by the theater's hydraulic lifts, those ingenious contraptions that whisk away scenery through a hole in the stage floor. Press a button, and that messy, football-and-beer vignette would sink out of sight; in its place would rise an elegant cocktail scene. Press again, and you'd get a child-proofed, waterproofed table safe for a raucous toddler playdate. One can only dream . . .

The most convenient table is a continuous, low surface nearly as long as the sofa it serves. Since those proportions—long slab, short legs— seldom form an attractive object, it's best to opt for a table that will disappear under the spread of your prized possessions. Small nesting and stacking tables, all the vogue, may promise a bit of flexibility, but nothing draws everyone together into the communal fire circle better than the old, clichéd, coffee-table-shaped coffee table.

The width of the table should be proportional to both the living room and sofa: a long, benchlike rectangle suits a small room; a square fits a bigger one. The smaller the table, the better your guests can huddle together. The wider the table, the larger the snack buffet.

The ideal height remains the same, whatever the surface area: eighteen to twenty inches—low enough for party guests to sit on the floor and surround the table, high enough for sofa sitters to easily reach their cocktails.

Since holding drinks is the main role of the table, it's wise to choose surface materials that can withstand flooding and bruising. A solid hardwood top with a water-resistant finish will keep looking better over the years, as you use it au naturel—sans coasters, padding, and finicky rules. Wood improves a room's acoustics, softens the sound of glasses plunked down, and treats one's shins better than metal or stone. All hardwoods are suitable, but a clear, light coating will show fewer scratches than a heavy dark stain.

Stick with a simple, slim design (no lumbering slabs of tree), and you'll end up with a lightweight table that's easier to move for cleaning or rearranging when the need for a dance party strikes.

Most important of all: Make sure there's enough room for a large pizza.

Floor Lamp

Set the Mood

Wearing a lampshade on your head was easier in your parents' day, when every living room was lit by a sofa-flanking pair of matching table lamps with fancy shades. Their sheer fabric shades turned the glare of old-fashioned incandescent bulbs, into a homey yellowish glow. Today those power-sucking bulbs are the enemy, and frilly lampshades are passé. So how are you going to light your living room?

In a few years, our dens will be transformed into stage sets full of dramatic possibilities. Controlled by a microprocessor, those economical, long-lasting LEDs will wash the walls with cascades of flowing light in all colors on weekends, then settle down during the work week to shine bright pools of reading light wherever we need them. Changeable colored light will supply the mood and sparkle once provided by paints and fabrics. (And unlike my fantasy hydraulic coffee table, these inventions are almost here.)

For the moment, the right light sources for the living room are three-way CFLs (compact fluorescent lightbulbs) just like the ones recommended for the bedroom.

The lamp itself should also be the same kind of basic, three-way model as the one used in the bedroom—clean, simple lines and a heavy base. A translucent shade in a warm off-white will diffuse light while maintaining the bulb's cozy temperature. (A pure white shade creates a harsh, blue-white glow.) Shades made of smooth recycled plastics will be much easier to dust and clean than fabric or paper ones.

The larger the room, the more lamps you need. The goal is to create adjustable ambience without glare, the contrast between a bright light and a dark background that tires the eyes. Omit bare decorative bulbs and chandeliers. But bring on the soy candles for the kind of poetic lighting electricity cannot surpass.

Vase

Bring the Outdoors In

A vase holds flowers, but flowers are not a necessity, unless you're a woman who loves flowers, or a person who lives with such a woman. (Political correctness be damned: Flower-coveting men are rare.) A vase can hold other things too, but none so precious as the roses brought by a grateful guest, or the daffodils you buy yourself on the day the snow melts.

As for those who disapprove of cut flowers—and the violence of plucking up living things for the fleeting, selfish pleasure of sniffing at them indoors only to watch them shrivel and die—read on. Having fresh flowers around achieves more than you know.

When emotions swell, there is no better token of love, longing, regret, remorse, joy, or gratitude. Flowers make potent symbols. They are very good at expressing poignant, contradictory feelings that sound vapid in words. They often mark the arrival of special holidays or events—Valentine's Day, Mother's Day, shower, wedding, or birthday.

Carnations may be funeral props in one culture, and party decor in another. In North America, flowers are subject to fast changes in fashion. Species can become hip or outré from one season to the next: Red roses may go from classic to déclassé, rare orchids from exotic to maudlin.

No matter the species, blooms are the most convincing reminder of the dependable beauty of nature and its heartening guarantee: Things grow. And among growing things, nothing is more spectacularly arbitrary than a flower, an intricate geometry of colors with an invisible cloud of perfume.

Fragrance is the flower's mysterious message, and smell is the most persuasive, primitive, and least understood of all human senses—capable of making us act without understanding our true, unconscious motivations. Fragrance can intensify experience, trigger memories, and change moods.

How do you harness the power of these biochemical catalysts? It's not hard. Pour lukewarm water into vase; insert flowers.

What vase? It doesn't have to be a wildly expensive wedding gift; any water-holding container can qualify. In fact, the contrast between improvised vase and perfect blossoms can be lovely. What's more endearing than a young man arranging roadside daisies in little green Rolling Rock pony bottles for a girlfriend's first visit?

A vase is no more than a primitive irrigation device used to keep flowers alive for a week or so, after they've been clipped from their source of water and food, the roots and leaves that take in sun, water, and nutrients. The more nutritious the water, the longer the plants will survive. Rain and spring waters buy more time than city water. Florist-supplied vitamin powder encourages plant life while discouraging the bacteria that cloud vase water.

Vase-bound flowers stay healthiest when they stand in just enough fresh water to cover a couple inches of stem, since flowers sip water upward via their hollow, porous stalks. If the stem bottoms are mushy, it's best to recut them, diagonally, using sharp scissors (see page 81) to make a large, clean slice. It's also a good idea to snap off the lower leaves to keep the water fresher.

The form of the vase informs the shape of the bouquet. Vase anatomy has three parts: the base, the mouth, and the neck, the narrowest section. A curvaceous shape—wide base, narrow neck, flared mouth—expands a bouquet into a wide, X-shaped bundle. A modern, cylindrical vase creates a tighter, more vertical arrangement.

The perfectly adequate vase is a clear glass container, about eight inches high, shaped with proportions that appeal to you in an inexplicable way. Transparent vases remind you to change or refill the water as plants drink it up.

The best vase is also priceless. Ideally, it costs nothing to acquire, and the conditions of the acquisition are impossible to reproduce. It may be a lowly florist's vase delivered with a surprise bouquet from someone you like, or a voluptuous pitcher ceremoniously purchased or presented.

The humbler the vase, the more likely you are to use it weekly and fearlessly. Vases take a beating. They bang around in the sink as they're filled with stems, then dumped and washed. Vases get in the way of kids and pets, and chip, crack, or crash.

The all-purpose utilitarian vase has only one problem, however. The less interesting the vase, the emptier and more forlorn it looks when it's not flaunting something. The simple solution? Keep it filled.

Filled with what?

In winter, exotic flowers are flown in from southern continents. They are expensive, breathtakingly flawless, and unreal. For more character, the piney fragrance of local greenery clipped from evergreen junipers and boxwood promotes cheer and a spirit of tenacity. You can even kill two birds with one stone by treating kitchen herbs like cut flowers: Buy bunches of parsley, chives, or basil and flaunt them as decoration.

In early spring, harvested tree branches will bloom indoors, creating a sense of hope that will last until tulips and daffodils finally pop up.

By late summer, flowers are bountiful. Roadside stands sell rough wildflower bouquets next to perfect, juicy tomatoes. And the roadsides themselves grow tall flowering weeds, free for the picking and lovely as any hothouse hybrids.

In the fall, hardy mums seem to prolong summer, fallen red leaves supply that last bit of color, and dried wheat and berries begin to take on a floral look.

There's nothing new about this horticultural parade of events. But it takes a vase, holding a small souvenir, to make us see it for the first time, all over again.

Music Device
The Best Sound Quality Yet . . .

A weird thing happened to music lately. It became a private activity. People started assembling personal snippets of digital music, storing them on plastic wafers, and listening to the music wherever they went, via ear-budded wires. Suddenly, teenagers were incommunicado. Touted as the next era in music, iPods and other MP3 players allowed everyone to carry huge personal files of music around anywhere. The trade-off for all this convenient mobility was sound quality.

Eventually, owners of tiny music players started parking their gadgets into still newer gadgets called docks—receiver/speakers designed to turn private music into more public ambience (sound that can be enjoyed wirelessly by anyone within a room).

Audio experts were appalled. To them, MP3 docks perverted the mission of audio electronics: the painstaking reproduction of sound for the purpose of blowing one's mind with the ecstasy of music. The idea of selling those docks as domestic music machines to hapless consumers was, and still is, unconscionable: The docks rob an unsuspecting public of the true, pleasurable potential of recorded music and diminish the labor of the recording artists by putting out inferior sound, over a short life span, at considerable expense.

According to audiophiles, the earliest digital recordings transferred to CDs removed indispensable higher frequencies. But the little discs' convenience seemed to outweigh their flaws. The digitizing of music, still more aggressively, for MP3 technology added another dimension of convenience, but it removed still more sound quality. The act of processing the compressed, distorted music as amplified environmental sound adds insult to injury. It's like serving up reconstituted, freeze-dried backpacking food to dinner guests. Much is lost—it's just not the same.

Audio experts claim that there's only one way to go at this point—backward. Vinyl records are still the best way to enjoy music, they say. They capture more incalculable and indescribable nuances of sound than any recording medium around. And there's something very cool about owning a big circle of grooved plastic enclosed in an artwork-covered cardboard sleeve. Widely available, used or new, albeit in offbeat places, vinyl is destined to outlive CDs—ergo, it's a better investment. Sounds hard to believe, but think of a car's manual transmission: Automatic is simpler and easier to handle, but real drivers prefer manual, and car manufacturers continue to offer it.

To make a vinyl record produce ambient music, put together a system à la carte, using a combination of new and period equipment. Start with a receiver, connect the receiver to a turntable, and attach the receiver to speakers. For greater simplicity but lesser sound quality, buy a device that combines all three components— turntable, receiver, and speakers—in one body. To learn where these pieces can be found, and how price influences their quality, it's advisable either to become an audiophile or befriend one.

Just think of all the vinyl out there waiting to be rescued. What goes around comes around. And around . . .

~~~~~~~~~~~

Desk

For the Office that Isn't

The desk you need is really a table. Anything sold as home office furniture is bound to be small and apologetic, trying to pretend it's something it's not. The typical home office desk is either too quaint (modeled after old-school ladies' letter-writing tables with fussy drawers), too commercial (styled after mahogany lawyers' desks), or too toy-like and makeshift (spindly metal computer stations). The latter's specialized compartments (for printer, hard drive, and so on) may seem convenient until you bring the thing home and realize that your hard drive is half an inch too high to fit in the allotted space. And it allows little room for paying paper bills, sorting receipts, and doing all manner of other grown-up business.

Its materials are bound to be imitative too. Wood composites covered with foils and other veneers. "Metals" that may actually be plastics. And flimsy aluminum and thin-gauge steel that look far more durable than they are.

The fact is, we're still not comfortable with the idea of working at home. Work brings stress, strangers (now via webcam), and homely storage issues into a family's only refuge. A corporate home office pollutes the sanctity of home. A homey-looking home office degrades the dignity of work. You can't win.

In their advertising, computer manufacturers skirt this dilemma by showing laptop users lounging on elegant sofas, sprawling on fireside carpets, curling up in fluffy beds, sunning by the pool. See? Now you can fit your home office into a sleek little mobile box, they're saying. Who needs office furniture, anyway?

In fact, just like a city needs its suburbs, every home needs a back office, a space where all our miniaturized and multitasking electronic equipment can work together with ancient mechanical office gear like desktop files, file cabinets, files, stapler, scissors, and paper clips.

Nothing organizes this ever-growing collection of gear better than a good, solid dining table. Not the one in the dining room, but a second dining table that is rectangular, as narrow as possible (30 to 36 inches), and no longer than needed (roughly 60 inches is good). This leaves a good amount of free space for inserting a rapidly changing array of rolling file cabinets, electronics, and wastebaskets below. Solid wood or bamboo provides a warm leaning surface for wrists and forearms and takes on more character as it is scratched, gouged, and soaked with spilled coffee. It also doesn't look so grim and officey.

Demand is the only downside to making a desk of a dining table. Over the years it may be recruited for parties, holidays, and other events that round up all the chairs in the house. That means unplugging a lot of wires, of course, but it's a good excuse, in the interim, to lounge with the laptop in bed, just as they do in those ads.

~~~~~~~~~~~~~~~~~~~

Reading Chair

Create a Sanctuary

Reading is a sport. It's a leisure-time, self-improvement activity that exercises the uppermost part of the body (its gray matter). And since all sports require gear—task-specific, ergonomically designed equipment that reveals the sportsman's skill and commitment—why shouldn't reading have its own?

A reader's main piece of equipment, the reading chair, should not only perform properly but also display the important features of the gearhead aesthetic: seasoning. Serious athletes prefer equipment that's visibly broken in and weathered by steady use. Impeccably new gear is the mark of a rank amateur or weekend warrior.

To survive the seasoning process, a reading chair must be constructed like gear, not decor: well engineered with high-quality materials designed to perform well under duress. It should mellow and improve with time, not fall apart. After a couple of decades, its cushions should be molded by readers' backs and bottoms, its arms roughened up by the sprawling of their legs. A well-honed reading chair says, quietly, "In this house, people read for pleasure."

To some, this tableau will look like a dowdy vignette from Colonial Williamsburg. But other visitors will see it as an oasis of calm in a tawdry world and make envious comments: "Gee, I wish I had time to read." Others still may be intimidated by a household of avid readers using antique reading equipment like members of some Luddite cult.

In truth, offscreen readers are a disappearing demographic. And traditional reading chairs are no longer called reading chairs. Salespeople may claim that reading chairs no longer exist and direct you instead to loungers, recliners, armchairs, wing chairs, and club chairs, any of which might, indeed, become a workable reading chair.

The dimensions of a decent reading chair can vary widely. Good examples show up in the realm of upholstered furniture, somewhere between the large sofa and the small occasional chair. The elusive formula for comfort will factor in immeasurable qualities such as the squishiness of the cushions, the tilt of the arms and back, and the reader's proportions. Consequently, the only trustworthy measure is the reader herself, field-testing a chair with her favorite reading positions.

Here is a list of four common postures any reading chair should accommodate. (Remember, reading is like air travel. Squirming in place not only prevents deep vein thrombosis, but it also aids circulation by speeding blood flow to the brain. The more you move around, the longer you can read alertly without cramping.)

Waiting room position. Sit up straight, with both feet on the floor or one leg crossed, as if you're cooling your heels in a doctor's office. Does the chair support your back? Can you use a throw pillow to improve the fit? How does the seat cushion feel on your buttocks and thighs? Soft but firm? It should be firm enough to keep you awake, but soft enough to feel homey.

Full backward stretch. Lean back and put your feet up on an ottoman or coffee table. Does your behind sink deep enough into the chair for comfort? Look at the chair's profile. The back should be angled. (A slightly angled back is not to be confused with a recliner; more on that in a bit.)

Sideways sprawl. Lift both legs over one chair arm while using the other as a back rest. Wide, "rolled" arms

work best. Warning: This posture is not ergonomically beneficial, but if it feels good, do it.

Kid lift. Reading to rapt children is one of life's great pleasures, and their literature is an unsung art form. If you have a houseful of kids, ask

> Salespeople may claim that reading chairs no longer exist and direct you instead to recliners or club chairs.

them to help choose a friendly chair. Try out various postures: child-on-lap, or child squished in next to you, depending on your sizes. Consider the extra-wide "chair-and-a-half" (also called "man-and-a-dog chair").

The anatomy of a good reading chair follows that of a sofa: a well-made hardwood frame, well-connected springs, and well-layered cushioning. Unless the chair has a slipcover that is easily cleaned, its upholstery should be even more durable than a sofa's. Although you might want to shout "Not on the couch!" to kids bearing chocolate, you should not ban children and snacks from the reading chair. Snacks promote reading. The less precious the chair, the better it will serve as an escape from reality.

Well-tanned leather pays off as a long-term investment, since leather repairs and patinas add to its rustic charm. A less costly alternative is faux suede, made of microfiber; it takes abuse nicely and feels pleasantly warm and nonsticky on bare skin.

Eventually the search will lead to recliners, and someone will say: Hey, why not? Just pull a lever, and the chair buckles into a snoozing position, its skirt morphing into an ottoman. Unfortunately, recliners promote zombielike behavior, a limbo that is neither fully relaxing nor productive. When sleepy, indulge in full horizontality elsewhere. Moving parts also promote breakage, and when the mechanism gives out, you're stuck.

One more note of caution about zoning out: Keep reading chairs away from all glowing screens, especially those connected to satellite dishes.

If space doesn't allow for a comfortable distance, noise cancelling headphones make a nice gift for the beleaguered reader.

Bookholder

The Story File

With computers fulfilling your every wish, why would you want books clogging your home? The heavy, space-hogging dust magnets cost you over the long haul, what with the real estate they occupy, the heating and cooling they enjoy, and the moving expenses they incur.

But book hoarding is not a matter of logic, and it's not often you hear book owners complaining about the cost-benefit ratio. Mostly, they get emotional over the old things.

"Oh, I just love my books!"

"I could never part with them!"

"They're like old friends!"

"I want more!"

The most voracious of true readers have the seediest books: a mishmash of white and yellowed hardbacks and paperbacks, obscure and tattered, dust-jacketed and bare, acquired over decades, piled helter-skelter. A devoted reader would much rather finish a book than straighten the bookshelves. "Lite" readers have the newest and glossiest books arrayed neatly, well contained on their shelves and coffee tables. Hardback bestsellers are mixed with fat new art books.

In predigital days, bookshelves held three kinds of books. There were new books you bought because you wanted to read them. Lined up together, they formed a horizontal to-do list—countries you longed to visit, languages you intended to learn, famous authors you wanted to know better. There were books you had already read, or reread, but continued to hang on to. Both kinds of books, read and unread, were joined by household reference books (the sort gifted at graduations).

Why bother with those anymore? After all, if you seek information, Google will find it. Well, world atlases, dictionaries, travel guides, and cookbooks have become anachronisms of a strange sort, no longer indispensable but still desirable, not necessarily for their information but for their mechanical charm. They carry information you *don't* need along with material you seek. They invite you to browse aimlessly. It's a friendlier and often more rewarding alternative to using a global search engine—would you ever have stumbled across that fantastic bouillabaisse recipe while performing an Internet search for veggie lasagna?

Those are the sorts of books you may very well open on a rainy afternoon. What about inherited books of value, or meaning, that must be passed on to future generations? That's what storage lockers are for. Or siblings. Or antiquarian book dealers. You don't hang on to memorable bottles of wine, so why not just consume books, remember them fondly, and recycle? That goes for great fiction you'll never have time to reread. Pass it along for others to enjoy.

The only people who really need plenty of bookshelves, and books to fill them, are the owners of 5,000- to 10,000-square-foot suburban Tudors with wordy floor plans (master suite, formal dining room, library) and rooms that swallow up furniture. They need books, and lots of them, to appear properly stately and all-around old-fashioned. Mansionettes aside, surrounding yourself with too many defunct books is like living with excess cats. There's something elderly and eccentric about it. (Unless, of course, the surplus is mercantile or avocational: You collect books, or breed cats.)

> Countries you longed to visit, languages you truly intended to learn, classics you always meant to reread . . .

But a slimmed-down collection of books is another matter altogether. A house without books seems cold and confining, no matter what its dimensions. A long-forgotten tome can be entirely transporting. A stack of books—like a collection of family photographs or artwork—represents the owner's memories, good intentions, and curiosity about people. From a purely visual standpoint, books create a swath of scenery, with depth and shape.

Books hold many things. But what things should we use to hold books?

Bookshelves and bookcases are problematic. Steel and plastic feel like office equipment. Solid wood is expensive, whether it's hardwood (cherry, oak, maple) or softwood (which needs a costly coat of paint). That's why the standard bookcase is made of particleboard. It arrives flat, and you assemble it with simple tools.

Longevity is the problem there. Laminate glues lose their stickiness, and hardware tends to wiggle out of particleboard holes.

A bookcase should be built to last. And the most lasting construction is the kind built into a house by a bona fide cabinetmaker. The ideal case is low—chair back, or "chair rail," level. It's two or three adjustable shelves high and as long as it needs to be, running the available length. (A tall, five-shelf bookcase has a way of looming over a room.) The ideal material is stained hardwood or painted pine.

The top of a low bookcase can be used as a display surface for propped-up photos and paintings, candles, keepsakes, or flowers. No, you can't take this furniture with you when you move—it's not really furniture at all, being a set of book*shelves* as opposed to a book*case*. But hopefully, if you do move, it will be into a house with bookshelves of its own.

A cabinetmaker will be out of the question for some—it's a considerable expense and may not be feasible for renters—but there is another recourse. Buy a bookcase that is a virtuous piece of furniture, with permanent joinery. It may be new, or old, or antique. It should be a stable hardwood box with just a couple of adjustable shelves. Its width of 40 inches or so will be no longer than its wood shelves can span without bowing.

A bookcase that size won't hold all the books you want to store, but it will force you to pluck out books you really care about, line them up, confront the absurdity of hoarding those old things for so long, and maybe even read the things all over again. Just like you said you would.

Phone

Only Connect

W hat an amazing time. The landline telephone is toast. The cell phone has become a computer. And the laptop, with built-in mic, works as a free international phone. So, now that we're Web-surfing on our phones, phone-calling on our laptops, and taking photographs and playing music on both, why aren't we happy?

Cell phones require too much "techno-mettle": the tenacity needed to learn how to use the phone, upgrade it often, and keep learning the new features located on each new model.

Young people must prove their techno-mettle by mastering the most complex phones and using them while walking or driving, only to junk them ASAP for upgraded models with more intricate features.

Geezers must prove their techno-mettle by using keypads they can't see or press easily, on new phones and with services explained by pages and pages of barely decipherable fine print. Cell phones test many of the faculties everyone loses as they age: hearing, near vision, manual dexterity, and patience for juvenile obsessions like rapid obsolescence, bogus innovation, and competitive consumerism.

To show their ubiquity, business-people of all ages must demonstrate that they are available instantly, and constantly, via a digital device like the BlackBerry.

Once we've proven our techno-mettle, we're still left hungry. Kids nag their parents for ever-expanding service plans on new phones with ever-expanding media features: more minutes, more messaging, more battery, more pixels! Older people want more volume and bigger keys. Everyone expects the industry to astound them with magical advances from one month to the next.

We're left insecure too. Have we mastered it all? Is there already a better phone out there—are we out of the loop? And once we buy a fresh model, how can we rest assured it is the optimal phone for our aspirations? Will we cook our brains with EMF radiation using the phone too much? And what happens if we drop the precious thing on an icy sidewalk? (The iPhone, launched in 2007 with a touch-sensitive screen of glass, doesn't like freezing temperatures or collisions and, incidentally, must be used with warm, glove-free flesh.) When we finally acquire that state-of-the-art phone, will it still drop calls, fail to connect, or fade out due to lack of service?

The next era of mobile technology will bring blazing speed and acuity to the cellular phone/computer, but it

---

What happens if we drop the precious thing on an icy sidewalk?

---

may not bring any more serenity than we have now. We're going to have to supply that ourselves, in the way we buy and deploy cell phones.

This will require a process of elimination still more vigilant than the one used to choose the other items in this book. The process starts with a choice of carrier, or lack of carrier—a pay-as-you-go phone. And the choice of carrier starts with a map.

Everyone has his own calling profile: a pattern of making and receiving certain kinds of messages within a certain geography. (Do you send nightly text messages to Macau, or call your mom on the next block?) Once you've mapped your expected cell phone use, you can look at a matrix—a comparison chart showing which companies cover what territories in and out of the country.

Consumer Reports is one source of this information. They poll cell users about their experiences with cell service providers and publish a comparison survey each January.

Once you find the right provider, visit their website, scan the options, then call up a live customer service representative and tell him how you want to use your phone.

Choose your service option, and take it with you to the retail store where the phones are lined up in mind-boggling profusion. Different phones are compatible with different carriers' special bandwidths, and some of them come free with the service contract. It's not the only place to find a compatible phone, but it's certainly the easiest.

It's also where you must use extreme vigilance. The salesman will present the phones in terms of electronic features, for example: "This phone offers many more options like [list of amazing things] for just a bit more money."

Ignore all the options for a moment, and think of the phone as a pair of eyeglasses. For everyday seeing, you don't need infrared night vision, telescoping magnification, or rearview mirrors. You need normal lenses that won't fall off your head too easily, or break when they do. They should be relatively au courant, but able to last a few years without embarrassing you. In other words, they should be as simple and practical as any extension of your body ought to be. The cell phone should be more like a durable body part, and less like a fragile little machine!

Fortunately, equipment manufacturers are starting to build extra-durable phones. Marketed toward adventurous sportsmen and hard-working he-men, the basic model is a sturdy shell of reinforced plastic coated with polyurethane over a cavity further cushioned by a bed of silicone rubber; the whole is assembled with water-resistant screws, filters, and O-rings. These "ruggedized" phones are fully immersible and resistant to humidity, dust, shock, and vibration. Each has a hook for hanging on belts and bags, making it easy to find.

Though the phones are aimed at tough guys in a hurry, the extra-wide keys turn out to be perfectly visible to middle-aged eyes, male or female. Beefed-up phones are still costlier than no-frills models, but their prices will come down if the category catches on.

Meanwhile, a website advertising one brand of durable cell phones shows videos of hikers, bikers, skiers, and whitewater rafters aggressively *not* using their cell phones.

What a great message. Unintentionally, it says: Stop text messaging gibberish, watching tiny sitcoms, and photographing your nose. Finish your work, pocket that cell, and go out and play in the sunshine!

Laptop

The Globalizing, Time-Traveling Wonder

The laptop is the most magnificent machine in the house. Via the Internet, it collects the best things from all over the world, translates them into any language, and delivers them to any place you happen to be. It also records your own creations—novels, documentaries, decisive memos—and dispatches them to the continent of your choice.

Many tasks in work and school are fungible now; they don't need to be connected to the permanent architecture of office buildings and classrooms. Some are better off without it. Working at home, sans distraction, may be more productive than working in bull pens. Anyone can take several briefcases of anything to any time zone, while working on the plane. Students can travel the world while using their laptops as portable classrooms, linked up with "long-distance learning" programs.

Although the connected computer has changed the geography and timing of every human exchange, we haven't even begun to take full creative advantage of the upheaval. We're no longer tied down to living in one particular place in the world, all year long, to be near the immovable institutions that used to attach

Can the laptop replace the TV? Yes. And it will.

us to one house, in one neighborhood, in one country. But for most people, that idea is still too radical to translate into real estate, scheduling, and contractual life as we know it.

U sing its most primitive functions, the laptop can replace every conceivable household directory of names, facts, and numbers: phone book, Rolodex, calendar, dictionary, textbooks, appliance manuals, and so on.

It can be a repository for a vault of precious information: your life's work, photo documentaries on everyone you know and everywhere you've been, a

complete history of your financial life. If you wish, it can replace the landline and cell phone. Via the Internet, it brings merchandise into the house— at your fingertips, you've got an international marketplace of retailing, wholesaling, trading, haggling, bartering, or auctioning websites.

Can the laptop replace the main machinery of home entertainment, TV and DVD player? Yes. And in all likelihood, eventually it truly will.

How can such an expensive machine be considered indispensable? Using a computer is a measure of literacy for just about every field of work. Increasingly, it's also used to transfer funds, instantly, from one place to another, or to order dinner or research home remedies.

Every household will need at least one computer to participate fully in this new kind of citizenry. A laptop, or miniaturized computer, is a better investment than any other configuration, simply because it can go wherever you need it to go. (A laptop also uses less energy and takes up less real estate than a desktop computer, making it cost-effective and environmentally saner in the long run.)

The high price that made the laptop a luxury only a few years ago has dwindled—and will continue to drop until the personal laptop becomes as common as the personal cell phone, and laptops are arrayed throughout the house like reference books. Building a basic, cheap, no-frills laptop is very possible. (The nonprofit group One Laptop Per Child is determined to provide such machines, to children all over the world, at a cost of $100 each.)

No matter what the coming technological advances—and there will be many—a laptop is not a long-term investment, so buying the best you can afford does not pay. (And know that even if you're seduced by a feature that represents real progress, a new, better version of that feature is likely to be just around the corner.)

The costliest laptop will allow you to do a million things really fast. Is that what you need? If not, list the tasks you want the machine to perform. Visit stores and get physical with the laptops on display. Check out the screen sizes and shapes. Small is portable; big is visible. Strike a compromise at about 15 inches. Stroke the touch pad textures. Feel the weight and bulk of the whole machine.

Next, find a geek—that's a young person obsessed with new electronic releases. Ask him to match your desires to the specs of a machine in your price range; go online and buy a machine customized to your specs, and endeavor not to spend *too* much time in front of it.

Printer

Be Your Own Copy Shop

What next? It once took a village to produce all the things home printers make today. Photofinishers, stationers, post offices, offset printers, copy shops, and bookstores used to sell snapshots, wedding invitations, business cards, signage, mailing labels, postcards, bumper stickers, and faxes to everyone in town. Now one desktop machine can do it all with a few changes of paper.

The next frontier in printers will produce everything else, futurists claim. Every household will become a miniature factory, using 3-D printing and cutting machines to make its own necessities on demand. Need a new toothbrush? Four more soup-spoons? A picture frame? You can design them yourself. Just pop in a digital file and watch the machine create the products by depositing, melting, or slicing layers of thermo-plastics, photopolymers, and tita-nium alloys into precise shapes right before your eyes.

> Every household will become a miniature factory, making its own necessities on demand.

The process already exists in the industrial world, where it's used to create prototypes (hence the name "rapid prototyping") or to make spe-cialized products like medical parts on a small scale. New rapid proto-typing methods are emerging with amazing speed: stereolithography, multijet modeling, laminated object manufacturing, selective laser sinter-ing, to name a few.

Imagine shopping for one of those, then breathe easy knowing all *you* have to do is choose a printer. Still, it's not so easy. More than other electronics—certainly more than the laptop—the printer presents a mael-strom of options. A visit to the elec-tronics store will bring you face-to-face with an array of products ranging from slow to fast, simple to complex, single function to multifunction. There's the inkjet-scanner-fax-copier combo. There are printers specially designed

for photo-frame-size printing. There are black and white printers, and there are color printers—two-process color printers, four-process color printers, color printers that take ten minutes to spew out a single page. And since the average printer is, after all, so much cheaper, ounce for ounce, than its neighboring electronics—laptops, TVs, and PDAs—it almost ends up seeming foolish to buy a basic printer.

Cut down on the confu-sion by narrowing in on your needs before you set foot inside an electronics store. Just as you did with the cell phone, figure out what *you* need. What do you want to print, how many copies do you want, and how fast do you want those things to appear? Documents? Photos? Documents with photos? Next, figure out what other officelike tasks you simply must do at home. Scan? Copy? Fax? Unless you really need those functions, stay away from the AIOs (all-in-ones). When one func-tion breaks—and it will—you'll have to replace the whole hulking machine.

Then, to get an idea of what the options are, trawl the websites of big-box stores specializing in office equipment. Because they sell to small businesses as well as households, they have a wider selection of more serious printers and tend to be staffed by sav-vier salespeople than the stores selling every conceivable sort of consumer electronics. Then proceed, unafraid, to one of those biz stores. Resist the lure of more than you need; find a friendly salesperson and inform him of your personal spec sheet.

Then make sure you put that printer to use. Be your own greeting card factory, scrapbooking company, and personalized stationery store. (Just be sure to find a second use for every scrap of paper you use, before you send it to the recycling bin.)

~~~~~~~~~~~~

Picture Frame

Capture a Moment

Nothing reveals more about a household than the people in the picture frames. No object is more precious, expressive, and possibly haunting than a photograph conserved in a sandwich of glass, wood, and paper and put on proud display. We frame likenesses of the people we love, and those who love us, not because we need to remember their looks, but because framing each one captures a moment in time, and the way the relationship felt on that day, in that year. Photos also function a bit like amulets, assuring us that we're being protected by someone out there, alive or not, and reminding us of the people who need us.

It's hard enough to single out a few photos from the hundreds (thousands?) we've yet to sort. Framing raises a new question: Should we rely on the new digital photo frames to convey all this emotion? Or, should we carry on as usual sans batteries and cords?

True, the digital frame puts on a good show, flashing one glowing photo after another with PowerPoint-like efficiency. And it's certainly a way of the future. Those radiant photographs might one day double as room lighting as they mimic sunrises, sunsets, and anything in between. The traditional wall of framed family photos could be transformed into a big screen showing a family documentary video or freeze-framed into a single, mural-like image.

In twenty years, the custom of framing photographs—encasing printed paper images in glass-topped boxes—may seem adorably historic.

Or maybe not. *Tempus fugit.* That's the point of keeping a photo: to pretend you can stop time. The digital frame *fugit* too much—the parade of images is fleeting, and their pixellization unsatisfying. The paper photograph in a traditional frame is comfortably unchangeable and unchanging.

What frame to choose? Frames are like furniture. Unless the pieces are well joined, they will eventually loosen. Conventional, mass-produced frames are made of prefinished molding, and connected at their corners with nails and/or various plastic or metal fasteners. Expensive wood frames are made the old-fashioned way, interlocked by wood joinery, then sanded and finished.

Ask for a compromise: a well-made factory model of solid hardwood molding, with well-mitered corners that look tight and smooth. The frame should hold a rectangle of glass, along with an acid-free cardboard mat; the backing should include an "easel" flap to hold the frame stand vertically or horizontally.

Then go ahead and flaunt those baby pictures, travelogues, and graduation pics. (And yes, if you must, give Fido's mug a place in the mix as well.)

Archives

A Place for All the Stuff

On New York City's Ellis Island, the streamlined exhibits in the Immigration Museum show how millions of one-way travelers each packed their worldly goods into a couple of suitcases and reduced their family histories to a handful of objects—a few photographs, lockets, or prayer beads—before sailing off to a strange new homeland. Some museum-goers choke up at the sight of such meager possessions. Some make jokes: Dude, talk about downsizing! Others begin to make lists.

"What would you take if you had to flee your house right now?" Americans also ask themselves that question as they watch the upheavals—

hurricanes, floods, earthquakes, fires, or acts of war—they're privy to every day, thanks to live news.

Though we may have more worldly goods than our ancestors, it turns out that if push came to shove, our choices of mementos might be very similar to theirs: tokens of love, religious amulets, and family likenesses. In order to ensure their safe passage, as well as their intermittent airing and admiring—a process best accompanied by a good bout of storytelling—it's important to decide where those irreplaceable piles should go.

S adly, archiving is a household task seldom crossed off the annual to-do list. We may feel a gnawing obligation to collect and protect family history from the elements. But we're not really sure what those elements are, what kind of container will keep them out, and where to put such a thing anyway. Who's got the time?

And who's got the strength? Being your own archivist stirs emotion. There are the memories, good and bad, and also the wrenching process of elimination. Should you keep one teddy bear or three? The second wedding dress, just the first, or none at all? What about all those adorable grade school masterpieces? If they don't make the archival cut, how can you trash them? Sure, the kids don't care about this stuff now, but maybe they'll be starved for nostalgia in fifty years.

In this nation obsessed with insurance, home security, and portable storage, it's surprising that marketers haven't fully exploited the need to protect our domestic archives from our most feared invisible dangers (mildew, mites, germs, radon, and foreign invasion). Enterprising scrapbookers create visual documentation of their memories, but that's just for flat things. There are pieces of furniture for books, DVDs, clothing—why not memories? Well, there's the old-fashioned, glass-fronted armoire, but that hulking specimen evokes spooky, frilly doll collections, and it's essentially a dust trap.

The only solution is to create an expandable system of three-dimensional files. Start with an archival box, sized at 11 inches by 14 inches by 2 inches. Such boxes, in a great range of specs, are easy to buy online from distributors of art supplies or big-box home design stores.

Archival boxes look like common cardboard but are actually acid free, made with high alpha-cellulose fiber, and buffered with calcium carbonate to neutralize their pH level. Metal corners prolong the life of the boxes.

These are presentable enough to be stacked anywhere, especially on bookshelves. Larger keepsakes do well in the archival garment boxes, 40 inches by 19 inches by 6.5 inches, sold by container stores online and designed to hide under beds.

READING,
WRITING, LIVING

IN THE LIVING ROOM, you can live well without buying much of anything new, or particularly newfangled. But for the electronics, the room needs a few humble pieces of furniture. If you rescue and revamp all the pieces from lists, auctions, thrift stores, antique dealers, and relatives, pride yourself on saving lots of wool, wood, and fuel. If you buy new, however, invest in the kind of quality that will endure for as long as possible. Landfills don't need any more bad sofas!

DOORMAT

- Plain coir mat the width of your doorway
- Eco-note: The mat can be composted when it begins to show signs of wear and tear.
- Find it: Hardware stores, big-box stores; or order it to fit from an industrial flooring company

Cost: $10 to $20

RUG

- Wool, handmade, flat-woven
- Shopping tip: Always buy a rug in person; if the seller allows returns, try out the rug in your home.
- Find it: Design, department, or big-box stores; online auctions and bulletin boards; rug importers

Cost: $200 and (way) up for a 5' x 7' rug

SOFA

- Kiln-dried hardwood frame with good joinery
- Seat and back cushions filled with high resilience (HR) polyurethane foam, aka poly-foam
- Commercial (contract) grade fabrics in synthetics (microfiber) or synthetic/natural blends
- Shopping tip: Upholstered furniture in the United States is usually "bench-made"— handmade in workshops small or large. In other words, the manufacturer is, in a sense, an artisan. Buy as close to the manufacturer as possible, and you'll have more choices about components, and more information about how the piece is made.
- Find it: LEE Industries manufactures and sells to stores like Crate and Barrel. Search styles and fabrics (they'll send swatches) through their website, then buy through a local dealer/retailer.

Cost: Spend $800 to $2,000 for a new, traditionally built commercial sofa; spend the same amount reupholstering a used sofa in better materials; or buy gently used.

COFFEE TABLE

- Solid hardwood, with real wood joinery
- 18" to 20" high, with proportions that fit the room size, furniture layout, and sofa
- Find it: Home design stores, or buy used/antique

Cost: $200 and up

MUSIC DEVICE

- Stereo receiver, record turntable, set of speakers. (Or you buy an all-in-one system.)
- Find it: Stores specializing in audio equipment, or buy used

Cost: Each component starts at about $200 and goes way up. Buy new or used.

DESK

- Skip the desk. Instead use a solid hardwood dining table, approximately 30" x 60", with real wood joinery and a water-resistant finish.
- Try: A Parsons table
- Find it: Better home design stores; Room and Board offers custom and semicustom Parsons tables in all-wood, as well as an à la carte choice of metal bases with wood tops; a Minnesota steel shop produces the handmade, hand-lacquered steel table frames. Around $750 for the finished product. For the best deals in town, buy used.

Cost: $50 to $800

FLOOR LAMP

- Three-way standing floor lamp with a heavy base
- Lamp should be rated for 50/100/150 watts standard incandescent bulbs. Use a three-way CFL rated for 12/19/28 watts.
- Eco-rating: CFLs save energy and burn cool.
- Find it: The lamp: IKEA, lighting supply stores, home design stores, big-box stores. The bulb: lighting supply counters

Cost: Lamp, less than $200; CFL, less than $10

READING CHAIR

- Armchair selected to suit your favored reading positions
- Upholstered in leather, microfiber, or contract-quality synthetic/natural fiber blend
- Find it: See Sofa, opposite page.

Cost: $700 to $1,000 in leather; $400 to $800 in fabric

VASE

- Clear glass
- About 8" high

Cost: Buy new or used, $5 to $20, or wait for florist to deliver.

BOOKHOLDER

- Fully assembled, solid hardwood bookcase
- Low and small (40" wide x 30" high) with two shelves, 12" deep with 12" clearance
- Find it: A local woodworker (furniture maker or carpenter) will make a bookcase using proper wood joinery (rather than nails and glue) and a beautiful finish.

Cost: Stores charge $500 to $1,000; a woodworker can make an excellent piece within that range or below it.

PHONE

- A rugged cell phone, immersible and resistant to humidity, dust, shock, and vibration
- Sturdy shell of reinforced plastic assembled with water-resistant screws, filters, and O-rings
- Try: G'zOne phone by Casio
- Shopping tip: Figure out your calling profile, then look to *Consumer Reports* or online to find the right cell phone carrier for you. Once you find the right provider, visit their website or go directly to one of their local stores.

Cost: About $150 with a two-year service plan

LAPTOP

- A laptop computer, PC or Mac, acquired in four steps. (1) Chat. Ask friends and colleagues about their laptops. (2) Research. Based on your design preferences, budget, and typical needs, narrow the field to a couple of manufacturers; visit their websites and use their "Product Advisor" or "Laptop Finder" features. Pin down screen size and weight before choosing the techier stuff. (3) Visit. At local electronics stores, handle the laptops

and grill the sales geeks. (4) Buy only the features you actually use, with the speed and performance you truly need.
- Find it: Buy at the stores or on the websites with the best price.

Cost: $900 to $1,600

PRINTER

- Home-office quality ink-jet printer
- Shopping tip: Print quality is more important than speed or capacity.
- Find it: Go to the HP (Hewlett-Packard) website and click "Help me choose a printer." (Helpful even if you aren't buying an HP.)
- Economize: Call around to find a good price on recently outdated models predating the model you want. You won't be missing much.

Cost: About $100 for a new model, much less for its precursor

PICTURE FRAME

- 5" x 7" hardwood, well-crafted frame with interlocking joinery and hand finishing
- Find it: Art supply retailer/distributor, local frame shop

Cost: $10 to $30

ARCHIVES

- Household-quality archival cardboard box
- Dimensions may vary to correspond to your needs, but start with the basic size: 11" x 14" x 2".
- Find it: Art supply retailer/distributor.

Cost: About $10 each, less if purchased in bulk

Acknowledgments

Diane Zipperstein and Steve Zipperstein made the writing of this book possible in several different ways. Thank you.

The writing was made better by Workman's editor-in-chief, Susan Bolotin, the best editor I've ever worked with but for Savannah Ashour, who reeled in all the pages with skill and wholehearted focus. They are not only smart and funny, these editors, but also nice.

Thanks, Eric Epstein, for introducing me to the crew.

At Workman, I'm also grateful to Peter Workman, David Matt, Anne Kerman, Gary Montalvo, Kim Small, Beth Levy, and Luke Bumgarner.

Thanks to Jerry Couture for counsel.

A series of talented Lehigh University students and graduates have passed through my studio. All have contributed to this book in some measure: Christina Kazakia (come back!), Jennifer Claire Steacy, Gregory Heller-Labelle, Erica Dollhopf, Bridget Snow Bruning, and Daniel W. Pfautz. Thanks also to Professor Anthony Viscardi, chair of the department of art and architecture at Lehigh.

Deni Thurman-Eyer lent advice and research. Faith Baum, Bathsheba Monk, Diane Labelle, Lyn Godley, Barbara Fraust, Leanne Graeff, and Cheryl Dougan brought welcome candor.

More appreciation goes to Kevin Lichten, Seok-Hee Lee, Pamela Shaw, Dan Blom, Pam Boyer, Holly Sachdev, Barbara Pearson, Angelika Cornelius, Barbara Diamond, Cher Ashcroft, Sally Handlon, Robin Beatty, Diane Davison, Olivier Mikhailoff, Jeff Fleeman, and Elizabeth Miller.

Gillian Weiner, Nat Weiner, and Emily, Margot, and Hilary Zipperstein helped in ways they do and don't know about.

Hundreds of people—working in the product development, engineering, marketing, and sales divisions of many different companies—patiently took the time to help me understand how their products work. I only wish I could thank each one individually.

Finally, I'd like to thank Richard Master.

SPECIAL THANKS TO THE FOLLOWING:

Front Cover—Broom: PHOTOS.COM; scissors: FISKARS; blanket: PERFECT FIT INDUSTRIES; mirror: CSNMIRRORS; pepper mill: PEUGEOT; duster: BECKNER FEATHER; computer: SHUTTERSTOCK; chair: LEE INDUSTRIES; knife: SANELLI; lamp: CRATE AND BARREL; tea pot: BODUM; stock pot: SHUTTERSTOCK; measuring cup: OXO; trashcan: BRABANTIA; chair: DESIGN WITHIN REACH; creamer, mattress pad, coffee maker: SOPHIA SU/LUKE BUMGARNER; *Spine*—lamp: GRACIOUS HOME; fork: SOPHIA SU/LUKE BUMGARNER; *Back Cover*—cleaning cloth, pillow: SOPHIA SU/LUKE BUMGARNER; Dutch oven: LODGE MANUFACTURING CO. Author photo by SCOTT JONES

Interior—2HYYP, www.2hyyp.com: 46; ACE MART, www.acemart.com: 152, 161; ALIBABA, www.alibaba.com: 75, 123; BAUHAUS2YOURHOUSE, www.bauhaus2yourhouse.com: 132; BECKNER FEATHER, www.becknerfeather.com: 172, 180; BODUM, www.bodumusa.com: 108, 109, 115, 125, 126, 149, 161; BRABANTIA, www.brabantia.com: 42, 57, 118, 126; BUY THE THINGS, www.buythethings.com: 113, 125; CASIO, www.casio.com: 203, 214; CRATE AND BARREL, www.crateandbarrel.com: 2, 6, 33, 83, 123, 138, 140, 142, 143, 147, 160, 191, 192, 200, 213, 214; CSNMIRRORS, www.csnmirrors.com: 43, 58; DALLA PIAZZA, www.dallapiazza.com: 69, 122; DEAN & DELUCA, www.deandeluca.com: 65, 117, 122, 126; DESIGN WITHIN REACH, www.dwr.com: 10, 34, 131, 15a9, 196, 213; DICK BLICK, www.dickblick.com: 210, 216; DOUBLE KNOT, www.double-knot.com: 30, 35, 184, 212; DRANNAN COOKWARE CO., www.waterbroiler.com: 100, 125; EPICUREAN, www.epicurean.com: 66, 122; FISKARS, www.fiskars.com: 81, 123; GRACIOUS HOME, www.gracioushome.com: 7, 33; KRUPS, www.krupsusa.com: 106, 125; LEE INDUSTRIES, www.leeindustries.com: 186, 198, 213, 214; LEIFHEIT, www.leifheitusa.com: 54, 58; LIBBEY, www.libbey.com: 144, 160; LODGE MANUFACTURING CO., www.lodgemfg.com: 93, 95, 124; MICROPLANE, www.microplane.com: 88, 124; MIELE, www.miele.com: 174, 180; OLISO, www.oliso.com: 51, 58; OXO, www.oxo.com: 70, 84, 86, 122, 123, 124, 171, 180; PERFECT FIT INDUSTRIES, www.perfectfitindustries.com: 26, 35; PETZL, www.petzl.com: 8, 34; PEUGEOT, www.swissmar.com: 78, 123; RESTORATION HARDWARE, www.restorationhardware.com: 45, 58; ROOM & BOARD, www.roomandboard.com: 9, 13, 34, 129, 159, 189, 213; SANELLI, www.sanelliknives.com: 61, 64, 122; SHARP, www.sharpusa.com: 103, 125; SONY, www.sony.com: 2, 33; STANLEY HARDWARE, www.stanleyhardware.com: 176, 178, 180; STARWEST BOTANICALS, www.starwest-botanicals.com: 17; SWING-A-WAY, www.focuspg.com: 80, 123; THERMO WORKS, www.thermoworks.com: 91, 124; WRAPABLES, www.wrapables.com: 56, 58; ZYLISS, www.zylissusa.com: 72, 123; PHOTO RESEARCHERS, INC.: 17, 166; PHOTOS.COM: 74, 123, 151, 161, 170, 180; PHOTOSPIN: 71, 123; SHUTTERSTOCK: 17, 85, 89, 97, 99, 124, 155, 161, 183, 195, 213, 205, 214, 207, 214; ORIGINAL PHOTOGRAPHY BY SOPHIA SU/LUKE BUMGARNER: 2, 16, 20, 22, 29, 34, 35, 38, 39, 41, 50, 57, 58, 111, 125, 133, 136, 137, 154, 157, 159, 160, 161, 164, 167, 169, 179, 180, 209, 210, 214